D1498163

Making Sense of
Everyday Life

Making Sense of Everyday Life

SUSIE SCOTT

polity

First published in 2009 by Polity Press

Polity Press
65 Bridge Street
Cambridge CB2 1UR, UK

Polity Press
350 Main Street
Malden, MA 02148, USA

ISBN-13: 978-0-7456-4267-3
ISBN-13: 978-0-7456-4268-0 (pb)

A catalogue record for this book is available from the British Library.

Typeset in 11 on 13 pt Scala
by Servis Filmsetting Ltd, Stockport, Cheshire
Printed and bound in Great Britain by
MPG Books Limited, Bodmin, Cornwall

The publisher has used its best endeavours to ensure that the URLs for external websites referred to in this book are correct and active at the time of going to press. However, the publisher has no responsibility for the websites and can make no guarantee that a site will remain live or that the content is or will remain appropriate.

Every effort has been made to trace all copyright holders, but if any have been inadvertently overlooked the publisher will be pleased to include any necessary credits in any subsequent reprint or edition.

For further information on Polity, visit our website: www.politybooks.com

Citations and photographs from Mass Observation reproduced with permission of Curtis Brown Group Ltd, London, on behalf of The Trustees of the Mass Observation Archive Copyright © The Trustees of the Mass Observation Archive.

The publishers would like to thank the following for permission to reproduce copyright material: Figures 1.1, 5.1, 5.2, 8.2, 9.1, 9.2, author; 2.1, TommL at iStock; 3.1, vgstudio at iStock; 3.2, Silvia Jansen; 4.1, Eric Vega; 4.2, Iain Hemmings; 6.1, sjlocke at iStock; 6.2, iofoto at iStock; 6.3, Dreamstime; 7.1, Myerson Photo; 8.1, Jonathon McIntosh; 9.3, naphtalina at iStock.

Contents

Detailed Contents

Acknowledgements

The inspiration for this book came from a course I taught with Jenny Shaw at the University of Sussex, which dovetailed perfectly with my research interests in self-identity and interaction. I would like to thank Jenny for her many valuable comments, her encouragement, and the fascinating conversations we have had about the subject matter of this book. My colleagues in the Sociology Department at Sussex have been similarly supportive during the writing process, and successive cohorts of students have provided useful feedback on the subject matter (as well as being good sports about doing breaching experiments for homework). Emma Longstaff and Jonathan Skerrett at Polity have been extremely helpful in providing prompt and informative guidance on the preparation of the manuscript, as have the three anonymous reviewers of the first draft. I would like to extend particular thanks to the staff and trustees of the Mass Observation Archive, who kindly gave permission to reprint both pictures (figures 10.1 and 10.2) and text (Quotations in chapter 4 are taken from the Autumn 2006 Directive), as well as of course the original respondents to the directives. Finally, a big thank you to my family and friends – especially Lily, Iain, Alison, Sarah, Paul and Michelle – for being as fabulous as always.

1 What is Everyday Life?

The sociology of everyday life is a bundle of paradoxes. As social scientists, we often assume that our role is to explain matters of great importance: cultural trends, historical events, social divisions and changes that affect large numbers of people over a significant amount of time. Against this research agenda, the idea of studying everyday life seems at best counter-intuitive and at worst deeply immoral: why should we waste our time examining 'trivial' matters like this when there are wars being fought, discrimination suffered and inequalities endured? Aren't we simply missing the wider picture?

The answer to this, put simply, is that everyday life *is* the wider picture. None of these larger scale events could occur without there being individual people doing little things in local places. One of the aims of this book is to show how these 'micro'-level, small-scale practices relate to, and are shaped by, 'macro'-level patterns. Social order, disorder and change are at once reflections of the relationship between individual and society, agency and structure, process and regularity.

Defining the everyday

The subject matter of everyday life is wide and varied; this book looks at seven substantive topics – emotions, home, time, eating, health, shopping and leisure – but there are many more we could consider. What they have in common is that they represent sites in which people do (perform, reproduce, and occasionally challenge) social life, day to day. Moran (2005) refers to four types of 'quotidian space' in this respect: workspaces, urban/mobile spaces, living spaces and non-places, wherein one is suspended between two different contexts (such as buses or service stations). Silva and Bennett (2004), meanwhile, suggest that we observe the everyday cultures surrounding home, family and community; sexuality, 'race' and age; and uses of technology. Thus one way of understanding everyday life is as a cluster of topic areas or fields of activity.

Nevertheless, there are some key themes that pervade each of these sites, and which characterize the practices we find in them. Firstly, everyday life is that which we presume to be mundane, familiar and unremarkable: 'the daily lives of ordinary people' (Bennett and Watson 2002: x). Questions such as 'How do we compose a shopping list?' or 'Why do we queue?' might seem ridiculously trivial but, once unpacked, reveal intriguing sets of rules. Secondly, it is that which is routine, repetitive and rhythmic: we do the same things in the same places at the same time, day after day, and this is what reproduces social life. Everyday life is habitual in nature (Felski 1999), and it is this very thing that makes it feel so familiar: think about the domestic routines of 'cooking the dinner' or 'going to bed'. Thirdly, our everyday lives appear to us as private and personal, the product of our individual choices, and so we find ourselves studying phenomena that are not obviously social, such as eating, sleeping or falling in love. As C. Wright Mills (1959) famously argued, to think sociologically is to relate 'private troubles' to 'public issues' – to look for the social patterns reflected in the lives of individuals.

If we define everyday life in terms of such conceptual features, we discover that it can be applied to innumerable different settings: what is mundane and ordinary to one person might be quite extra-ordinary for another. Indeed, this is part of the problem in trying to pin down what we mean by 'everyday'. These phenomena are nebulous, pervasive and ambiguous: obvious to the point of elusiveness (Martin 2003). They form the background against which we see more concrete life experiences, the 'connective tissue' (Bennett 2004) that holds everything together. However, this does not mean that they are trivial, benign or insignificant: Martin (2003) reminds us that the everyday world is infused with power, politics and historical significance. Thus, throughout the book, readers are encouraged to think critically about the origins of social practices and the interests that they serve.

How did the sociology of everyday life develop?

We tend to think of the sociology of everyday life as a relatively recent development, but its subject matter was implicitly addressed in many earlier texts. Classic studies of poverty (Rowntree 1901), the family and kinship (Willmott and Young 1960) and deviance (Becker 1963) may have sought to demonstrate general social trends, but they did so by examining their effects on people's lived experiences. We might then say that everyday life enjoyed an 'absent presence' in the discipline but has recently become recognized as worthy of study in its own right, like the sociology of the body (Turner 1996). Bennett and Watson (2002) offer three perspectives on why this happened, focusing on significant changes in the twentieth century. The first is our understanding of what is worthy of public representation: whereas in pre-modern times only monarchy and figures of high status would be pictured or discussed, we have since become increasingly interested in more 'ordinary' people's domestic lives, as evidenced by the rise of photojournalism, published diaries and reality TV. Secondly, there is the Foucauldian argument that we are living in a 'disciplinary society', where every move we make is subject to control, surveillance and regulation. The mass media are particularly culpable here, as paparazzi photographers follow celebrities into the most mundane locations, hoping to snatch a precious insight into their 'real' lives. Social research is also implicated, for the twentieth century saw the emergence of new methods for documenting everyday life, such as the methods of ethnographic fieldwork and social surveys. Thirdly, the rise of social movements in this period, such as feminism, black civil rights and Gay Pride, brought questions of identity and lifestyle differences to the forefront of political consciousness, and changed the way we thought about the social world. All of these changes meant that individual, private lives became increasingly visible to academics as objects worthy of study.

The most prominent theorists in this new mode of inquiry were Georg Lukács, Henri Lefebvre and Michel de Certeau. Lukács was a Hungarian Marxist and existentialist who warned against the dangers of being too immersed in one's daily routines (1977 [1923]). This attitude of 'pre-reflective acceptance' towards the world, he suggested, prevented people from realizing their potential and living 'authentically'. Lefebvre was influenced by Lukács and of course Marx, when he applied the former's ideas to the situation of the working class under Western industrial capitalism. Lefebvre (1971 [1968]) argued that capitalist workplaces, such as the factory, with its dreary, repetitive cycles, alienated people from the true conditions of their existence, and kept them in a state of false consciousness (cf. Marx 1959 [1844]). This had a pervasive effect upon everyday life: *la vie quotidienne* was characterized by routine, repetition and regularity, punctuated by the occasional break that made this bearable. Consequently, Lefebvre argued that everyday life was not just a benign, residual category that remained after the major institutions of society had been understood, but rather it was an important realm to study in its own right. This view was developed by Michel de Certeau (1984), who pointed to the significance of how people 'do', or 'practise', everyday life. These acts might involve following norms, but equally could be creative, adaptive and defiant. Writing in the aftermath of much political, historical and social change in the twentieth century, de Certeau argued that resistance need not entail grand gestures of political uprising, but rather that individuals could subvert authority by breaking minor rules in their everyday lives; he called this 'making do'. We look in more detail at Lefebvre and de Certeau's work in chapter 2, and return throughout the book to this question of the mutuality of rule-following and rule-breaking.

Contemporary social theorists have drawn upon these ideas to inform their studies, either implicitly or explicitly. Jack Douglas (1981 [1971]) believed that understanding everyday life was an essential part of any theory about the social world, and so the task of the researcher was to examine the common-sense meanings individuals gave to their actions. Berger and Luckmann (1967) famously argued that we construct our own social reality in the course of our daily lives, through our encounters with others. There is no underlying, objective reality to discover, but rather an infinite number of local, subjective realities, which must be studied from the perspective of those who inhabit them. This is a central tenet of interpretivist sociology, which has informed the work of Symbolic Interactionists, phenomenologists, ethnomethodologists, ethnographers and action theorists throughout the twentieth and twenty-first centuries (see chapter 2). In a similar way, Cultural Studies theorists consider how different versions of reality are conveyed by the places, images and artefacts we encounter in everyday life: these can be read critically as 'texts' that transmit particular interests or ideologies (Moran 2005). It is interesting to consider, then, how people engage with these texts, more or less knowingly, to make sense of the social world.

How do we study everyday life?

Interpreting everyday life means viewing social behaviour through a particular kind of lens. Firstly, it is essential to make the familiar strange (Garfinkel 1967), or to look more objectively at phenomena that we would otherwise dismiss as unremarkable: mundane conversations, bedtime rituals, decisions about what to eat, and so on. This means bracketing out our prior assumptions about what is normal, natural and inevitable, as well as any value judgements we might make as to which is the most desirable option. For example, you might compare notes with a friend on how much television you watch and how it is integrated into your day, but this is not a moral question of whether TV is 'bad' or of how much you 'should' be watching. Rather, you would be thinking about how, when and why you decide to engage in this activity over others, and what purpose it serves in your everyday life. Do you watch TV with others and use it to bond with them? When in the day do you watch the most – does this coincide with mealtimes, leisure time or boredom? These are morally neutral questions that seek to find out 'what is going on here?' in social terms: how decisions are made, how routines are created, how rules are followed or broken. Like the conceptual 'anthropologist on Mars' (Sacks 1996), you should stand back and scrutinize familiar settings, as if you had never seen them before, from the perspective of a detached observer. This process is descriptive and analytical, as examples are documented and their features are mapped out, but it is not morally evaluative. Highmore (2002) makes an analogy with the detective story, suggesting that we investigate the 'mysteries' of seemingly innocuous social behaviour to see what lies beneath.

The second technique is to search for underlying rules, routines and regularities in the behaviour you observe, insofar as these tell us something about how the settings are socially organized. This means going beyond the surface of the immediately observable, digging deeper to identify the meanings behind it. Remembering that we are concerned with the routine, mundane and repetitive aspects of people's day-to-day lives, we must then relate these micro-level processes to the macro-level of social order. How do the specific daily activities of individuals combine to create and sustain a sense of order, stability and predictability in their local worlds, and how do these worlds combine to form a larger scale culture? We can examine the hints of structure that we find in small-scale practices: the norms, conventions, habits and rituals that make social behaviour appear orderly. Why do we have rules for different situations, how were they established, and why do we (most of us, most of the time) follow them?

Thirdly, it is important to challenge our taken for granted assumptions (Garfinkel 1967) about the world by considering what happens when these rules are broken. Throughout the book we will look not only at why social norms are upheld, but also at instances of norm-breaking. Deviant cases can be as interesting to study as normative

Figure 1.1 *Studying everyday life involves 'making the familiar strange' and identifying the norms that govern social behaviour. What are the rules of waiting in public places?*

cases, insofar as they reveal the underlying values and assumptions that have been challenged. Some social rules only become visible when they are broken, because they are so implicit: this is evident in subtle *faux pas*, such as misjudging a dress code or addressing someone too informally. Other rules are more explicitly acknowledged, but become more visible when broken, for example the noisy neighbour who plays music late at night. Rule-breaking acts are significant not only in terms of their implications for the individual (losing face, feeling ashamed, making amends), but also in terms of the social reactions they evoke. The classical theorist Durkheim (1893) argued that deviance was actually functional for society, in that it unites 'us' against 'them' and reinforces 'our' adherence to a common set of values (1984 [1893]). By identifying the rule-breaker as a deviant individual, the behaviour is safely contained and disassociated from the group, which becomes more cohesive. Throughout the book, we shall consider how people respond to rule-breaking acts, which values are brought to light, and how social order is restored.

The chapters of the book are organized around these principles, and you will find each topic discussed in relation to three corresponding themes. Rituals and routines refer to descriptions of specific practices, codes of behaviour, habits and other examples that serve to illustrate the theoretical arguments. They are designed to 'make the familiar strange' and encourage analytical thinking about how the everyday world is performed, (re)produced and experienced. Social order refers to the underlying structures of rules and expectations that organize these practices. This helps us to understand why we engage in rule-following behaviour so much of the time, and how this creates a sense of social order and continuity. Finally, challenges refers to the instances of norm-breaking outlined above: the 'exceptions that prove the rule' and that elucidate the values of a group. These rule-breaking acts and the reactions they evoke will help us to understand who is seen as deviant or conformist, which values are important and how they are sustained.

Outline of the book

In the chapters that follow, we take a look at several different sites in which the everyday world is reproduced and unpack some of the features that enable this to happen. Firstly, however, chapter 2 reviews some of the key theoretical perspectives on everyday life, such as Symbolic Interactionism, ethnomethodology and phenomenology, Structural Functionalism and Cultural Studies. This constitutes a theoretical toolkit, to complement the methodological toolkit presented in chapter 10; you may wish to read both of these chapters initially, and refer back to them when you come to research specific topics. The remainder of the book applies these theories to a range of substantive topic areas. These can be read independently and in any order, although there is a logical progression from the micro- to the macro-level: beginning with the most private, subjective experiences, we move through questions of self-identity and embodiment, to social interaction, lifestyle practices and different fields of activity, and finally to opportunities for transcending social structure.

Thus, in chapter 3, we consider the extent to which the apparently private world of the emotions is shaped by the public realm of interaction, norms, values and discourses. To illustrate this, we look at three contrasting states of mind: love, shyness and embarrassment. In chapter 4, we explore the meaning of the home and the importance of domestic routines in our everyday lives. How do we make a home and present it to others? Why is gardening important and home decorating such a popular pastime? Chapter 5 considers time and scheduling as a pervasive feature of everyday life, from the temporal order imposed by clock time to the ways in which we try to subvert this, by making, spending and wasting time. How do our daily schedules impose structure on our lives and regulate our behaviour?

In chapter 6, we look at practices of eating and drinking, insofar as these are socially shaped: why do we often eat together, and what purpose does this serve? What constitutes a 'proper meal' as opposed to a 'snack', and where do such ideas come from? What are the rules of drinking alcohol, and how does the non-drinker challenge others' expectations? Chapter 7 considers health, illness and disability as factors that affect our experience of everyday life. What has previously been normal and routine can easily be disrupted by periods of ill health, with dramatic effects on the way we manage social situations. But is this simply a matter of physical impairment, or is it also about the attitudes of others and the design of the social world? In this chapter, we question how people decide that they are ill, how they experience their conditions, and how appearing 'different' can evoke some interesting social reactions. Chapter 8 focuses on shopping and the 'consuming' nature of everyday life. What are the rituals and routines of shopping for the household, as compared to going to the mall with friends? Are these orderly, structured processes? How and why do we make shopping lists, or deviate from them? This chapter also considers the significance of the gift exchange, which helps to cement social relationships: what are the rules of buying gifts, and what do we expect in return? In chapter 9, we look at holidays, leisure and recreation as examples of the way in which we try to escape the routines of everyday life. How do we use breaks, treats and other rewards to punctuate high points of the day, week or year?

Finally, in chapter 10, we take a look at the methods social scientists have used to study the everyday world, from the ethnographic observations of the Chicago School to official statistics, photojournalism, and the in-depth interviews of interpretivist sociology. Each method is discussed in relation to empirical studies mentioned earlier in the book, which readers are encouraged to revisit and evaluate. What does each one reveal about the social world that cannot be gleaned from other sources? Why is it important to listen to the voices of 'ordinary folk' as well as to read official accounts? This chapter is intended to help students who are about to embark upon social research projects of their own, by raising some important questions to consider when designing an appropriate methodology.

Throughout the book, we shall remain focused on the question of how the practices found in everyday settings help to create, sustain and reproduce the social world. The substantive topics covered in each chapter are explored in terms of our three themes: social order, structures and underlying rules; interactive rituals and routines; and challenges to the taken for granted. Put together, these help us to see how we can make sense of our everyday lives, and why it is important to do so.

2 Theorizing the Mundane

In this chapter we examine some of the key theoretical perspectives that inform our understanding of everyday life. These theories cut across the disciplines of the social sciences, from psychology to philosophy and sociology, and from the macro- to the micro-level of analysis. The latter distinction is often overstated as a simple dichotomy (Scott 2006), but in fact there are many points of overlap between the two branches of theory – particularly in relation to our three themes of social order, rituals and routines, and challenging the taken for granted.

Accordingly, this chapter is divided into three sections, but the theories presented within each should be read as interlinked and complementary. Readers are encouraged to use this chapter as a toolkit (in conjunction with the methodological toolkit presented in chapter 10) from which you may select the most appropriate theory, or range of theories, for the topic at hand. Although you may find some approaches more palatable than others (my own preference is for dramaturgy and Symbolic Interactionism), each perspective offers its own unique insights into different dimensions of social life.

We begin with the questions of social order raised by psychoanalysis, social psychology, Structural Functionalism and anthropology, then explore the significance of rituals and routines through the theories of phenomenology, ethnomethodology and Symbolic Interactionism. Finally, we consider the more explicitly critical approaches found in neo-Marxism, Cultural Studies, and the work of Lefebvre and de Certeau. In subsequent chapters, we shall return to these theories, using one or more to investigate the substantive topics that comprise the subject matter of everyday life.

Theorizing social order

Psychoanalysis

Psychoanalytic theories centre upon the idea that we have an unconscious mind, full of instincts, desires and drives, which motivate our behaviour. This stemmed from Freud's (1984 [1923]) topographical model of the human mind being divided into three distinct layers, or levels of consciousness. At the tip of the iceberg was our conscious mind, through which we perform social actions with an awareness of their implications. Beneath this lay the pre-conscious mind and, beneath that, the unconscious mind, which was the largest part. Freud believed that the surface-level behaviours we could observe in everyday life reflected deeper emotional drives and conflicts in this latter part of the mind.

The effects of this upon social life were explored in many of Freud's works, including *The Psychopathology of Everyday Life* (1975a [1901]), *Beyond the Pleasure Principle* (1975b [1920]) and *Civilization and its Discontents* (2004 [1930]). Freud wrote about three competing forces within the personality: the id demanded instant gratification of our appetites for love, aggression, sex, and so on; the ego was a voice of reason, which recognized the constraints of living alongside others and with limited resources; and the superego acted as a moral guardian, reminding us of how we ought to behave according to the values of our culture. Everyday life involved a constant battle between these forces, as people tried to reconcile the pleasure principle (what we want to do) with the reality principle (what we can and should do).

Related to this is the concept of 'civilization': the process by which the raw and wild emotions of the unconscious mind come to be 'tamed' by our experiences of the social world. For example, in chapter 3, we consider how strong feelings of lustful passion have been repackaged into the idea of romantic love. Negative emotions such as envy, rage and anxiety may also have been 'civilized' as they are channelled into more socially acceptable forms of expression, such as football fandom or celebrity worship. In chapter 6 we see how Norbert Elias (1994) took this Freudian concept further with his notion of the civilizing process. He questioned how and why the need to 'civilize' our primitive instincts came about, and what social purposes these codes of etiquette served.

Freud believed that socially unacceptable thoughts and feelings would be repressed into the unconscious, where they could be kept hidden, but at the expense of one's mental and emotional wellbeing.

In *Civilization and its Discontents*, Freud (2004 [1930]) warned against the dangers of restricting our most intense unconscious urges, such as those for sex and for aggression, insofar as they would inevitably leak out in one way or another. In his clinical work, Freud sought to demonstrate how some repressed feelings were expressed through 'neurotic' symptoms of anxiety, depression and obsession. More commonly, he suggested, unconscious feelings would leak out in everyday behaviours, such as slips of the tongue (mispronouncing a word in a significant way), jokes, and 'lustful' passions for work or play (Freud 1975a [1901]).

Repression was one of several defence mechanisms that Freud identified as ways in which we seek to manage our unconscious urges and survive in civilized society. Many of these defences were depicted as unhealthy, insofar as they prevented us from forging deep, authentic bonds with other people. For example, projection occurs when we identify our own feelings in others and criticize them for it, while reaction formation can be identified in prejudicial attitudes such as homophobia, whereby someone who finds homosexuality repulsive is thought to be harbouring unconscious homosexual feelings themselves. Other defence mechanisms can be seen as neutral or even positive in their effects upon social life. Displacement, for example, may involve redirecting aggressive instincts away from people and onto objects or activities, such as extreme sports. One of the most interesting and pro-social defences that we use in everyday life is humour: telling jokes can help us to deal with certain feelings that cannot be consciously acknowledged, such as extreme grief or terror. We sometimes talk about having a 'gallows humour' that enables us to cope with difficult life experiences, and this of course also oils the wheels of social interaction.

Social psychology

One of many branches of its discipline, social psychology involves the study of how the mind is shaped by its social context. From this perspective, the social world is understood as an external environment that impacts upon the individual: other people are effectively 'stimuli' to which we react and, in turn, our responses comprise stimuli in their social worlds. Experiencing everyday life is therefore a matter of encountering and dealing with these stimuli, by processing the information they provide. Social psychology is aligned with cognitive psychology, insofar as it examines how we interpret, store and retrieve these data in order to make sense of the world and find our place within it. The social self is seen as rational, as it selectively attends to stimuli according to their perceived importance to our goals.

Interpersonal behaviour is seen as driven by a number of social motivations, which are universal among humankind. Michael Argyle (1994) identifies eight of these, which lead us to seek relationships with others. At one extreme, there are basic biological needs (to eat, drink and gain physical comfort), which are often met by other people. Then we have dependency on others to provide help and protection, and a drive for affiliation, or friendship and social acceptability. Alongside these pro-social motives, we may have desires for dominance and power over others, sex and physical intimacy, and aggression. We also have higher order motivations, such as a need for self-esteem and ego-identity, which comes from being liked and accepted by others. Argyle's final category is of miscellaneous other motivations, such as money, personal values and the need for achievement. These various factors can affect the way that we approach situations in our everyday lives: the drive for affiliation might make us seek out friends in a new place, while the need for dominance might make someone keen to be a team leader in their job.

Once we are engaged in social interaction, we have to read the verbal and non-verbal cues that other people give us. We may interpret people's emotional states from their tone of voice or bodily posture (Scherer 1974), for example: some psychologists argue that facial expressions of emotion are universally understood (Izard 1972). We may decide that someone is lying from their averted gaze or quavering voice (Ekman and Friesen 1969), or that their uncrossed arms and 'open' posture shows a willingness to interact. Goffman (1963b) similarly argued that we demonstrate our 'accessibility' (or lack thereof) to others by the way we use our bodies, although his focus was on the social consequences of this. Social interaction is not simply about the perception of others, however, for we must also consider how they are perceiving us. We use meta-cognitive processes to work this out by reflecting on our own perceptions, and, as Laing et al. (1966) showed, these can occur in endless chains: my perception of your perception of me. These processes are important in mediating feelings of self-consciousness, as we shall see in chapter 3.

Social psychologists talk of a repertoire of social skills that we build up, which can help us to deal with other people more or less effectively. Argyle (1994) identifies some of these as the ability to keep conversations flowing, make small talk, or use humour to be a rewarding interaction partner. These skills are seen as indices of a person's wider social competence, their knowledge of the unwritten rules of interaction within a particular culture, which help us to communicate and act appropriately (Summer Institute of Linguistics 2006). This competence is developed through the process of socialization, as we learn how to become members of a shared culture, and as such it is learned through our experiences of interaction. However, we do not always feel confident that we have this knowledge, or that we can use it appropriately in a given situation; in the next chapter, we shall see how the perception of one's own interactional incompetence shapes the experience of shyness and embarrassment.

Related to this, social psychologists are also interested in the mistakes we make in our perceptions of others. They describe these as cognitive errors in the processing of information, and argue that they are fundamental to our experience of social life. For example, the Fundamental Attribution Error (Heider 1958; cf. Jones and Nisbett 1971) occurs when we assume that someone else's behaviour in a situation reflects their stable traits of personality, despite being aware of how our own behaviour changes between situations. Meanwhile, the False Consensus Effect (Kelly 1967) describes a tendency to see one's own behaviour as typical and assume that others will behave in the same way.

But are these purely psychological phenomena, existing in a social vacuum? Many sociologists would argue that the self is a malleable entity, which changes form according to the normative demands of each situation: variations in behaviour reflect as much about cultural rules and expectations as they do about individual cognition. This is not to deny the reality of mental processes, but simply to locate them in a wider context of social forces, norms and values. The interplay between self and society can be understood at the micro-level, through interpretivist perspectives such as symbolic interactionism (see below), or at the macro-level, through the approaches to which we now turn.

Structural Functionalism

Within sociology, the approach most commonly associated with social order is that of Structural Functionalism. This perspective developed out of the work of Emile Durkheim (1893, 1895, 1912), who argued for a positivistic science of society: individual behaviour was governed by law-like social forces, emanating from society as an external entity. For

Durkheim (1982 [1895]), the patterns we observe in everyday life are interesting only insofar as they reveal these underlying forces and the social functions that they serve. For example, acts of religious worship involve collective practices, which create a sense of social solidarity through members' shared commitment to common values (Durkheim 1976 [1912]). The emphasis here is on consensus, conformity and regularity in social behaviour, which, though criticized for its 'oversocialized' conception of humankind (Wrong 1961), does explain how and why social order is upheld most of the time, by most people.

A second key theorist in this tradition was Talcott Parsons, who concentrated on the functionality of social systems, but argued that this operates through the voluntaristic action of individuals (1951). Thus although cultural norms and values constrained people's behaviour, they did have some choice in how they responded to structures, forces and institutions. Parsons and Bales (1956) argued that socialization was a key mechanism in this regard: members of a society were taught about the rules, norms and expectations of behaviour in their culture, and learned how to adhere to them. Thus social life was orderly because of people's expressions of commitment to common goals. This suggests a link to our theme of rituals and routines: social order can be seen not merely as an abstract concept, but rather as a dynamic, ongoing process, reproduced through human action. More recently, Randall Collins (2005) has argued that selves are constituted by 'interaction ritual chains' (cf. Goffman 1967a, 1967b), as we flow from one situation to another. We do not simply deal with the immediacies of each encounter, but rather link these together in our minds to create a sense of meaning, purpose and identity over time. This suggests an interesting complementarity between Structural Functionalism and Symbolic Interactionism (an approach discussed below), which is paradoxical and so often overlooked, but which opens up exciting new directions for theorizing.

A related approach that developed in the twentieth century was structural anthropology. Lévi-Strauss (1963) echoed Durkheim in pointing to the rule-governed nature of human behaviour, but saw the origins of this as lying not in dynamic social forces, but rather in the more static notion of a culture's 'deep structure'. This operated like a language or grammar, setting out rules and principles that were culturally universal but expressed in different surface level manifestations (Scott 2006). In particular, there was a tendency for societies to be organized around binary themes, such as raw/cooked or living/dead, and to have rituals that managed the transition from one to another. We revisit this idea throughout the book by reference to food and drink rituals (chapter 6), becoming sick (chapter 7) and moving between the spheres of work and leisure (chapter 9). More generally, a recurring theme is that macro-level social order is dependent on micro-level (inter)action for its accomplishment and reproduction.

Theorizing rituals and routines

Interpretivist sociology

Many of the theorists of everyday life can be located in the interpretivist tradition. This is a branch of social theory that emerged in opposition to the positivist, 'scientific' approach of the Enlightenment. Interpretivism is based upon the idea that the social world cannot be studied in an objective, scientific manner, because its subject matter is human beings, who have free will and act in unpredictable ways. Furthermore, researchers are themselves part of the social world that they are studying, which on the one hand puts them in a privileged position to understand it from the inside, but on the other hand complicates the process of making the familiar strange.

The German sociologist Max Weber (1949 [1904]) is often regarded as a founder of interpretivism, although he was in turn influenced by the philosophers Kant and Dilthey. Weber made a distinction between action (which is meaningful to the person) and mere behaviour (which is instinctive and unreflexive), and argued that the role of sociology was to interpret social action – that which took into account other people's meanings and motivations. The tool he offered for doing this was *verstehen*, or interpretative understanding: we should attempt to understand the local, subjective reality experienced by a particular person or group, by stepping into their shoes and taking their view of the social world.

This idea was later developed by Peter Winch (1958), who applied it to debates about ethnocentrism in cross-cultural research. Winch argued that it was only possible to understand another culture fully from the inside, and so Western theorists should be wary of imposing their interpretations upon 'other' cultures. It is for this reason that I ask you to bracket out any assumptions or value judgements you may have about your own way of life being normal, natural or 'right', because, if we adopt Winch's relativist approach, we can view all cultures (including our own) as equally 'strange'. No set of rules, norms or conventions is inherently 'right' or superior to any other, and so we cannot make any meaningful distinctions between them on the basis of these surface-level practices. What we can do, however, is to look for the common themes that recur across cultural contexts and which tell us something about the organization of social life. Lévi-Strauss (1963) called these 'structural universals', while Winch (1958) spoke of the 'grammar' underlying rule-following behaviour. Thus we might find that various cultures have different ways of exchanging gifts, preparing meals, treating illnesses, and so on, but that they all recognize these as important social activities and have a system in place to deal with them.

A third figure in this early interpretivist tradition was Georg Simmel, a German sociologist and contemporary of Weber. Simmel (1950c [1917]) believed that society was nothing more than individuals interacting in regular, patterned ways: individual motives became social motives through this process of 'sociation'. Simmel was interested in collective forms of action that were taken by groups, and emphasized the power that they had over the individual. He argued that we could study society by looking at the composition of different social groups (from the smallest partnership to the largest organization) and the effects of their activities on members and non-members. This 'formal' sociology involved studying both the forms and the contents of social life (ibid.). Forms were the general organizing principles of group action, such as proximity, conflict, subordination/domination, play and the division of labour. Contents were the manifestations of social forms that could be observed in specific contexts, such as subordination within a marriage or the division of labour within a household.

Phenomenology

Alfred Schütz was a German theorist who was interested in the way that we interpret outside events and objects (*noumena*, in Kant's (2003 [1781]) terms) and mentally impose definitions on them (*phenomena*). This set of symbolic representations constituted the 'lifeworld', a subjective impression of reality. Schütz argued that we experience the world as an ongoing stream of consciousness, and so have to decide how to divide this flow into meaningful sections. For example, in a typical day, we move between different physical settings and encounter different people, so we think of these as distinct situations or events that each mean different things and require different responses. In this way, we create our own subjective realities, which enable us to go about our everyday lives with a degree of confidence:

we think we know what the world is like, at least for the purposes of our own immediate behaviour within it. Schütz (1962, 1964) referred to this as the 'natural attitude', suggesting that, most of the time, we are not self-consciously aware of how or why we are constructing the world; we simply get on with doing it.

However, this is also a social world, filled with other people who each have their own interpretations of reality, so how do we manage to live alongside them? Rather than each living within our own separate bubbles, Schütz (1972) argued, we try to align our streams of consciousness with those of other people, to reach 'intersubjective agreement'. This is similar to the interactionist notion of the 'definition of the situation' (see below): all of the participants in a given situation share an understanding of what is going on and how they are expected to behave. We attribute meanings to each other's behaviour, which may be 'because' motives (referring to why someone has decided to do something) or 'in-order-to' motives (identifying what they hope to achieve by doing it). Meanwhile, these other people will be making the same interpretations of our own behaviour, and so there is a constant process of exchange as meanings are negotiated.

Once we have achieved our intersubjective agreement, Schütz argued, we tend to apply the same interpretations to other, similar scenarios that we encounter in future. It becomes a kind of template, or a lens through which we view new situations and make sense of other people's actions. It would be very tiring and time-consuming if we had to establish intersubjective agreement afresh every time we entered a new situation, and so we try to make the process more efficient. Schütz (1972) suggested the term 'recipe knowledge' to describe the information that we use in this way: on the basis of our prior experiences of similar situations, we develop an idea of their key 'ingredients' – what is going on, which roles people are playing, what will happen, and so on. For example, in a shop, we expect to find the goods we want, identify the staff, and carry out a transaction. Holding this recipe in our minds, we can fit the information from the new situation into the existing template and decide on an appropriate response. Schütz sometimes referred to these recipe ingredients as 'typifications', or beliefs about what will typically happen in this kind of situation. This provides us with a set of background expectations and assumptions, which enable us to enter them without thinking about how or why we should behave – they allow us to adopt the natural attitude.

The typifications of the lifeworld exert a powerful force upon us

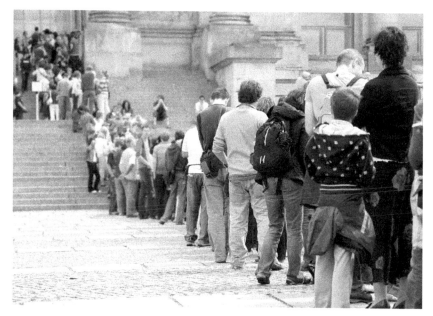

Figure 2.1 *Queuing is an interesting behaviour to observe. Unspoken rules dictate how close people stand, where they look and how they manage their bodies in social space. Queue jumpers break these rules – how are they sanctioned?*

because we forget that they are socially constructed: they appear to us as objective and external. It becomes difficult to 'think outside the box' once we have become accustomed to doing things in a certain way, and to seeing other people do the same. For example, in chapter 5, we see how clock time is an essentially arbitrary frame of reference that we have created to measure and allocate time, and yet we feel tied to our schedules. Such phenomena are reified social 'facts' (Berger and Luckmann 1967) that keep us committed to norm-following behaviour and reproduce the order of society. In some cases, however, our expectations are confounded or we are otherwise unable to act on the basis of our recipe knowledge, and so must 'suspend' the natural attitude. We shall see how this happens in the various discussions of challenges and rule-breaking throughout the book, for example the rituals of queuing (see chapter 5).

Ethnomethodology

This latter issue interested Harold Garfinkel, an American social scientist who developed an approach called ethnomethodology. For

Garfinkel, like Winch, social life was all about rule-following, which created a semblance of social order and made most situations flow smoothly. However, Garfinkel (1967) saw this orderliness as an interactional accomplishment: something that did not simply exist in the social world as a structure, imposing itself on individuals, but rather was created by these individuals in the course of their everyday lives. It was something to be constantly worked at – achieved and reachieved through actors' definitions of reality. He was famously critical of the 'cultural dopes' depicted in Structural Functionalism, whose behaviour was passively determined.

Consequently, Garfinkel argued that social order was precarious: it was upheld by routines, rituals and habits, but could easily be disrupted if such rules were not observed. As social behaviour was not determined by structural forces, and individuals were free to act as they chose, there was always the potential for rules to be broken and for the threads of social reality to be unravelled. From this perspective, it suddenly seems remarkable that most of everyday life is so ordered and predictable: why do we tend to play along by the rules and so rarely challenge them?

Garfinkel's answer to this was that we have a vested interest in upholding social order because of the benefits it provides, and so we effectively choose to follow rules – but always with the (implicit) awareness that we could do otherwise. This makes the social world appear stable and predictable, which in turn helps us to fit into it: we can bracket out uncertainties, adopt the natural attitude, and get on with our everyday lives. How exhausting would our lives become if we deliberated over everything we chose to say and do? We can therefore see social life as an implicit bargain: individuals trade some of their autonomy for the benefits of order and predictability, and this is a matter of skilful rule-following action and careful negotiation. The term 'ethnomethodology' reflects this, as it literally means 'the study of the methods used by people' to construct and make sense of their own everyday worlds.

Garfinkel was interested in the extent to which people are aware of the implicit rules they are following in interaction. He argued that, most often, these are 'seen but unnoticed' social norms, to which we do not consciously attend, but rather learn and then bracket out. This creates an unreflexive state of practical consciousness in everyday life, as we routinely apply the same methods to accomplish the same order. Like Schütz, Garfinkel thought that social encounters tend to run smoothly because we rely on the 'expected background features of everyday scenes' (Garfinkel 1967: 36). We have a set of taken for granted assumptions about how certain types of situation will proceed, and most of the time these are honoured by everyone involved. Social order thereby appears to us as an objective reality, and we forget that we created it: 'if men define situations as real, they are real in their consequences' (Thomas 1923: 572). However, when a rule is broken, we suddenly become aware of its existence, and of the precarious nature of the order around us. This means that, if we want to understand how a social group experiences its world, we should examine how it makes sense to its members. Which rules are they following – or breaking? What kind of shared, background knowledge do they have of each other and of the situation? How do these expectations help them to interpret what is going on? Garfinkel's approach is sometimes called the 'documentary method', because he collected examples of surface-level, mundane behaviours in this way and presented them as evidence (or documents) of underlying social rules.

One of the most important rules Garfinkel identified was indexicality. This is the idea that, in everyday encounters, we rely on a great deal of shared, tacit background knowledge about the situations we encounter, and do not need explicitly to address these points. We presume (or take for granted) that other people will share our understanding of a situation and follow the unspoken rules that govern it. We use speech figuratively rather than literally, include abbreviated or vernacular terms, and refer to people or objects that are not immediately present. As listeners, we also fill in the gaps of other people's speech to infer its meaning: Garfinkel called this the 'et cetera clause'. Non-verbal language can be used in the same way, of course, as we may use gestures to refer to concepts, actions or characteristics. In this way, Garfinkel said that most everyday interaction is indexical: the actual words that are uttered and gestures that are made on the surface serve as mere indices (indirect references) of a set of shared understandings. They can be regarded as 'the document of, as pointing to, as standing on behalf of an underlying pattern of matters that the person, by his speaking, could be telling the other about' (1967: 40). If we made all of this knowledge explicit, not only would our conversations become incredibly laborious and dreary but, more generally, social encounters would be impractical and take forever to complete; the smooth flow of interaction would grind to a halt. Interaction is therefore based as much upon what is left unspoken as what is explicitly said, and can be viewed as a document of underlying norms and values.

To illustrate this, Garfinkel examined an everyday conversation between a married couple, showing on one side what was actually said, and on the other, what this indexical speech referred to:

Husband: Dana succeeded in putting a penny in a parking meter today without being picked up.	This afternoon as I was bringing Dana, our four year old son, home from the nursery school, he succeeded in reaching high enough to put a penny in a parking meter when we parked in a meter parking zone, whereas before he has always had to be picked up to reach that high.
Wife: Did you take him to the record store?	Since he put a penny in a meter that means that you stopped while he was with you. I know that you stopped at the record store either on the way to get him or on the way back. Was it on the way back, so that he was with you, or did you stop there on the way to get him and somewhere else on the way back?

(Garfinkel 1967: 38–9)

Garfinkel then went on to look at instances of actual rule-breaking, which he engineered to demonstrate this point. He asked his students to conduct a series of 'breaching experiments', whereby they would challenge some of the taken for granted assumptions others had about a situation, and observe what happened. Garfinkel was much more interested in social reactions to rule-breaking than in the acts themselves, insofar as they revealed the group's normative expectations. One of his breaching experiments involved students acting as if they were lodgers in their own homes, observing the action from a position of detached neutrality that 'made the familiar strange'. They reported that it was difficult to maintain this charade for long, because it meant resisting their 'natural' inclination to join in with indexical conversations and help their families to sustain their definitions of reality: 'I was glad when the hour was up and I could return to the real me' (1967: 46), one student reported.

Another breaching experiment involved pedantic questioning, which directly challenged the rule of indexicality. Students were asked, when engaged in conversation, to bracket out all of the tacit, shared, background information that they would normally use to make sense of other people's speech, and to quiz their interlocutor about the precise meaning of their utterances:

S: Hi, Ray. How is your girl friend feeling?
E: What do you mean, 'How is she feeling?' Do you mean physical or mental?
S: I mean how is she feeling? What's the matter with you? (He looked peeved.)
E: Nothing. Just explain a little clearer what do you mean?
S: Skip it. How are your Med School applications coming?
E: What do you mean, 'How are they?'
S: You know what I mean.
E: I really don't.
S: What's the matter with you? Are you sick?

(Garfinkel 1967: 42)

The reaction of the poor, unsuspecting subject (S) here is typical of those reported by Garfinkel's experimenters (E). At first perplexed, the person assumes this is a temporary aberration from an otherwise 'normal' character, and tries to proceed with the encounter. Disruptions of the taken for granted make us feel uncomfortable by challenging our sense of personal identity and social reality, and so we are reluctant to acknowledge them. Eventually, however, as the experimenter continually refuses to play by the rules, the victim becomes angry and defensive, reacting with moral indignation to the breaches they observe. 'Why can't "E" just behave "normally" and make life easier for everyone?', they think. It must be the individual who has the problem ('Are you sick?') because the rules are beyond refute. This demonstrates the coercive power of social norms and rules: whenever they are seriously challenged, people move in to defend them, because our priority as social actors is to maintain the interaction order. We explore this idea more throughout the book, as we consider social reactions to rule-breaking behaviour in different social contexts.

Symbolic Interactionism

Interpretivist theory in general, and the Weberian concepts of *verstehen* and social action in particular, fuelled the development of American sociology in the twentieth century. Central to this body of work was the notion of the social self, proposed by James, Mead and Cooley. James (1890) made a distinction between the 'I', the agent of thought and action, and the 'Me', a version of the self presented to others; in this way we could have many different social selves. Mead (1934) developed this idea further, arguing that mind, self and society are all intertwined in a collective social process, and so the social self James talked about emerged from interaction. In Mead's view, the 'I' was the creative, impulsive agent of social action, while the 'Me' was an image of oneself as seen from the perspective of others, and these were two alternating phases of the self. However, Cooley (1983 [1902]) argued that the 'I' was equally socially shaped, for it was impossible to think of oneself without also considering other people and our relationship to them. Cooley wrote about the 'self-feelings' and 'self-sentiments' that defined the 'I', most famously in his concept of the 'Looking Glass Self'. This had three elements: imagining how we must appear to others, imagining how others might judge us, and the resultant self-feelings, such as pride or shame. We return to these ideas in chapter 3, when we discuss how emotions are shaped by social relationships: shyness and embarrassment are 'self-feelings' that emerge in exactly this way when we worry about how other people perceive us.

Symbolic Interactionism retained the idea of a dialectical relationship between self and society, but reversed the focus of inquiry. Instead of looking at the effects of group interaction on the self, the emphasis was on the processes of interaction themselves, how they were shaped by the different motivations of the participants, and the implications for social order. The term 'Symbolic Interactionism' was coined by Herbert Blumer (1969), who identified three basic principles: people act on the basis of meanings, these meanings emerge from interaction with others, and they have to be interpreted by the individuals concerned. Interactionists believe that the outcome of a social situation depends on the way that each person perceives and responds to it, because this affects everybody else's perceptions and behaviour, in an ongoing cycle.

Social life is therefore messy, complex, unpredictable and open-ended: people 'make' rather than passively 'take' their roles, and are constantly revising their behaviour in light of the behaviour of others. This is why interpretivists argue that we cannot have a pure science of society: human behaviour is not predictable or law governed, but rather contingent on the way that people interpret situations and influence each other. Thomas and Thomas (1970 [1928]) called this the 'definition of the situation', and emphasized that it was a collective understanding that emerged from each unique site of interaction. For example, one group of people sitting in a doctor's waiting room one day might have a completely different view of each other and of the situation from the group that sits there the next day.

What is interesting about these kinds of micro-level interactions is that, almost inevitably, the participants will strive to achieve a sense of order, to make the situation flow more smoothly. Whatever is going on, and however much conflict there may be between different people's interests, each individual wants to know some basic facts about the situation that will enable them to act: What is going on here? Which roles are other people playing? How do I fit in? When action is co-ordinated in this way, it creates what Strauss (1978) called a 'negotiated order': a higgledy-piggledy working definition of reality that remains open to reinterpretation. This reflects another paradox: everyday life is at once messy, complex and multiperspectival, and smooth, orderly and rule-governed. There is order in the chaos.

These ideas were consolidated in the work of the Chicago School, named after the university department of sociology in which its proponents worked. William Thomas and Everett Hughes were among these, as were Robert Park and Ernest Burgess, who championed the cause of empirical field research. It was only possible to understand the social world by getting out there and being in it, they said, because this allows us to obtain an insider's perspective on each social setting. This also reflected a pragmatist philosophy: meaning was identified in the way that people put their knowledge into action in their everyday lives. The Chicago School was responsible for a great number of empirical studies, including Becker's (1951) account of jazz musicians, Thrasher's (1927) ethnography of a street gang, and Thomas and Znaniecki's (1958 [1918–20]) analysis of the experiences of Polish immigrants to the United States. We continue to study everyday life in this tradition, by examining the local, subjective worlds of particular social groups or settings, and trying to identify the norms and values that shape behaviour in that context (see chapter 10).

Dramaturgy

One of the most famous figures in the symbolic interactionist tradition, although he did not define himself as such, was Erving Goffman. His social theory was built upon a dramaturgical metaphor: society could be compared to a theatre in which teams of actors performed different roles, like the characters in a play. Like James, Goffman (1959) believed that we have many social selves, as we tailor our performances to the audiences we meet in each situation and try to influence their view of us. Goffman called this 'impression management' and said that it involved techniques of 'self-presentation': we might use props, costumes, setting and scenery to create a particular character, but there would always be an underlying 'real self' in the actor.

Goffman made a distinction between two regions of the self that corresponded to the regions of the theatre. Frontstage was where performances were given, characters were presented, and the situation would flow smoothly: if anybody made an embarrassing blunder, others in the team would step in to conceal it, for 'the show must go on'. Backstage, however, actors could step out of character, let their masks slip and contradict the impressions they had given frontstage. For example, in a shop, we can distinguish between the shopfloor (frontstage), where customers are politely greeted, and the stockroom (backstage), where staff can drop their smiles, be themselves and insult the customers. The backstage area can be a source of great relief and comfort for the actors, as it provides valuable time for relaxation, practising techniques and reflecting on past performances, which in turn makes it more likely that future performances will be more smooth and orderly.

Goffman (1961b) wrote about interaction as occurring through 'encounters' between social actors. These might involve focused interaction, when people come together with a common purpose or shared focus of attention (such as a party or a seminar), or unfocused interaction, when people simply happen to be in each other's presence (for example, on the street). In both cases, the actors will be trying to establish a common definition of the situation, but they will each have their own agendas in terms of the characters they want to perform. For example, in a classroom, although everyone is there to learn and is studying the same subject matter, individual students may assume the roles of the class clown, the swot, the reluctant attendee, and so on. Nevertheless, these roles complement each other and so, together, the team gives a collective performance. With these performances occurring in each micro-level social encounter, Goffman argued, the overall effect is one of stability; he called this the interaction order. The latter notion goes some way towards addressing criticisms of Symbolic Interactionism for neglecting structural factors (see, for example, Stryker 1980).

In order for this to work, Goffman (1963b) said that actors must demonstrate their 'accessibility', or openness to interaction. This involves both a practical preparedness and a moral willingness to co-operate with others and establish a shared definition of the situation. We usually display this by default whenever we are out in public: a polite smile and cheerful countenance lets those around us know that we can be co-opted into their performances. In some cases, however, we try to give the impression that we cannot be interrupted: have you ever avoided eye contact with a *Big Issue* seller, market researcher or homeless person asking for 'spare change'? Rather than experience the embarrassment of an awkward encounter, we avoid such inter-action altogether. We sometimes use 'involvement shields' to show such inaccessibility to others, for example by burying one's head in a newspaper or playing with a mobile phone. Indeed, more gener-ally, Goffman suggested that we use material 'props' to perform our characters in everyday life.

Normally, however, actors do work harmoniously together and strive to keep a situation flowing smoothly. Goffman (1967a) said that we support our team-mates' performances by keeping each other 'in face' – that is, accepting the impression they are trying to convey (even if we do not really believe in it) and playing along with the game. Goffman identified two kinds of 'facework' that we perform in this way: defensive strategies sustain our own public characters, while protective strategies sustain those of other people. For example, if Jack were to ask Jill out on a date but she turned him down, he might try (defensively) to save face by pretending that he was 'not that inter-ested anyway', while she might try (protectively) to keep him in face by pretending that she was dating someone else. Facework can extend to whole groups of people, too, as we shall see in chapters 3 and 7.

Structuration theory

A more comprehensive approach, which developed in the late twen-tieth century through the work of the British sociologist Anthony Giddens, was structuration theory. While he endorsed Garfinkel's insights into the minutiae of social action, Giddens (1984) criticized ethnomethodology for its neglect of social structure; similar criticisms have been levelled at Symbolic Interactionism (Stryker 1980; Ritzer 1996). If we are all, most of the time, following social rules, where do these rules come from and how are they established? Giddens envis-aged an ongoing cycle of structure and agency, whereby each fed back into the other. In terms of agency, Giddens argued that social actors are skilled and knowledgeable, and that we operate on two distinct levels of consciousness. Practical consciousness (Garfinkel's term) is what we use to perform routine, habitual actions without thinking about them, using Schütz's 'recipe knowledge'. Discursive conscious-ness is a state of mind into which we can suddenly shift when our expectations are confounded: like the unwitting subjects in Garfinkel's breaching experiments, we may suddenly become aware of a rule's existence when it is broken. For example, Giddens suggested that, most of the time, we follow routines without thinking about them: they are unreflective and habitual. It is only when something out of the ordinary happens that we realize we have these routines, and how much we rely upon them. Routines provide comfort and familiarity, so we feel anxious if prevented from following them.

Meanwhile, structure, for Giddens, did not mean abstract social forces, but rather everyday rules and routines, which, when adhered to, reproduce social reality. Structure is present both before an action (by providing the conditions for it) and afterwards (as actions have intended or unintended consequences) (Stones 2005). As we have seen, structure shapes individuals' behaviour, because we perceive these rules and routines to be real, objective and beyond question, and so we (usually) follow them. Three categories of rule (semantic, regulative and transformative) suggest three corresponding types of action (discourse and ideology, sanctioning, and resource allocation). These actions in turn feed back into the social structure, because they reinforce our assumptions about what is normal in our culture and how other people should behave. Even rule-breaking actions feed back into the structure, either by evoking a reaction of moral indignation to defend it (as Garfinkel's experiments showed) or by leading to its modification (as, for example, laws are changed to reflect changing social attitudes). This reminds us of the interplay between the micro and the macro – or how small-scale interactions in our everyday lives reflect wider issues of social order.

However, Giddens's theory has been criticized by the realist Margaret Archer (1995), who claimed that it was misleading to conflate structure and agency. She argued for a relationship of dualism rather than duality: the two aspects of the process should remain analytically separate, because this is how they appeared in the real world. This raises the important question of where society ends and individuals begin: to what extent are our actions constrained by external forces (even socially constructed ones), and how much power do we have to resist them?

Theorizing challenges

Cultural Studies

Our final set of theories builds upon these questions by examining where social norms and rules come from, and whose interests they might serve. Critical theories have been widely applied at the macro-level, most famously in the work of Marx, but also have implications for understanding conflict at the micro-level (cf. Mellinger 2008). Cultural Studies is a discipline that is concerned with the ways in which powerful groups' ideologies (interests, ideas and values) are transmitted through the 'texts' of the everyday world (Farmer 2003; Moran 2005). These might include literary or visual scripts from the mass media, but equally may be places, scenes or sites of interaction, such as the queue (Schwartz 1975) or bus shelter (Moran 2005).

The researcher's role is then to deconstruct and critically read such texts, identifying any subtle messages within them. The semiologist Barthes (1972 [1957]) made a distinction between the denotative meaning evident in the manifest appearance of a cultural sign and its connotative, underlying meaning, found once it had been critically decoded. However, lay people were also adept at interpreting the meaning of these signs, albeit unknowingly, and thus 'mythologies' (encoded ideologies) were transmitted through music, fashion, advertising and other texts of popular culture.

Ideologies are enormously powerful in shaping our understanding of the world and our place within it (Hall 1997), which in turn shapes social action. For example, in chapter 8, we consider how consumer culture has created a new set of reasons for and places in which to go 'lifestyle shopping', while chapter 9 discusses Urry's (2002) argument that the 'tourist gaze' has changed the way that we design vacations.

Post-structuralism

A related approach, which has influenced many Cultural Studies theorists in recent years, is that of post-structuralism. Here the aim is also to critically deconstruct the messages implicit in cultural texts, but, rather than revealing the interests of a powerful group, these are thought to reveal more nebulous power relations. For example, Derrida (1978 [1967]) pointed to the ways in which some social groups were 'erased' or written out of popular consciousness because of their absence from historical accounts. It is therefore important to consider what cultural texts both do and do not include. For example, in chapter 7, we examine the social model of disability, which points to the way in which physical and social settings feature disabling barriers to participation for less able-bodied people.

This is a vision of power as being dispersed throughout society, rather than concentrated in the hands of a few. Foucault (1980 [1976]) argued that power operated through discourses, or ways of seeing, thinking and representing social phenomena, which come to be seen as natural. A parallel can be drawn here with Berger and Luckmann's (1967) notion of reification, whereby socially constructed ideas define the phenomenological reality of the lifeworld (Schütz 1972; see above). As we shall see throughout the book, one of the most significant mechanisms of social control in modern societies is disciplinary power (Foucault 1977 [1975]), whereby people internalize the discourses surrounding them and begin to impose these on themselves. If we believe that we are choosing to conform to normative expectations, then we do not feel controlled. Examples of this are discussed in chapter 3 (discourses of romantic love and the pressure to overcome shyness) and chapter 6 (discourses of healthy eating), among others. However, it is also worth remembering Foucault's argument that, where there is power, there will also be resistance: we shall therefore be considering many counter-discourses that challenge these taken for granted assumptions, such as the aforementioned social model of disability (chapter 7), 'Shy Pride' (Scott 2007) and the pro-anorexia movement (chapter 6).

New sociologies of everyday life

As we saw in chapter 1, these critical approaches culminated in the development of a more explicit social scientific study of everyday life in the twentieth century. *La vie quotidienne* was recognized as an important object of study in its own right, rather than just a residual category of mundane trivia (Lefebvre 2008 [1947]; de Certeau 1984). Although the sites of everyday life were characterized by repetition, routine and familiarity, this did not mean that they were devoid of political interests, ideologies and subtle forms of social control. Lefebvre (2008 [1947]) argued that the routines in which we take comfort keep us trapped in a state of pre-reflective consciousness, which prevent us from realizing the true, exploitative conditions of our existence. These theories have been criticized for expressing an air of middle-class complacency: the 'enlightened' intellectuals were claiming privileged insights into how society really worked and how 'the masses' were being duped (Bennett 2004). Nevertheless, insofar as Lefebvre and de Certeau were urging their readers to think more critically, there was a definite spirit of resistance to their work. For example, de Certeau (1984) argued for the agentic ways in which we practise, or 'do', everyday life, which may either reproduce or resist social norms.

This underlines the connections between our three themes: the rituals we observe in everyday practices, the social control that they indicate, and the opportunities they afford for challenge and resistance. In de Certeau's (1984) view, there were many opportunities for 'making do' with subversive practices, such as adapting, appropriating or reassembling materials: graffiti-ing a wall, taking an alternative route around an urban space, refusing to conform to the 9–5 working day, and so on. While each of these acts may seem inconsequential in isolation, they are significant in reminding us that we do have some choice, that the world is not as natural and inevitable as it appears. Lefebvre (2008 [1947]) called these 'moments': sudden flashes of insight into how the everyday world is socially constructed, and how precarious this definition of reality is. This book is intended both to demonstrate how such processes occur and to encourage a more critical awareness that lends itself to interpretative 'moments'.

Summary points

- The self is embedded in the social world, and so our private thoughts and feelings are related to cultural norms, values and interaction.
- Psychoanalytic theories claim that our social behaviour is driven by unconscious emotional forces that have to be tamed or 'civilized'.
- Social psychologists study the way in which we cognitively process information about other people and their relation to us.
- Structural Functionalism focuses on 'society' as an entity that exerts social forces upon individuals' behaviour. This suggests consensus, conformity and, arguably, passivity.
- Symbolic Interactionism considers how the social self is shaped through the exchange of symbolic gestures between actors, and how these people work as 'teams' to keep a situation flowing smoothly. One branch of this is Goffman's dramaturgical perspective.
- Phenomenology examines the ways in which people construct their own social realities through the 'lifeworld', using recipe knowledge and typifications.
- Ethnomethodology addresses the precariousness of these techniques by challenging people's taken for granted assumptions.
- Structuration theory recognizes the interplay between structure and agency in reproducing the social world.

- Cultural Studies involves decoding and deciphering the messages implicit in cultural texts, which include places, sites or ritual practices. These messages are usually read critically as political discourses or ideologies.
- Post-structuralist theorists such as Foucault saw power as dispersed through insidious discourses and disciplinary regimes.
- Lefebvre and de Certeau argued for a critical analysis of everyday life in terms of its ritual practices, mechanisms of control and opportunities for resistance.

3   Emotions

The sociology of emotions is a relatively new area of social theory that has emerged since the late twentieth century, through the world of Hochschild (1983), Bendelow and Williams (1998) and Denzin (2007). This served as a challenge to existing psychological and biological theories of emotion (e.g. Tomkins 1962, 1963; Izard 1972), which had referred to innate cognitive or neurological mental processes of 'affect'. Sociologists put these individual experiences in their wider cultural context by considering how we make sense of emotions and regulate their impact on our everyday lives. For example, Lupton (1998) talks about the 'emotional self' as something that emerges out of the relationship between the individual and society. Similarly, Bendelow and Williams (1998) argue that the emotions lie at the juncture of many dichotomies in Western thought, such as mind/body, culture/nature, reason/passion, public/private – and perhaps even masculinity/femininity. Because they lie on the boundaries of these realms, emotions pose a possible threat to the orderly divisions in society, and so have to be 'managed' and controlled.

A famous example of this is Arlie Hochschild's (1983) study of 'emotion work' in the service industry. Her interviews with air stewardesses revealed that they were trained to suppress certain emotions (such as anger, boredom or resentment) and display others (cheerfulness and generosity), for example by smiling and being polite to customers who were annoying them. Hochschild called this the performance of 'emotional labour', and argued that, eventually, the employees began genuinely to feel the emotions they were trying to convey: they gave what Goffman (1959) called 'sincere performances', as they believed in the parts that they were playing. However, the employees said that they felt empty and depressed as a result: it was as if their emotions had been taken away from them and sold to the organization for which they worked. Hochschild used this case to demonstrate how emotions were becoming increasingly commercialized – repackaged as commodities and sold to a market of demanding consumers. The study also illustrates the interplay between micro-level rituals and routines and macro-level social order.

We should be wary of being too 'social determinist' in our arguments, however. Ian Craib (1997), a psychoanalyst and sociologist, criticized the latter discipline for trying to explain too much about emotions. He argued strongly for the view that emotions have a private, inner life of their own, although the ways in which they are expressed, defined and managed may be shaped by cultural factors (or, as he called them, 'social scaffolding'). He suggested that, as well as the external emotion work that Hochschild described, there was internal emotion work that goes on at an unconscious level. This chapter explores this complex relationship between the two realms through the examples of love, embarrassment and shyness, which are broadly indicative of our three themes: respectively, social order, rituals and routines, and challenges to the taken for granted.

Love and social order

A biological necessity?

What does it mean to fall in love? Hollywood movies and romantic novels convey the message that love is mysterious and enchanting: we all have a 'soul-mate' out there, waiting to be found, and with whom we will live 'happily ever after'. Social scientists, however, are more sceptical. The Darwinian theory of evolution led some sociobiologists, such as Dawkins (2006 [1976]), to argue that we pursue relationship partners simply to procreate, or spread our 'selfish gene'. However, Jolly (1999) pointed out that this may explain sex, but not love: perhaps we have an equally instinctive urge to co-operate, be altruistic and form lasting bonds with others?

This is the view taken by many social psychologists, who seek to identify the factors that shape 'interpersonal attraction': what do individuals stand to gain from entering into relationships, and what makes these partnerships last? According to Gross (2005), we are more likely to be attracted to someone if they meet certain criteria. At the simplest level, mere proximity, exposure and familiarity are important: the most common way of meeting a relationship partner is through work, where we spend a large proportion of our everyday lives (Lever 2006).

Another factor is the perceived similarity of our values, attitudes and beliefs: we like people who endorse and validate our views, thereby building our self-esteem (Rubin 1973). Paradoxically, this can also occur when 'opposites attract', because we define ourselves relative to others and gain a stronger sense of identity from knowing what makes us distinct. Gross goes on to say that we like people who are competent yet fallible (seemingly 'perfect' people are intimidating), and who are of a similar level of physical attractiveness to ourselves, but that our perceptions of what constitutes male and female beauty depend on the cultural context.

Orderly routines

Once we have met a prospective partner, the process of courtship begins, and this, too, seems patterned and orderly. Courtship rituals are shaped by norms and values, which are heavily gendered: for example, we sometimes hear people refer to the (now rather outdated) 'rules' of dating etiquette, which prescribe female modesty and self-restraint (Fein and Schneider 1995). Within academia, too, Duck (1988) suggests that much of the research into courtship is value-laden. For example, there is an assumption that the longevity of a relationship is a measure of its success, and that conflict and relationship breakdown is necessarily a bad thing. By contrast, the recent trend towards serial monogamy (see below) suggests that we expect to try and fail at several relationships before 'settling down', and actually think of success in terms of short-term individual happiness. Duck also criticizes the assumption that love develops gradually and naturally through increasing levels of intimacy, because this depends on sociodemographic factors. Couples who marry relatively young (before age twenty) are more likely to divorce (Norton and Moorman 1987), as are those who cohabit before marrying (Newcomb 1986). Duck therefore concludes that the mass media's depiction of romantic love has given us unrealistic ideas about finding and maintaining the 'perfect', conflict-free relationship.

As for what makes relationships last, a social psychological explanation comes from Homans's (1974) exchange theory: we rationally weigh up the costs and benefits of being with someone, and only remain in the relationship if we feel that we are getting out as much as we are putting in. Gross (2005) suggests that this is indicative of a wider principle of equity: relationships should be fair, and we are only prepared to invest in one emotionally if we believe that our feelings will be reciprocated (cf. Brown 1986). This may sound rather cold-hearted and calculating, but, as Kate Fox (2004) argues, the rule of fairness is ultimately a moral one that governs everyday life. We select our relationship partners within a cultural context of discourses, myths and ideals about normal, desirable behaviour, and so we compare what is actually happening with our 'recipe knowledge' (see chapter 2) about human relationships. Like Duck, Fox reminds us that the rationality and free will that we supposedly exercise when managing our feelings is in fact shaped by the 'seen but unnoticed' rules of social convention.

Valentine's Day: structured spontaneity?

We can see this from an examination of some of the rituals and routines through which romantic love is demonstrated. Think of Valentine's Day, for example. This is often celebrated by couples in Western societies through an elaborate set of rituals. The day might begin with an exchange of cards (adorned with pictures symbolizing love, such as hearts and flowers) and presents (also on a romantic theme – red roses, chocolates or 'sexy' lingerie). One partner might make the other breakfast in bed, run a bubble bath, or find other ways of 'pampering' their loved one. Throughout the day, the couple might take a romantic stroll through the park (more flowers) or, if at work, exchange secret messages by text or email, giving them a sense of exclusivity: the value of a dyadic relationship comes from its perceived uniqueness and rarity (Simmel 1950b [1908]: 125–6). In the evening, they will typically go out for a 'romantic' meal, for which they will 'make an effort' to 'get dressed up', and which is symbolized by certain signifiers: candlelight, soft music, luxurious food and wine. To the actors involved, each of these things may seem spontaneous and natural: we think that we are making an individual choice to select a particular card, present or meal, even though we might grumble about Valentine's Day being 'so commercialized'. But what about the wider cultural values embedded in these symbols of romantic love: where do these ideas come from? What makes flowers – and roses in particular – so important, and why are certain foods 'sexier' than others? Are these really spontaneous displays of heartfelt emotion, or are we swayed by social convention? Is the idea of romance gendered, or heterosexually biased? What would happen if we expressed these lustful feelings every day of the year instead of saving them for February 14th?

Figure 3.1 *Valentine's Day celebrations involve certain stylized ingredients: flowers, wine, a meal ... but is romantic love just a matter of social rituals?*

Power, ideology and discourses of romance

Sociologists have been largely critical of the notion of romantic love, arguing that it is a socially constructed, culturally defined concept. Sullivan (1999), for example, suggests that falling in love is a socially learned experience: we are socialized into ways of thinking about and expressing this emotion, rather than its being an instinctive force of nature. We learn what it means to be 'in love' and how to perform this appropriately, as evidenced by the culturally specific rituals of Valentine's Day, dating, wedding ceremonies, and so on. Jackson (1993) similarly argues that the subjective experience of emotions such as love is always connected to wider discourses and ideologies. She criticizes the cultural construction of romantic love as something that oppresses women by its emphasis on female passivity and help-lessness. Romantic novels, films and soap operas often employ narra-tives of seduction and enchantment, with couples being overwhelmed by the 'mysterious force' of love. Evans (2003) agrees that we are socialized into the discourses of romantic love, and that this helps us to 'tame' our sexual drives: for example, we learn that promiscuity is deviant and liable to sanction, which leads us into more conventional, monogamous relationships. This relates to the more psychoanalyti-cally informed view of Marcuse (1955) that our unconscious lustful feelings have been 'civilized' by modern culture: we are permitted to express desire only in socially acceptable ways.

Of course, this is changing, and Evans (2003) points to the greater sexual freedom we now have to experience serial monogamy, experiment with different sexual identities, and indulge in casual sex without emotional attachment. The gendered rules of courtship have become less rigid, too, with more women initiating (and ending) relationships, proposing marriage, and asserting their right to choose whether, when and how often to have sex. This suggests that the everyday experience of love may be diversifying, although the structural impact of this may be slower to change.

If our relationship behaviour is rule-governed in this way, we might think about the consequences that this has for social order. For example, the modern nuclear family (a married couple and their children) was understood by functionalist sociologists Parsons and Bales (1956) to have emerged as an institution of industrial society, whose main functions were to socialize children and stabilize adult personalities. Conjugal roles within this family were gendered, with the man playing an 'instrumental' role (bringing home money to provide for his dependants) and the woman playing an 'expressive' role (as the supportive nurturer of her family's emotional needs). Between them, husband and wife sustained a steady flow of healthy workers for industrial capitalist society. Of course, this theory has since been criticized for justifying an exploitative patriarchal division of domestic labour (see, for example, Barrett and McIntosh 1991) and for being outdated in terms of women's growing participation in paid employment, but it is interesting to consider how pervasive such an ideology remains. For example, Duncombe and Marsden's (1993) interviews with sixty married or cohabiting heterosexual couples in the UK revealed that women bore the burden of performing most of the emotional labour (Hochschild 1983) in the relationship, while men were reluctant to discuss their feelings. Heterosexual marriage is often assumed to be the logical, desired endpoint of most courtship rituals, but it is an institution that is structured by quite rigid gender roles.

Furthermore, we can also witness many challenges to this 'heteronormativity' (Butler 1999 [1990]). Following the Divorce Reform Act of 1969, the number of divorces in the UK rose from 27,224 in 1961 to a peak of 180,018 in 1993, and remained steady at around 150,000 for most of the period 1985–2004; however, the rate has actually begun to decline since then (ONS 2007a). A similar pattern has been noted in the USA (US Census Bureau 2000) and Australia (Australian Bureau of Statistics 2006). Consequently, there has been a threefold increase in the number of families headed by lone parents in the UK, from 8 per cent in 1972 to nearly 24 per cent in 2006 (ONS 2007a, 2007b). Again, a similar trend can be found in Australia, where the corresponding figure had increased to 22 per cent in 2003 (Australian Bureau of Statistics 2006). Cohabitation before marriage, and increasingly instead of it, is now very common, and the introduction of gay and lesbian civil partnerships in some Western societies has challenged certain taken for granted assumptions about what it means to be in love.

Giddens (1992) suggests that the cultural climate of 'late modern' Western societies has changed our understanding of the role of intimacy in relationships. No longer seeking to settle down and reproduce as quickly as possible, he says, we now proceed with caution. Serial monogamy has become the norm, as we 'test drive' various relationships, one after another, until we find the right one. The late modern self is ontologically insecure and highly self-reflexive, and so, in each relationship, the individual will be constantly weighing up the costs and benefits of staying versus going. If the relationship is deemed unsatisfying, they are free to cut their losses and walk away. This kind of 'pure relationship', Giddens argues, epitomizes contemporary attitudes to love and explains the apparent fragmentation of the stable, nuclear family. On the other hand, sociologists have argued that the high rates of remarriage, cohabitation and non-heterosexual unions indicate that we remain committed to an ideal of relationship stability (Fulcher and Scott 2007). Love may be a powerful subjective feeling, but it is undeniably shaped by social factors.

Embarrassment and ritual performances

Disrupted routines

Embarrassment is one of the most common emotional states that we experience in everyday life. It is also one of the 'self-conscious emotions' (Tangney and Fischer 1995) – the others being shame, guilt, pride and shyness – that occur when we reflect upon our own behaviour or status. We feel embarrassed when we perceive that we have broken a social rule, but, as Harré (1990) points out, these are infractions of relatively minor rules or norms. An actor who breaks a more serious, formal rule will often be committing a crime, and is more likely to feel guilt or shame than embarrassment. The latter therefore suggests concerns about self-presentation (Goffman 1959): it is not that we think we have actually done something terribly wrong, but rather that we might appear to others as immoral, stupid, rude, and so on. This requires the presence of an audience, who are thought to be critically evaluating one's (poor) performance; embarrassment occurs when we are in public, not in private (unless we are imagining an audience). Edelmann (1987) argues that a defining feature of embarrassment is a perceived discrepancy between the self-image that we would like to convey and the one that we believe we have conveyed: in Goffman's (1959) terms, between expressions 'given' and 'given off'. Miller similarly defines embarrassment as 'that state of awkward abashment and chagrin that results from public events that disrupt our expectations and communicate unwanted impressions of ourselves to others' (Miller 1996: 10).

What is going on when we make these minor blunders? Ethnomethodologists would say that they constitute a breach of taken for granted assumptions (Garfinkel 1967) or residual rules (Scheff 1984 [1966]). In chapter 2 we saw how these are tacit expectations that we share about how people will behave in a given situation, based on typifications and shared background knowledge (Schütz 1972). Residual rules reflect 'common sense' or 'what everyone knows', and are so deeply entrenched in our everyday lives that we rarely question them. Gross and Stone therefore suggest that embarrassment occurs 'whenever some *central* assumption in a transaction has been unexpectedly and unqualifiedly discredited' (1973: 102, emphasis in original): one person acts so surprisingly that the smooth flow of action is disturbed and the encounter grinds to an awkward halt. They go on to say that this is most likely to happen when a situation requires continuous and co-ordinated role performances, for there is a greater potential for someone to slip up. A traditional Christian wedding ceremony, for example, demands carefully choreographed displays from the bride, groom, best wo/man, bridesmaids, vicar and church congregation, and if any one of these actors makes a blunder, it will affect all the others and the show as a whole.

However, we can identify patterns in this behaviour that suggest traces of social order. For example, social psychologists have attempted to categorize the types of situation that might cause embarrassment. Gross and Stone (1973) suggest that the presentation of an 'inappropriate identity' is embarrassing, and this can be due to inconsistency, mistakes or unsupported claims. As an example of inconsistent identity, a student might behave quite differently in the company of his friends than in the company of his family, and so when his parents visit him at university he does not know how to act and becomes embarrassed. Cases of mistaken identity occur when we forget someone's name, address them wrongly or confuse them with someone else; we feel embarrassed when our incompetence is revealed. Unsupported identity claims embarrass actors who have tried to present themselves as one thing but are exposed as something else: for example, a dinner party guest tries to impress her upper-class hosts but uses the 'wrong' cutlery.

Miller (1996) offers a typology of four kinds of situation that evoke embarrassment. Firstly, individual behaviours include trips, falls, slips of the tongue, or mere conspicuousness – for example, realizing that you are dressed inappropriately for a social gathering. Interactive behaviours involve a collective loss of script that is embarrassing for everybody, as in the wedding example above. Audience provocation occurs when someone tries deliberately to embarrass someone else, by teasing, praising or criticizing them. Finally, bystander behaviour is embarrassing insofar as witnessing someone else's mistakes can be uncomfortable to watch. This may be either because empathizing with them makes us cringe on their behalf (vicarious embarrassment) or because they are associated with us and their behaviour reflects on our own status (team transgressions). An example of the latter is the child who has a tantrum in the supermarket, thus embarrassing his parents (see chapter 7).

Displays and strategies

Embarrassment is a social emotion not only in its origins but also in its effects. These can be seen in the way that both the individuals themselves and those around them react to the embarrassing act. Firstly, the embarrassed actor is self-consciously aware of their predicament, and this may be expressed in different ways. The feelings may leak out non-verbally through bodily signs, most notably blushing. Leary et al. (1992) argue that this is a response to *unwanted* social attention: we do not see models blushing, or performing artists doing so when in character. Crozier (2006) suggests that blushing occurs when private information about the self is exposed to public scrutiny, resulting in self-consciousness. He describes a shift in perspective to the standpoint of 'the other', as we suddenly see ourselves as the (real or imagined) audience would see us. This is an example of Cooley's (1983 [1902]) Looking Glass Self (see chapter 2): the blush reflects an awareness of how one is appearing to others and how they are judging that appearance. Writing in *The Guardian*, Cherry Nixon recalls, 'I wanted to be seen as cool and calm but my reddening cheeks were forever misrepresenting me' (Nixon 2007: 2).

Social reactions

People use various tactics to deal with embarrassment. The culpable individual may try to escape the scrutiny they face, either by evading the issue (pretending it didn't happen or glossing over it), fleeing the immediate situation, or avoiding similar situations in future. In Scott and Lyman's (1968) terms, they may try to account for the mistake by providing either an excuse (agreeing that the behaviour was wrong but denying responsibility for it) or a justification (accepting responsibility but denying that it was wrong). They may also offer an apology, which often serves to appease a disgruntled audience: it reassures onlookers that, while this action was undesirable, it was out of character for the individual, who recognizes their mistake and is unlikely to repeat it (Goffman 1956). Finally, the individual may use humour to deal with their embarrassment: 'laughing it off' is perhaps the most common technique we use to ameliorate the seriousness of a blunder and to show that no real harm has been done. Humour makes the audience warm to an embarrassed actor, who can then be trusted to remain in play.

A second set of reactions to embarrassment come from other people, who observe the incident. Goffman (1956) argued that, because we are all dramaturgical team-mates in the theatre of social life, when we see someone looking flustered and uncomfortable, we try to help them out. Although they may endure good-natured teasing or 'ribbing' by their friends, it is rare to see embarrassed people being left to flounder in the spotlight. Goffman said that team-mates step in to 'repair' embarrassing situations and to keep the individual in face; he later called this behaviour protective facework (Goffman 1967a). For example, a man who trips over will be helped to his feet and dusted down, while an audience will laugh along with a woman who makes a joke about her own *faux pas*, to reassure her that it does not matter. Sometimes team-mates show what Goffman (1959) called 'tact' or discretion, by politely pretending not to notice a mistake and carrying on with what they had been doing. We often see this with speech errors and lapses of control over the body: observers will 'gloss over' the mistake and 'carry' the situation for the next few moments until the blunderer has regained her composure and can come back into play. Goffman (1956) said that these kinds of social reactions are crucial in maintaining the interaction order, for they restore a damaged situation to 'normal appearances' and allow the performance to continue.

Embarrassing acts, therefore, are those that occur within the rituals and routines of interaction and pose a challenge to taken for granted assumptions. They evoke supportive social reactions that keep the actor in face, thereby helping to maintain micro-level social order.

Shyness: challenging expectations

By contrast to embarrassment, shyness is a form of self-consciousness that appears to serve no social function. It involves a feeling of apprehension about embarrassing events that may not even occur and prevents people from participating as much as they would like in social life. Nevertheless, a study that I conducted (Scott 2004a, 2004b, 2005, 2007) revealed that this too is a social emotion, not just a property of certain individuals' minds. Through in-depth interviews and an email-based discussion list, I collected data from forty self-defined 'shy' people in the form of narratives about their personal experiences of shyness. Using a Symbolic Interactionist perspective, I investigated which kinds of social encounters evoked feelings of shyness (cf. Zimbardo 1977), how shy behaviour challenged social norms and expectations, and how other people reacted to this deviance.

Perceptions of self and others

Mead's (1934) model of the social self (see chapter 2) can be applied to shyness, insofar as the shy self comprises two phases: the Shy 'I' and the Shy 'Me' (Scott 2004a). The first refers to the subjective experience of feeling shy – an emotional state of anxiety and inhibition. The second term refers to an image of oneself as shy, viewed from the perspective of others. These phases work in a cycle, reinforcing each other: we feel shy, realize that we appear shy to others, and feel increasingly self-conscious. Blushing may occur, as we perceive private thoughts and feelings to be 'leaking' out to public scrutiny (Crozier 2006). Shyness emerges from interaction when an actor defines themselves as lacking the 'social skills' necessary to perform as they would wish, and worries that they will give the impression of incompetence. This self-image is defined by contrast to those around the individual, who are seen as relatively skilled and poised for action. Adapting Mead's notion of the Generalized Other, I suggest that shy actors see their team-mates and audiences as a 'Competent Other': they believe that everyone else understands the unspoken rules of behaviour in the situation and that it is only they who do not (Scott 2004a, 2007). For example, one of my respondents, Emma, said, 'I think people are more confident and can handle situations better than I can ... they don't seem to be worried [about] what others think' (Scott 2007: 63).

Team players and impostors

How does shyness emerge out of social interaction? My research suggested that it is a common response to dramaturgical stress (cf. Goffman 1959): if we perceive a situation to require a particular role performance that we feel ill-equipped to give, we worry about making an embarrassing mistake, appearing 'stupid' and creating an atmosphere of awkwardness for everyone (Scott 2005). Insofar as the shy actor is already in the situation, they cannot avoid it, and so must try to behave appropriately. This is stressful because the individual feels like an impostor who may be exposed at any moment. Furthermore, the shy actor fears that their team-mates will not provide protective facework if they do make such a blunder, and so they will be left alone to flounder under the spotlight. Shyness therefore emerges from interaction when a person anticipates giving an incompetent performance that will lead to criticism, embarrassment and rejection (Scott 2007). As another respondent, Nook, explained, 'It's like I'm being asked not to be myself but to put on an act. I don't really know what the act should be, and when I try, I just feel like I'm lying to everyone and being dishonest' (ibid.: 97).

Disguises and concealment

Interestingly, shyness is not only a response to performative situations, but it can also be a performance in itself. Managing shyness day to day involves preparing 'lines' of action (Goffman 1967b) that enable the individual to survive each difficult situation with the minimum unwanted attention. There are a number of dramaturgical strategies that can be employed to achieve this, either by allowing the shy actor to 'pass' (Goffman 1963a) as non-shy or by minimizing their involvement in the situation. In the latter case, we find these individuals 'hovering on the fringes' of a gathering, trying to fade into the background and not be noticed; they may decide to remain quiet rather than risk saying the 'wrong' thing. Meanwhile, in order to 'pass', actors may learn tactics for disguising their shyness (Scott 2005). They can conduct 'backstage rehearsals' by planning out what they will do and say in a particular situation, often to the point of literally writing a script. My participant Connie remembered doing this before getting on the bus, 'to make the situation as short as possible, talking to the bus driver', while Georgia wrote herself some notes before telephoning the gas company. Another strategy for passing is to use props that function as what Goffman (1963b) called 'side involvements'. These are subsidiary activities, such as smoking, drinking or checking a mobile phone, which accompany the main focus of an encounter and can help to distract the audience's attention from a poor performance. For example, Urchin explained how

> eating in a social situation gives me something to do with my hands and face, and takes the pressure off me to interact with other people. So, at a drinks-party type of affair, I'll spend much of the time at the food table, stuffing myself with crisps and Twiglets ... I find coping with other people easier if I'm doing something else at the same time – if socialising and conversation aren't the only purpose of our being together. (Scott 2007: 112)

Each of these dramaturgical strategies is carefully devised, practised and performed by social actors, and is designed either to convey a particular impression or to prevent an undesired one leaking out. Even the blush that often accompanies shyness is a communicative gesture, which can sometimes be anticipated and disguised. This suggests that shyness is not simply a passive, psychological response to certain situations, but rather is an actively constructed social role (Scott 2007).

Sanctioning deviance

The reactions of other people to shy behaviour reflect the way that it breaks the residual rules of interaction. As Scheff (1984 [1966]) explained, those who break these fundamental, common-sense assumptions shared by the majority will be regarded as strange, sick or antisocial. In this way, shyness is a form of deviant behaviour, but is only defined as such within a certain cultural and historical context. 'Failing' to speak one's mind, initiate social encounters or 'pull one's weight' in conversation defies the values of assertiveness, vocality, extroversion and competitive individualism that are significant in contemporary Western societies, but may be quite acceptable in many Asian societies. In the West, shyness confounds the expectations of many audiences, who must then try to make sense of this behaviour.

Figure 3.2 *Shyness is often perceived as deviant in relation to contemporary Western values of assertiveness and extroversion. However, in many non-Western cultures, shyness suggests modesty, a virtue.*

Social reactions to shyness determine whether or not it is defined as deviant. In some cases, shy behaviour can be normalized – disregarded as a temporary aberration from an otherwise 'normal' person's character. Certain kinds of situation are often presumed likely to 'make anyone feel shy': for example, attending a job interview or giving a wedding speech. Shyness can also be normalized with reference to a person's age or gender: we tend to think of shy children as 'cute' but expect them to 'grow out of it', while shyness in women may be more socially acceptable than it is in men because of its association with stereotypically 'feminine' traits of modesty and passivity (McDaniel 2003; Scott 2007). In other cases, however, shy behaviour breaks a residual rule of interaction and cannot be excused in this way. The actor is then seen as deviant and held individually responsible. For example, Etta described how she had inadvertently offended someone simply by allowing her shyness to leak out: 'One particular lady with a loud voice shouted one day at me, down the length of the bus, "Who do you think you are tossing your head at? You think you are too good to sit near me". I was mortified, as all I'd done was scuttle past her, pretending not to see her!' (Scott 2007: 134).

This example illustrates another facet of shyness as deviance: it is often misperceived as rudeness and aloofness. This is cruelly ironic, because 'shy' people are often highly sensitive and considerate to the needs of others – almost by definition, because the feeling comes from a fear of causing offence. Such reactions remind us of Garfinkel's (1967) reports of the responses to his breaching experiments (see chapter 2). Audience members who perceive one of their unspoken rules to have been broken will react with moral indignation, heaping blame upon the individual offender. This is not because the shy behaviour in itself was so terrible, but because it challenges some of the core values held by a group. As Titus explained, 'I think people don't like the idea [that] you are listening but not contributing because it's like stealing, like someone who uses your milk but never buys any … It must seem to these people that we are being aloof, like we won't talk to them because we think THEY aren't worth talking to. You can see why they'd get annoyed' (Scott 2007: 141–2).

Elsewhere (Scott 2007), I have argued that those who frequently encounter such reactions may gradually drift into a 'deviant career' (Becker 1963) of shyness. They become labelled as 'the shy one' of a group, and come to see themselves in such terms, often to the point of feeling unable to behave out of role on those occasions when they do feel more confident. As my participant Ruby said, 'once you're classified as a shy person … you can't do something just, like, drastic or outrageous, cos they'd say "Oh, what's wrong with you? Are you sick?" … I can't switch from being Little Miss Quiet in the corner and then to be Little Miss Loud' (Scott 2007: 149).

Shyness, then, is a social emotion that ostensibly suggests a challenge to social norms, but also reveals elements of social order, rituals and routines. Shy feelings occur when actors fear that they do not understand the rituals and routines of a particular context well enough to join in and give a credible performance. While these individuals may devise impressive dramaturgical strategies to manage their shyness, it often cannot be disguised completely and is expressed through rule-breaking behaviours that challenge the interaction order. Nevertheless, they evoke reactions of moral indignation that cast blame upon the individual and so ultimately defend and reinforce this social order.

Love, embarrassment and shyness are distinctly different emotions but share in common their relation to social processes. We make sense of these private experiences in terms of public rules and discourses, and find that their behavioural expressions are judged in terms of adherence to or deviance from cultural norms and values. This leaves us with the question of what is left if these social processes are taken away. Do emotions have a private, internal life of their own beneath the level of symbols, definitions and discourses? Do they (or we) have agency? Psychoanalysts such as Craib (1997) and social psychologists such as Brown (1986) or Leary (1996) would answer 'yes', and point to the complex processes that go on in the mind when we feel an emotion, which may be cognitive, neurological or unconsciously driven. Post-structuralist social theorists, on the other hand, might answer 'no', and, in its 'strong' form, this approach claims that emotions are socially constructed by discourses: we live in a 'post-emotional' society (Meštrović 1997) where it is impossible to experience a genuinely individual feeling. Other sociologists take a 'weak' post-structuralist view in arguing that emotions do have a life of their own but that their expressions tend to be 'disciplined' by cultural norms and discourses (Lupton 1998). The relationship between individual agency and social forces is a complex and changing one. In the next chapter, we explore how this is mediated by institutions such as the home, in which opportunities for self-expression are constrained by demographic factors, lifestyle trends and group identities.

Summary points

- Emotions are shaped by social processes of interaction, role performance and cultural norms.
- Love is often understood and performed in terms of romance and other modern, Western cultural discourses. These create patterns of orderly behaviour.
- Embarrassment occurs when we realize that we have broken a minor rule of interaction and created an undesirable impression upon others. It involves ritual displays that evoke others to 'repair' the situation.
- Shyness involves a fear of making such mistakes, expressed through feelings of self-consciousness and behavioural inhibition. However, these gestures can be read as deviant, evoking reactions of moral indignation.

4 Home

What makes a home? At the simplest level, the term refers to a physical place that provides us with shelter and residence (*Oxford English Dictionary* 2003); this may be a house or an apartment, a caravan, a boat, and so on. We often talk about 'going home' or 'being at home' to describe a feeling of comfort, familiarity and relaxation, whether this be associated with a geographical location, a physical building or a social group. However, as we saw in chapter 3, emotional experiences like this are influenced by cultural norms and powerful discourses. For some people, home is not a matter of choice but simply where they spend most of their time, such as a residential home, prison or hospital. The idea of home, then, holds many different meanings, which are interpreted by individuals in the context of their particular circumstances and everyday routines. In this chapter, we discuss some of these meanings and consider how social actors use the home differently to construct and perform their identities. We will explore the rituals and routines of domestic life, the role of the home in reproducing social order, and the challenges that some people face when their home takes on negative connotations.

The meaning of home

Viewing the home through an interpretivist lens, we can examine some of the meanings it has for people. Firstly, as a physical place in which we reside, home is fundamental to our experience of everyday life. Felski (1999) says that the home provides a base from which we start out each day and to which we return when our work or activities are done. This shapes the experience of 'everyday time' (that which is routine and ordinary rather than special and different) as being rhythmic, repetitive and based on routines. In phenomenological terms, such experiences create our sense of taken for granted reality – the background expectancies that we can (most of the time) bracket out (Schütz 1964). A second meaning of the home is familiarity: we derive comfort from returning to the same surroundings and following the same routines every day; it can be very unsettling to move house or leave home. Fox suggests that comfort and familiarity make the home a safe haven, a place to which we retreat from the outside world and where we can be ourselves. She refers to the old maxim 'An Englishman's home is his castle': we like to go home and lock ourselves into our own private space, following the 'moat and drawbridge rule' (2004: 111–13). For example, one of the Mass Observation respondents said, 'My home is my sanctuary – once I close the door and I'm safe, then I relax' (MO F218, female, aged 59).

Finally, the home is a place of privacy, a Goffmanesque 'backstage' region (Goffman 1959). This is where we remove our public masks and relax out of character, behaving in ways we would not want other people to see. We talk about 'going home' when we are tired, fed up, and have had enough of a social engagement, because home represents a place away from prying eyes. This may mean being absolutely alone, or being in the company of others whom we trust: Augé (1995) defines home as the ability to make oneself understood, and to understand others, within a social network. Thus Wardhaugh (1999) argues that 'home' is not simply a place but rather a state of mind, marking the boundaries between inside and outside, private and public. Another Mass Observation participant explained that, 'For me, the word "home" means somewhere you can feel safe, a sanctuary from the world, where you can totally relax and be yourself. It is somewhere to look forward to going back to and somewhere you can feel happy' (MO A2801, female, aged 41). Saunders encapsulates each of these meanings when he suggests that

> The home is a core institution in modern society. It shelters the smallest viable unit of social organisation – the household – and basic patterns of social relations are forged, reproduced and charged within it. It is the place with which individuals can most readily identify and it easily lends itself to the symbolic expression of personal identity. It offers both physical and psychological shelter and comfort. It is the place where the self can be expressed outside of social roles and where the individual can exert autonomy away from the coercive gaze of the employer and the state. It is the private realm in an increasingly public and intrusive world. (Saunders 1990: 60)

Ordering the home

The emergence of domesticity

This vision of the home as a place of belonging, familiarity, comfort, safety and privacy is connected with the rise of Western modernity. The Industrial Revolution of the eighteenth and nineteenth centuries moved the production process out of the home and into designated workplaces, such as factories and mills. This created a separation of home and work for most people, in terms of both the practicalities of their daily routines (travelling to work, working alongside others rather than alone, perhaps doing a different job altogether) and the meanings that each sphere held. Whereas, previously, the distinction between home and work had been blurred, suddenly going to work became a chore and coming home signified a retreat to a safe haven. This coincided with the rise of the nuclear family, which functionalists such as Parsons and Bales (1956) and Shorter (1976) described as well suited to the domestic sphere. Male breadwinners typically supported their wives and children by bringing home a wage, which was spent on food, consumer goods and leisure activities.

Alongside this came another separation: that of the private from the public sphere of everyday life. As Saunders's comment above shows, the home's association with the private sphere meant that it came to be seen as a safe retreat and a means of self-expression. This new sense of personal attachment to the home created a new trend in home ownership, together with what Gershuny (2000) called the 'self-service' or 'DIY' economy based upon home-centred activities. We prefer the convenience of travelling by car rather than using public transport, use washing machines instead of the launderette, and so on.

The historian Phillippe Ariès (1979) identifies this as the last in a sequence of stages that occurred with the rise of modernity: the private sphere was associated with domesticity, intimacy and privacy, while the public sphere remained tied to sociability, the market and the state. Kumar (1997), however, challenges this conventional view, asking whether the home belongs only to the private realm, or whether it might extend into spheres of public activity. For example, in political discourses we find the idea of returning to one's 'homeland' to restore a sense of shared religious or political identity. Thus the home is not synonymous with domesticity, even though we often assume this connotation.

Domestic divisions

Factors such as class, gender, ethnicity and age can make people feel more or less personally attached to their place of residence, and their status within the household will determine whether, where and to what extent they can enjoy privacy at home. Social order is therefore reflected and reproduced through the construction, display and organization of home life. In terms of age, young children may be expected to share bedrooms with their siblings, and their parents do not ask for permission to enter these spaces as they would do with older relatives. In terms of ethnicity, studies of migration have revealed power differentials operating even within supposedly multicultural communities. For example, the 'Great Migration' to Chicago in 1916–19 created a divide along the 'colour line', with black people concentrated in the city's ghettos with the poorest housing and the lowest paid jobs (Warner 1953). Similarly, Patterson's (1963) study of Brixton, London, revealed that its African Caribbean immigrants faced discrimination from the white population in being offered the worst quality, most expensive housing.

Class, status and hierarchy

According to historical sociologist Catherine Hall (1982), the idea of the home as a place of privacy is closely tied to the emergence of middle-class 'respectability' in the nineteenth century. The separation of home from work, in particular, was something that held more meaning for the upper and middle classes than for the working class. Hall gives the example of middle-class shopkeepers, who resented living in quarters above their shops; the wives in these families often refused to be seen on the shopfloor. Davidoff and Hall (1987) suggest that a 'culture of domesticity' emerged around this time, shaping in particular the lives of middle-class women. This gendered ideology centred on the idea of women being based within the home and living a moderate, rational and ascetic lifestyle. Women were expected to cultivate the 'feminine' qualities of grace, decorum, modesty and self-restraint in the way that they ran households and presented the domestic space to visitors.

Meanwhile, young working-class people would often be employed as domestic servants, bringing their labour into the homes of others. Studies such as Liz Stanley's (1984) analysis of the diaries of a Victorian maidservant, Hannah Cullwick, illustrate how the home could also be a workplace for such people, and how they fiercely protected what little privacy they had. Cullwick wrote in her diary of how she managed to conduct an illicit affair with a middle-class gentleman, Arthur Munby, and struggled to keep this a secret from her employers. By contrast, Leonore Davidoff (1990) describes the opulence of upper-class living in the eighteenth century: home life for this group meant entertaining guests at lavish balls and parties, where young women made their debut into high society. The smooth running of these events of course depended upon servants working below stairs, behind the scenes, who were regarded as invisible 'non-persons' (Goffman 1959). Social order within such households clearly depended on a rigid division of domestic labour, with the members of each social stratum knowing their places (Davidoff and Hawthorn 1976).

These values continued to influence the domestic lives of individuals throughout the twentieth and into twenty-first century. Packard (1959), for example, argued that, although the USA was ostensibly a classless society compared to Britain, over the twentieth century it became increasingly concerned with marking status differences. Packard suggested that the domestic home was a key site in which these class anxieties were played out, particularly in the 1950s, when there was a rise in disposable income. The purchase of new consumer goods became an exercise in self-presentation, as householders chose to display whichever items gave their home 'snob appeal', such as antique furniture and real fireplaces. We still see this in the current trend towards buying houses with 'original' or 'period features', suggesting that a core meaning of the home is how it will appear to others. This demonstrates what Veblen (2005 [1899]) called conspicuous consumption: in capitalist society, people seek to buy and display goods that will confer high status upon them, using their 'taste' to distinguish them from members of other social classes (cf. Bourdieu 1984).

Similarly, in the UK, scepticism about the idea that 'class is dead' (Scott 2001) is fuelled by Kate Fox's observations of how the home is constructed and displayed:

> Upper-class and upper-middle-class homes tend to be shabby, frayed and unkempt in a way no middle-middle or lower-middle would tolerate, and the homes of the wealthiest working class nouveaux-riches are full of extremely expensive items that the uppers and upper-middles regard as the height of vulgarity. The brand-new leather sofas and reproduction-antique dining chairs favoured by the middle-middles may cost ten times

as much as the equivalent items in the houses of upper-middles, who despise leather and 'repro'. (Fox 2004: 115)

Fox identifies such features as fitted carpets, matching furniture and display cabinets as indicators of middle-middle-class status, and net curtains, satellite dishes and widescreen televisions as indicators of upper-working-class values. Meanwhile, threadbare, shabby rugs and mismatched antique furniture are clear signifiers of upper-middle- and upper-class homes, for the truly aristocratic inherit their belongings. Fox therefore argues that these unspoken 'class rules' shape the way that people use the home to express and communicate their status, not only to others but to themselves. However, it is important to think critically about this, remembering de Certeau's (1984) argument about 'making do' with gestures of resistance (see chapter 2): how might 'poaching' status symbols from other class cultures help us deviate from the rules?

Gender and housework

The experience of home life is also mediated by gender, especially with regard to the division of domestic labour between heterosexual couples in nuclear families. A pervasive common-sense view is that women are associated with the domestic sphere, and thus with everyday life more generally. Bennett (2002) suggests that this may be because of the cyclical, repetitive nature of daily time within the household, which contrasts with the linear experience of time reported by those who work outside the home. Thus, in the traditional nuclear family, the male breadwinner would experience an unfolding of events, with each day introducing new challenges, while the female homemaker would find herself caught in a never-ending cycle of domestic chores. Lefebvre (2008 [1947]) argued that, because they were more likely to be housewives and caught up in stifling domestic routines, women experienced the habitual, mundane, repetitive nature of everyday life much more intensely and negatively than men.

Feminist accounts of housework posit that, far from being separated from the workplace, the home remains a site of invisible, unpaid labour. Oakley (1974) famously argued that housework is the most alienating form of work under capitalism. It meets each of Blauner's (1964) criteria for alienation (monotony, the fragmentation of tasks, time pressure and social isolation), and is particularly dissatisfying because household chores are never finished: there is always another meal to be cooked or more laundry to be done. The fact that house-work is not paid added insult to injury, Oakley argued, for, by keeping their husbands fed, clothed and in good health, housewives were pro-viding an invaluable service to the capitalist economy.

However, Felski (1999) counters that the repetitive rhythms and routines of domestic life can be interpreted more positively. Homemakers can decide when, how and in which order to do the domestic tasks they set themselves, and can derive contentment from some of these. Planning, shopping for, and cooking a family meal, for instance, can be experienced as an act of love and nurturance (Miller et al. 1998), which affords opportunities for creativity and self-expression. Felski argues that those engaged in domestic labour do not simply miss out on the excitement of life outside the home, but rather create meaningful worlds within it.

Oakley's depiction of housework may also be regarded as rather outdated: with more women in paid employment outside the home and technological advances helping to reduce the intensity of domes-tic labour, surely things have become more equal? Perhaps not: recent studies suggest that, while they may 'help out' more with housework, men do not take on an equal share, and so women find themselves working a 'dual burden' of paid and domestic labour (Stockman et al. 1995). Meanwhile, the supposedly liberating effects of new tech-nologies has been questioned by Wajcman (1995), who says that the amount of time spent on housework over the twentieth century actually remained constant. Modern devices such as the washing machine, electric iron and dishwasher may have made each task less physically arduous but have had little effect on the amount of work to be done. If anything, she argues, we have invented more tasks and expect them to be done more frequently: instead of one weekly wash, we divide clothes into piles by colour and fabric, and do several washes per week. Our expectations of what homemakers could and should achieve have risen, and so the work has become even more time consuming. Wajcman therefore argues that these apparently 'labour-saving' devices are in fact 'labour-enslaving'.

A related argument comes from Elizabeth Shove (2003), who sug-gests that, along with a rise in our expectations about the quantity of housework to be performed, we have set increasingly high stand-ards about its quality. Shove argues that the twentieth century saw a change in the meanings associated with domestic labour, centring on a shift away from comfort to cleanliness. We wash our clothes and our bodies much more than we used to, purchase increasingly powerful cleaning products, and have become quite 'germ-phobic' in our response to normal household dirt. Furthermore, Shove suggests, the notion of cleanliness is infused with moral values of goodness and purity: to make something clean requires hard work and results in a sense of achievement. Our standards of hygiene are rising, as we try to keep our homes more and more spotless, and the sense of competitiveness between homemakers may be no less than it was in the 1950s.

Interestingly, Shove relates these concerns to wider issues of social order, drawing on the anthropological work of Mary Douglas. Douglas (1966) argued that our concepts of dirt and defilement symbolize broader concerns about social contamination. We develop complex systems of classification and segregation, fed by rules about which objects or materials may mix, and become anxious if these are transgressed. Douglas famously made the relativist claim that what we think of as 'dirt' is no more than 'matter out of place' (1966: 36) and represents our concerns about social disorder. Similarly, Shove (2003) suggests that the modern rituals we have devised for washing, wiping, mopping, and so on, mirror the purification rites and rituals found in traditional societies. We control our environments by removing contaminating matter and placing boundaries between 'safe' and 'unsafe' places, which imposes order on the domestic world.

Homemaking rituals

Identity performances

What does your home say about you? If you own a property or have your own space within a shared residence, the chances are you will have decorated it according to your tastes – but where do these ideas come from? Do we choose furniture, furnishings and objects to display from an innate aesthetic sense, or are our preferences shaped by social trends and cultural values? In this section, we explore the idea that people construct and display their homes as an expression of self-identity and (dis)association from social groups.

In chapter 2, we saw how Goffman (1959) depicted social life as a series of theatrical performances. From this dramaturgical perspective, we can think about the home as a stage on which identities are played out, using settings and scenery, artefactual 'props', supportive team-mates, and so on. For example, a wealthy businesswoman

Figure 4.1 *What does your home say about you? The way that we decorate living space can be read as a form of self-presentation.*

wanting to create the impression of glamorous sophistication might choose solid wooden furniture, neutral colours and expensive artwork to display in her living room, while a young couple who want to make their home a happy place for children might use bold primary colours and wall murals. A teenager retreating to his bedroom may cover the walls with posters, rearrange his furniture and play loud music to express his sense of difference from his family. Each of these are situated identity performances: the people in question seek to convey a particular impression (either to themselves or to those around them), but as their circumstances change, so will their self-images and the messages they seek to communicate. The home therefore serves as an article of identity equipment that can be adapted to the changing motivations of the actor: the same space can be redesigned and redecorated to support different identity performances over time.

These frontstage performances (Goffman 1959), designed for public view, contrast with backstage regions of the home that are intended for private use, such as the bedroom and the bathroom. We use these backstage areas to construct our frontstage personae, for instance by getting dressed up to greet a visitor, or assembling furniture in a garden shed that will eventually be displayed in a smart hallway. Maleuvre (1999) says that it is the choice of items we display that turn a house into a home, and that express our self-identities.

One interesting example of this comes from Rachel Hurdley (2006), who looked at what people displayed on their mantelpieces. This small, narrow surface over a fireplace serves as an ideal repository for objects that, while seemingly innocuous, actually symbolize key features of a person's identity. Hurdley used 140 postal questionnaires to house-holders in Britain and interviewed thirty of these individuals and their families in depth. Her data reveal how people used the collection and display of valued objects to perform identity work, presenting different characters both to themselves and others. For example, Sylvia, a middle-aged woman, had two interesting objects on her mantelpiece. The first was a bronze statue of a man and woman embracing, which had been given to her as a present by her grown-up daughters. Sylvia explained that this was a particularly meaningful sculpture because it represented the love between herself and her husband, and she was touched that her children recognized that. Hurdley suggests that the emotional investment made by the two young women in choosing this gift was equalled by their mother's efforts to interpret and appreciate its meaning: she performed the identity of a beloved mother. The second object Sylvia displayed was an ugly, shapeless dough ball, created by her young grandson and also given to her as a gift: 'It's got a "G" for Grandma on it but I can't see it' (Hurdley 2006: 724). While this object was perhaps not as aesthetically pleasing as the bronze statue, Sylvia was equally keen to display it for several reasons. In part, she put it there to humour her grandson and protect his feelings, thus performing her love and gratitude towards him. In doing so, she felt that she was also performing the moral identity of the 'good grand-mother' to her daughters and any visitors to the home; she appeared kind, indulgent and appreciative. Hurdley comments that there may also have been a third level of performance going on in the context of the interview itself, whereby Sylvia tried to present herself in each of these ways by accounting for her actions, conscious of how she might be depicted in the researcher's writing.

Data from the Mass Observation archive (Autumn 2006 Directive) provide further insights into the ways in which the home can be used as a site of identity performance, both to oneself and to others. For example, a middle-aged, gay man living alone in a flat explained how he had decorated the flat to his own tastes because, as a writer, he spent so much time at home. He was suitably house-proud because he felt that the result expressed his character, which made it a comfortable place to be in, but he was also aware of how other people might interpret the statements he was making:

> It is very important to me how my flat looks. Everyone who visits seems to like it and often people say they are surprised by how it looks. Don't know why, they obviously have a different idea of how I would live. I like to buy good quality furniture that will last a long time. Solid hand-made things. I also like to collect paintings and have many on my walls. The flat is very small and I don't have space to display them properly but I buy them so that I can look at them, not to show off to others. (MO A3623, male, aged 48)

Similarly, a female academic explained how she had decorated her study at home to be not only a functional workspace but also a means of performing identity as a biographical narrative. The room was a museum of the self (Maleuvre 1999), festooned with objects and artefacts that represented memorable times in her career, significant friendships, and places she had visited:

> On top of one of the book cases is a CD player, and balanced on top of the speakers are 2 Aboriginal baskets woven out of grass and decorated with wool. There is a hook on the back of the door, where I hang my Acoubra hat I bought when I lived in Australia, and which I wore when I worked as an anthropologist, working with Aboriginal people. Along one wall there's my desk, at right angles to the window, and a book case. My desk has a computer, an African pot a friend gave me, which I use to store pens, and a printer ... I have my old school dictionary wedged between the monitor and the computer tower ... The book shelves have all sorts of ornaments, all given to me by others, and all from different parts of the world. They include a pottery bear from the Moscow 1980 Olympics, a brass Indian god (Shiva the destroyer I think), an Aboriginal lightning ancestor in wood, ochre and eagle feathers, an antique portable silver inkwell, 2 old blue poison bottles, and a wooden pot from Zimbabwe! I wouldn't part with any of them! (MO 3137, female, aged 38).

For others, however, home is a much more transient place, selected by necessity as much as choice, and comprising a far smaller repository of memories. Structural factors such as income, age, occupational stability, and so on, may influence the extent to which one can use the home to express individual identity. In particular, younger people, and those in temporary accommodation, may have less opportunity to make their home truly their own, but will nevertheless attempt to personalize it. This young woman, for example, shared a rented flat with her friend and reflected on how a tight budget had restricted, though not prevented, their ability to display their characters:

As we rent we wouldn't be able to make any major changes, but have cus-
tomised it in our own way, mainly with brightly coloured accessories such
as a fantastic turquoise spotted toaster! We are also extremely proud of
our book cupboard, which I think, if I'm honest, sold the flat to us. We've
filled it to the point of bursting and love showing off our book collection
to visitors! ... Our flat is mostly decked out in IKEA furniture. If we need
stuff we generally go to IKEA, as we both like their stuff, it's cheap and it's
not too far away. (MO C3210, female, aged 26)

Finally, it is worth recognizing that these identity performances can
be as much about who or what one is not as they are about who or what
one is. Just as we can associate ourselves with a particular social group
by adopting its tastes and styles, we may also seek to disassociate ourselves from other social groups (cf. Bourdieu 1984). For example, this
respondent explained how she had sought to distance herself from
stereotypes of the elderly:

I like modern styles which include wood, clean lines and 'less is more'
for me – no clutter. My taste is quite different from my sister (cosy but
very old fashioned) and several friends of similar age, who either live with
clutter or fill their every space with china, photos or even plastic flowers.
I like to think anyone stepping inside [my home] would not immediately
think 'old people live here' and my daughter keeps me up to date too! (MO
B786, female, aged 72)

Home improvements

This function of the home in expressing self-identity may explain why,
in Western cultures, 'home improvement' or DIY has become such a
popular trend. Not content merely to decorate our homes according
to our tastes when we move in, we seek constantly to update and rede-
sign them. The quest for the 'perfect' home is in some ways similar
to the quest for the 'perfect' body through diet, exercise and cosmetic
surgery: a reflection of the individualistic, anxiety-ridden climate of
late modernity (Giddens 1991). Like the perfect body, the perfect
home may never actually be attainable, as design trends constantly
change, along with personal tastes and priorities: the pink, fluffy
carpet and floral print sofa of a previous decorating spree may not go
down too well with a new partner who prefers minimalist black and
white. But perhaps to look for meaning in the goal of this activity is
to miss the point: the source of this addictive pleasure may lie in the
process, not the product. Home improvement is an ongoing activity,
full of meaningful rituals and routines.

Kate Fox says that the British are 'a nation of nestbuilders' (2004: 113), and that the rule underlying this growing obsession is one of territorial marking: we like to put our 'personal stamp' on a place as a way of turning a house into a home. We do not like to think that we have simply moved into somebody else's old home; decorating it according to our own tastes helps us to feel that we have chosen this place and that it expresses our individual identity. Fox jokes about people feeling driven to 'rip something out' when they move into a new house, as a kind of nesting ritual, and suggests that visiting DIY shops at the weekend has replaced church-going as a new religion of sorts. Redecorating a new home helps to supplant its previous identity with a statement about the new inhabitant's tastes and lifestyle. As one of the Mass Observation panellists demonstrated:

> the last room I finished decorating was the back bedroom. When I moved in, it had been a child's nursery, and there was still a frieze of cartoon cats beneath the picture rail. I have converted it to a study cum guest bedroom cum upstairs sitting room. I stripped the floorboards and stained them the same antique pine colour as the floorboards downstairs. In the middle of the room is a tufted cream rug with flecks of raspberry ... (MO B3227, male, aged 39)

Home improvement is not just a one-off activity, either. Baum and Hassan (1999) point out that, when a home no longer meets our needs, we will often renovate and redecorate it rather than move to a new property. This means that we may stay in the same property for many years but make it into several different, successive homes. Their analysis of data from the 1991 Housing and Location Preference Survey, conducted in Adelaide, South Australia, revealed that the motivations for doing renovation work differed between those who were relocating and those who were altering their current property. The latter group tended to be those in larger households, often with children, and with greater incomes: perhaps they needed more space, could afford to renovate, and did not want to disrupt the stability of their family life. Those who moved house, by contrast, were often young, single people with smaller incomes; many were in rented accommodation and had fewer ties to the location.

Furthermore, we can identify class and gender rules within this overall trend. Bennett, Emmison and Frow (1999) illustrate this in their study of 2,756 Australian men and women, which revealed the ways in which people used home improvements to make statements about their own class identity and to distinguish themselves from the members of other social classes (cf. Bourdieu 1984). For example, they draw a contrast between Gillian, a middle-class woman with a professional career, and Mary, a working-class housewife. Gillian's values centred on education, success and achievement through work, and she loved artwork, music and books. She wanted her home to express these ideas and to appear well designed, spacious and tidy: she did not like the euphemistic term 'lived in'. Painting over the pink walls with a cool blue and green, and refusing her husband's suggestions of other 'gaudy' features, Gillian sought to distance herself from what she saw as the signifiers of a working-class background. Meanwhile, Mary had a very different set of priorities. She was devoted to her husband and sons above all else, and was proud of her traditional working-class values. Mary wanted her home to be a comforting, welcoming place for the family, and had little patience for the 'airs and graces' suggested by home improvement. She believed that her home had no contrived style, but simply reflected her day-to-day life:

> I just buy what I like. If it matches something, it's good luck rather than good management, but I do try to make it a house, so when you come into it you feel comfortable and at home ... And you know it's not a house that's starchy, that you think, I won't sit there, I'll crush the cushion, or should I take my shoes off because everybody else's shoes are at the front door. (Bennett et al. 1999: 24)

Thus although Mary vehemently denied that she was making any conscious statement with her home, she was nevertheless expressing her working-class identity in the way that she talked about *not* doing certain things. Gillian and Mary were using their homes in similar ways to perform class identities, either by aspiring to one set of values or seeking to distance themselves from another.

Bennett, Emmison and Frow (1999) also suggest that gender differences are apparent in the way that we style our homes. They asked their respondents about how they perceived the 'ideal' home, and found that, whereas the women liked their homes to appear 'lived in', provided they were clean, comfortable and easy to maintain, the men preferred a more functional, spacious and modern look that would make their home distinctive. From this we might surmise that women care more about the emotional experience of being 'at home', whereas men are more concerned with the image of the home as it appears to others, an object on display. Of course, this distinction rests upon possibly outdated gender stereotypes; as we have seen, it is no longer necessarily the case that women spend more of their everyday lives at home while men spend more time in the workplace, nor that design styles can be categorized as masculine or feminine. Such trends merely reflect normative assumptions that are open to challenge.

Gardening routines

It is worth considering another activity associated with home design and decoration – gardening. As Fox (2004) notes, this may reflect another territorial attempt to carve out a patch of turf to call our own; she suggests that is more of a passion for 'island-dwellers' such as the British and Japanese than it is for those with more access to large open space, such as in parts of the USA, Canada and Australia. Fox observes a distinction between the way that we tend to our front gardens (prissily kept flowerbeds and ornamental features for display purposes) and our back gardens (overgrown lawns framed by hedges and fences). This echoes dramaturgical theory: front and back gardens correspond to Goffman's (1959) front and back regions, the first being visible to passers-by and the second being a more private, secluded space.

For Bhatti and Church (2001), meanwhile, gardens have a phe-nomenological significance in connecting 'cultures of nature' to the everyday world of the home. They draw upon Giddens's (1984) structuration theory (see chapter 2) to show how the social practices of domestic gardening are a form of human agency, mediated by inter-action with family and friends, which feeds into the wider structure of human–nature relations. Bhatti and Church use data from the Mass Observation archive to show how humans relate in a meaningful way to animals, insects and plants through gardening, which serves as a highly personalized (re)connection to nature. For example, many people spoke of tending the garden with parents or children as a way of enjoying family life: 'One year when the lawn mower was in pieces for several weeks, it pleased my father to issue us all with scissors – some of us with nail scissors – and we (five children and my mother) were all sent out to cut the grass with these implements. The result had best not be imagined.' (MO: M1201, female, aged 35, cited in Bhatti and Church 2001: 377). Others viewed the garden as a place in which to retreat from family and social pressures and to be 'at one with nature'. They strove to balance this desire for privacy with that for social interaction (cf. Allan and Crow 1991), by managing the bounda-ries of the garden: 'I hate it being open as our neighbours on both sides allow their weeds and dandelions and other ground-bugging weeds to grow flowers and seed, so it is an endless battle to keep our

Figure 4.2 *Gardening, once stereotypically the preserve of the elderly, is an increasingly popular pastime with people of all ages. How and why do gardening routines serve a social purpose?*

beds free [of weeds]' (MO: A883, male clerk, aged 63, cited in Bhatti and Church 2001: 379). Bhatti and Church therefore conclude that the domestic garden, 'provides opportunities and possibilities in relation to nature that may not exist elsewhere either in the rest of the home or in public spaces … [it] is a place in which – on a personal level – to engage, confront and understand the changing natural world' (2001: 380).

Challenging domesticity

The dark side of the home

The preceding discussion has focused on a conventional under-standing of the home as comprising one or more persons living in a private, relatively small dwelling, often with family or friends, and by choice. However, it is important to recognize that, for many people, 'home' means something quite different. Chapman and Hockey (1999) talk of the discrepancy between such idealistic rep-resentations and the reality faced by some. For example, the vision of harmonious living in a nuclear unit is thrown into question by studies of the 'dark side' of the family, namely violence and abuse. Data from the 2001 British Crime Survey revealed that 3.4 per cent of women and 2.2 per cent of men had experienced domestic violence within the past year (Walby 2004), and that, in 37 per cent of these cases, leaving home did not bring an end to the violence (Walby and Allen 2004). Women in particular are seen to be at risk of domestic violence although, far from experiencing it as helpless victims, they are often actively involved in seeking help, and find themselves in a cycle of staying, leaving and returning (Dobash and Dobash 1998). Rape within marriage is another serious issue that has only rela-tively recently been recognized in criminal law (Russell 1990). Other studies suggest that it is misleading to focus exclusively on male offenders: women may also initiate violence within relationships (Straus and Gelles 1986; Nazroo 1995) or perpetrate child abuse (Turton 2006). For the victims of these crimes, home can seem far from a place of retreat and safety, and being 'at home' may mean living in fear and despair.

Total institutions

Other people may live in places that are ostensibly safe and stable but distinctively un-homely. Goffman (1961a) used the term 'total insti-tution' to refer to residences in which people live, eat and sleep, day after day and around the clock, for a prolonged period: these include hospitals, boarding schools, military barracks and prisons. Those living in total institutions will often be there by coercion rather than choice, making their experience of everyday life one of regimented routines, schedules and predictability (we return to this in chapter 5). Foucault (1977 [1975]) talked about such institutions as one of the sites in which 'disciplinary power' was exercised over minds and bodies: a faceless set of rules and obligations could nevertheless determine how people behaved, when, where and why. Goffman (1961a) writes in particular about the lives of inmates at a psychiatric hospital, who, upon admission, underwent a symbolic 'mortification of the self' and 'degradation ceremony' (Garfinkel 1967). These patients were stripped of their identity equipment, such as clothes, toiletries and personal possessions, and issued the standard hospital kit (pyjamas, toothbrush, comb, and so on). They could not determine the structure of their days, the company they kept, the activities in which they partook or the surroundings in which they did so. Nevertheless, Goffman pointed to an underlife, or culture of resistance, that developed as patients devised ways of 'playing the system': they would sneak extra sachets of salt and pepper from the dining hall, carve plastic spoons into knives, and put rolled up newspapers under their seats to make them more comfortable. Such practices indicate that maintaining a sense of homeliness is an important human value that is resilient in the face of threat.

Other types of total institutions may be redesigned to protect the inmates' sense of home. The USA has the largest prison population in the world – 2.19 million, or 738 per 100,000 persons – followed by China, and within the EU the UK has the highest per capita imprisonment rate (Walmsley 2006; US Bureau of Justice Statistics 2007). In the UK, the Woolf Report (Woolf 1991) criticized the way in which prisons were designed to appear cold, austere and unwelcoming. Prisoners were effectively being punished twice, the report said, because not only were they deprived of their liberty, they were also made to endure poor living conditions. Woolf recommended treating prisoners with humanity, respecting their civil rights, and exposing them to no further hardship beyond the deprivation of liberty. Sociological research points to the negotiated order (Strauss 1978) found in day-to-day prison life, as inmates grudgingly consent to being given orders in exchange for being allowed to indulge the norms and values of their 'prison culture' (Morgan 2002). There are unwritten rules against 'grassing' on a fellow prisoner, for instance, or usurping the authority of the 'top dog' in the implicit hierarchy. As one prison minister recalls, 'On one level, prison can be viewed as a morality play in which those who have power exploit those who don't ... prison relationships are often utilitarian, and friendships ... are approached with caution (Atchison 2003).

Homelessness

Meanwhile, what of those who do not even have a home, in the conventional sense? Tom Hall's (2003) ethnography of young homeless people suggests that these are the victims of social exclusion – from family life, employment, leisure activities, and so on. An individual is defined as homeless if they do not have a fixed, regular place of night-time residence (US Department of Housing and Urban Development 2007), although they may live in temporary accommodation, a homeless shelter or halfway house. The term 'rooflessness' is sometimes used more literally to refer to people who have no shelter at all: those sleeping rough on city streets or park benches. Yet others may be 'voluntarily homeless', as nomads or travellers, but may not perceive themselves as such. A caravan, boat, converted ambulance, and so on, can become just as long term and 'homely' to its residents as a purpose-built house. The meaning of home therefore extends well beyond mere physicality, and may well be, as Wardhaugh (1999) claims, a state of mind.

'Home' is an interesting concept in revealing the connections between our three themes of social order, rituals and routines, and challenges to the taken for granted. On the one hand, as a backstage retreat, being at home suggests opportunities for self-expression that remind us of our freedom from external pressures, roles and responsibilities. On the other hand, the home, as an institution, often takes the form of daily routines, household chores and domestic divisions, which can appear as reified structures. Is there really such a difference between these self-imposed patterns of behaviour and the regimes enforced in total institutions? Are our homely routines a matter of choice or obligation? In the next chapter, we take this further by examining how temporal schedules fit into our daily lives, as socially constructed yet meaningful and 'real' phenomena.

Summary points

- The notion of home has many different meanings, such as its being a place of belonging, familiarity and privacy.
- The association of the home with privacy emerged with the rise of modernity and the nuclear family.

- The experience of home life is mediated by structural factors such as social class and gender.
- Identities are performed in the home through the selection, collection and display of objects and artefacts.
- The rituals and routines of home improvement show how individuals use their decorative styles to perform their membership of (or disassociation from) social groups.
- Gardens can function as a symbolic extension of the home, in which identities are performed.
- Common-sense assumptions about the meaning of home can be challenged by cases of abuse and domestic violence, total institutions and homelessness.

5   Time

Daily life is characterized by repetitive cycles of practices whose rhythms shape our experiences. Day after day we engage in the same mundane activities, at the same times and in the same order, and this routine predictability allows us to take the everyday world for granted. In the previous chapter, we explored how domestic routines represent one such juncture between structure and agency. In this chapter, we consider the role of time more generally: how do we perceive, experience and manage time socially, and what functions does this serve? We begin with some remarks about the experience of time, then consider the ways in which we measure and distribute it, through timetables, schedules and calendars. The next section looks at how the rituals and routines of daily life are shaped by these schedules, whether we are at home, at work, or managing the boundary between the two. We may devise ways of planning, saving and 'deepening' our time to be more productive, but not everyone is equally empowered to do so. Finally, we consider some of the ways in which taken for granted assumptions about time can be challenged by those who follow unconventional schedules, whether by obligation or choice. These incidences of norm-breaking, as ever, help us to see the unspoken rules of behaviour more clearly.

Experiencing time

As we saw in chapter 2, phenomenology is concerned with the way in which people construct their own subjective realities by making sense of the world they perceive. Schütz (1962, 1964) said that these lived experiences are what make social life meaningful, rather than any objective perception of reality. One example of this is the way in which we experience time subjectively: although we are immersed in a constant flow of experiences, we divide these into discrete and measurable temporal units, such as minutes, hours and days (Muzzetto 2006). However, we also seek to align our experience of time with those of other people in order to achieve 'intersubjective agreement' – a shared understanding of what is going on (Schütz 1962, 1964). For this reason, we devise what Simmel (1950a [1902–3]) called an 'objective culture' to which we can orient our individual perceptions. Clocks and watches are part of this objective culture, insofar as they help us to co-ordinate our schedules. For example, if a business meeting is scheduled for 9.00 a.m. on a Monday morning, then however tired Bill may be, or whatever Meena might prefer to be doing, neither can dispute that it is 'time for' the meeting, and so they must go there. Even though clock time, schedules and working hours are socially constructed, they can appear to us as objectively real, beyond question: time is a reified social structure (Berger and Luckmann 1967).

Barbara Adam (2004) identifies three main ways in which we experience this phenomenon. Body time reflects the cycles of birth, death and reproduction that shape the individual's passage through life. We experience certain life events in terms of their impact on our bodies. For example, we measure the ageing process by how fast and how drastically our bodies change: to age 'well' is to age slowly, with barely perceptible changes at any one time. By contrast, pregnancy introduces the body to a distinct, time-limited and shorter term process of change, which is often experienced by women in terms of time (Warren and Brewis 2004). Pregnant women may measure their progress towards the goal of childbirth in terms of days (280), weeks (forty) or months (nine). Clock time is an abstract representation of time, as it is measured in modern societies. It is a socially constructed idea, reflecting the urge rationally to measure, quantify and monitor progress in a linear fashion. Finally, social time is the most relevant to our study of everyday life: this is time as it is understood, used and controlled at a social level to shape individual lives. This includes the familiar themes of habit, repetition and rhythm that characterize daily life, and our concern with its tempo and pace; we seek to regulate this through schedules and routines. Adam suggests that social time is also apparent in the way that we think about our ancestors and cultural history: to have a sense of society extending into the past and the future is to understand more fully one's place within it.

Southerton (2006) points out that our experience of time is itself temporally organized, as we move between different activities, or practices, throughout the day. Drawing on Fine (1996), he suggests that there are five dimensions of time that shape our experience of it: periodicity (or rhythm), tempo (pace), synchronization (the co-ordination of tasks), duration (how long things take) and sequence (the order in which we do things). Put together, these dimensions constitute the temporal rhythms of daily life. For example, a student might begin the day working at home at her own rhythm and tempo, but then find herself 'multi-tasking' later in the day when she combines shopping with collecting children and walking the dog (synchronization). More often, a single activity will reflect several dimensions of time. Southerton suggests that we can analyse any social practice in these terms, measuring its position along the five dimensions.

Time and social order

Calendars

The social regulation of time occurs at many levels, reflecting the mutuality of orderly, macro-social patterns and experiential, micro-social routines. Firstly, we measure the passing of time over years, decades and centuries to put the present day in an historical context. In the Judaeo-Christian world, centuries are identified as either 'Before Christ' or 'Anno Domini' (in the year of our Lord, or after the birth of Christ), and so the meaning of individual years is determined by their temporal relation to a pivotal event. Centuries are divided into millennia (one thousand years) accordingly, and are observed by believers and non-believers alike as a taken for granted reality. For example, academic referencing uses this system to date studies, not because all researchers are Christian, but because this is 'how things are done'. Individual scholars must learn by the rules in order to fit into this culture, and failure to abide by them is not tolerated: 'poorly referenced' work is not published, and poorly referenced essays receive low marks. Normative conventions such as these shape our awareness of time and its passing and exert a 'seen but unnoticed' pressure upon us to follow the rules.

Calendars are used to measure the passing of time within a year, although the definition of 'one year' also varies between cultures, religions and social groups. The 365-day year may be the norm of Judaeo-Christian societies, but Chinese history is measured in terms of dynasties, political regimes and lunar cycles. The Chinese New Year occurs on the first day of the first lunar month, and so the date does not neatly map onto a recurring date on the 'civil calendar', as it is known.

Similarly, the Muslim festival of Eid ul-Fitr takes place at the end of the month of Ramadan, the ninth month of the Islamic calendar but, as this too is based upon lunar rather than solar months, the date of the festival moves around the civil calendar. Jewish culture follows the cycles of nature insofar as they correspond to significant events in the religion's historical development. The festival of Passover, for instance, commemorates the exodus of slaves from Israel to Egypt, and is celebrated in the spring, as a time that is symbolic of regrowth. Jewish months are also lunar and overlap the dates of the civil calendar (Solomon 1996).

Within each of these cultures, time is measured in a different but meaningful way that makes sense to its members. As Winch (1958) said, there is no single 'right' way of seeing the social world, for each culture has its own internal logic and rationality. For the social scientist, what is most interesting is the way that these systems are understood and adhered to by individuals, and the effects that this has on their everyday lives. The functionalist sociologist Emile Durkheim (1976 [1912]) argued that the significance of such traditions, particularly religious ones, lies in the way in which they create rituals, ceremonies and regular events that bring people together. Calendrical events reflect a culture's shared beliefs and values, and their observance every year reinforces its members' commitment to their society.

Schedules

With these ideas in mind, Zerubavel (1981) argues that our experience of time is conventional: we cannot understand it outside of our own culture's norms and conventions, which are socially constructed. There may be no objective underlying reality that is 'time' – only our representations and markers of it. For example, the seven-day week, with its conventional structure of five working days and two weekend days, is essentially an arbitrary division of time, created to serve human ends. This reminds us of the Kantian distinction found in interpretivist social theory between noumena, real objects in the world, and phenomena, human perceptions of these objects. Such phenomena are reified: they appear to us as objective, external social facts (Durkheim 1984 [1893]), obscuring the truth that we constructed them (Berger and Luckmann 1967).

This orderly structure operates at the micro-level through schedules that regulate our time. These 'microscopic temporal units' (Zerubavel 1981: 31) divide the day into hours, minutes and seconds, each of

Figure 5.1 *Ruled by the clock? Schedules shape our everyday activities, as we move from one activity to the next. They also help us to co-ordinate our routines with each other, which maintains social order.*

which has to be accounted for in relation to a designated set of tasks. Schedules are phenomena that embody the idea of rule-following action: we tend to think of them as guiding us towards our duties and responsibilities, which may impinge upon our sense of freedom. They also impose structure upon the day, by telling us where to be and at what time; schedules regulate the movement of individual bodies through time and space. Foucault (1977 [1975]) called these disciplinary regimes, insofar as they suggest a form of social control that is diffused and impersonal. There may be no specific person forcing us to get up, eat or work at certain times, but we do so anyway, because we have internalized a normative schedule.

Zerubavel (1981) suggests that the origins of the daily schedule can be traced back to the 'horarium' taught in the Benedictine monasteries of the sixth to the twelfth centuries AD. This was an hour-by-hour breakdown of strictly regulated activities that the monks were expected to observe every day, and which is still found in many convents and monasteries today. The horarium represents the epitome of the Foucauldian regime:

> The brethren ... must be occupied at stated hours in manual labor, and again at other hours in sacred reading ... the brethren shall start work in the morning and from the first hour until almost the fourth do the tasks that have to be done. From the fourth hour until about the sixth let them apply themselves to reading. After the sixth hour, having left the table, let them rest on their beds in perfect silence. (The Rule of Benedict, cited in Zerubavel 1981: 34)

At first glance, this may appear harsh and punitive: it suppresses individual interests and inclinations and puts social order above all else. Those confined to some 'total institutions' (Goffman 1961a; see chapter 4), such as prisons and psychiatric hospitals, might resent such regimes for this reason, experiencing them as a negative, repressive form of control. In other ways, however, this may be seen as a positive, enabling form of power: it can be comforting to follow an externally imposed schedule insofar as it removes responsibility from the individual to make choices about when, how and in what order they do things – there are no feelings of guilt about making poor use of one's time, or time-wasting (see below). The existentialist philosopher Sartre (1957 [1943]) argued that these kinds of action display an attitude of bad faith: they allow people to deny that they have an essential choice about how to live their lives. It is easier to believe that we must obey the rules imposed upon us simply because they are there, rather than to question how and why they were constructed and whether we want to follow them. We seek out regimes and timetables in this way because they put a comforting blanket over such existential questions, making life more routine and predictable. This may also explain why inmates of total institutions sometimes experience what Goffman (1961a) called 'release anxiety' shortly before being discharged. That is, they sabotage their own health (for example, by self-harming) in order to be detained for longer, because the idea of having to devise one's own rules and routines 'on the outside' is too frightening to contemplate.

Most of us follow some kind of regular daily schedule not completely unlike that of the Benedictine horarium, and it can be very unsettling not to have such a routine. Those who are self-employed or work in occupations that do not demand regular working hours (such as artists, writers and academics) often find that the pressure to discipline oneself, combined with the impossibility of knowing whether one is tackling work in the 'right' way or at the 'right' pace, is a source of great anxiety. They may envy those of their friends who work regular '9–5' hours, insofar as this clear demarcation between work and leisure allows them to take legitimate 'time off'.

Steger (2006) provides an interesting example of this in the context of Japanese work culture. While the stereotypical image of the Japanese worker is the male, middle-class employee of a company who puts in regular, long hours, the reality for many Japanese people is quite different. Housewives, for example, may work around the clock, while those women in paid employment often work part-time irregular hours to fit around their childcare duties. Steger's research focused on high-school students who experienced great anxiety about motivating themselves to study and devising their own daily time-table. The students' work ethic was so strong that they studied late into the night and, especially during exam periods, would replace nocturnal sleep with naps during daytime classes. In Steger's view, these various examples show that different social groups employ different strategies of time management to suit their needs, and that even in an apparently 'monochronic' society like Japan we can find 'polychronic' uses of time.

Queuing

At the micro-level of everyday interaction, the ritual of queuing helps to reproduce social order. Barry Schwartz (1975) argued that the distribution of waiting time reflects the power structure of a group: those with greater access to valued goods and services have more power, and vice versa. In the service industries of modern society, staff exercise power by making clients wait to be served (seeing their own time as more precious), while clients express deference through their willingness to wait. The queue is therefore a microcosmic social structure that ensures the smooth running of organizations.

For individual actors, queuing is also meaningful as a form of social action. Schwartz examines the normative codes to which actors adhere and the subjective meanings that these hold for them. In economic and psychological terms, queuing is costly for the individual: it is boring, frustrating and a waste of time. There must then be a social benefit that outweighs this cost and makes people willing to defer to the 'greater good'. Schwartz suggests that we rarely object to the principle of queuing, because we can see that everybody is being treated fairly: there is an unspoken rule of priority allocation, or 'first come, first served'.

We do object to violations of this rule, however: namely the queue jumper, who implies that their time is more precious than everybody else's. Kate Fox (2004) observes how people in line respond to queue jumpers with moral indignation, for the act breaches a fundamental rule of social order. Would-be queue jumpers are eyed with suspicion: a 'paranoid pantomime' occurs as those in line uneasily shift back and forth to prevent people from pushing in. In some cases, queue jumping is permitted because individuals are seen to have a greater or more urgent need: the medical emergency rushed into hospital, or the elderly woman offered a seat on a crowded bus. However, these exceptions are anticipated and planned for: they are authorized by a shared set of rules and values. Schwartz therefore argues that, although there is a potential for disorder inherent in any queue, this is pre-emptively managed by both the priority of allocation rule and its authorized exceptions.

Clock time

An interesting example of the conventionality of time lies in the idea of clock time – that which is measured by the twelve- or twenty-four-hour clock. This is an artificial unit of time, for although it appears to mirror the natural cycle of a day, sleep studies have shown that, when we do not have clocks or watches, our bodies naturally adopt a twenty-five hour schedule (Blakemore 1988). Clock time therefore represents a human desire to quantify, measure and control the world and facilitate the co-ordination of social activities.

E. P. Thompson (1963) suggested that adherence to clock time is a feature of modern Western societies, insofar as it embodies the values of rationality, efficiency and means–end calculation. Punctuality and timekeeping are revered as moral virtues, and it is considered bad form to be late or keep people waiting (Shaw 1994). As Weber (1985 [1904–5]) famously showed, these values were central to the Protestant work ethic that led to the rise of industrial capitalism in the West: Benjamin Franklin's maxim that 'time is money' led the early capitalists to work harder and for longer hours, to maximize their profits. With this came the associated values of punctuality and diligence: factory workers in particular learned to practise the ritual of 'clocking on' and 'clocking off' at the beginning and end of a shift, with harsh penalties for anyone who was late or caught slacking.

These values and their incumbent rituals continue to this day, as most people who work under supervision feel obliged to demonstrate that they are 'putting in the hours'. Sometimes techniques can be used strategically to demonstrate this, as for example an office worker emails his colleagues from home late one night, knowing that the time will be shown on the message. Such ritualized performances of the 'good worker' role illustrate Goffman's (1959) concept of 'make-work', discussed later on.

However, with changing patterns of work, adherence to clock time may be becoming less rigid. Westenholz (2006) found in her study of Danish IT workers that there were four different ways of responding to this norm. Clock timers followed the conventional, institutional structure of the working day, perceiving a clear division between the times when they were 'at work' (e.g. 9 a.m.–5 p.m.) and other times when they were not (in the early mornings, evenings and weekends). Task timers did not make such a distinction: they measured their work in terms of discrete tasks to be done and worked for as long or as short a time as their daily quota of tasks demanded. Blurred timers were the largest group and fell somewhere between these two extremes, mixing clock time and task time. For example, an employee might aim to complete at least eight tasks in a day, but only insofar as this is possible within conventional working hours and external, domestic commitments. Finally, invaded clock timers found it meaningful to distinguish between work and non-work time hypothetically, but, in practice, ended up working outside 'normal' working hours. Westenholz argues that these four patterns create distinct 'time identities', as employees come to define themselves by their attitude to work. An individual might switch between time identities if they move to a new job or if their priorities change: for example, an erstwhile single, professional 'career woman' who then has children learns to juggle the responsibilities of work and home life, moving from being a work-driven 'task timer' to being a multi-tasking 'blurred timer'.

Gender differences

Timetables, schedules and the experience of clock time are important in creating the rhythms of daily life. This is perhaps most evident in studies comparing men's and women's daily routines, which reflect patterns of paid and unpaid labour, respectively. Insofar as the sphere of everyday life has traditionally been associated with domesticity and femininity (Felski 1999), this will affect women's experience of time. Davies (1990) suggests that female homemakers' experience of time is cyclical, based upon the endless repetition of domestic chores throughout the week, whereas men who work outside the home experience time in linear terms, as a series of unique challenges to be met each day that provide opportunities for purposeful achievement.

However, with growing diversity in household structure and composition, it is important to question how applicable such models are to twenty-first-century society. Is the experience of time distinguished by essential sex differences, or by the socially defined roles of 'breadwinner' and 'homemaker', which may be adopted by either gender? Elizabeth Silva (1999) conducted semi-structured interviews in the UK with twenty women, seventeen men and forty-five children, who were asked to describe an average weekday. Silva argues that the differences in men's and women's use of time were owing not to gender per se, but rather to their different levels of involvement (both practical and emotional) in 'homely' activities, such as housework and childcare. Thus some men spent as much time as women at home, but this was because they were self-employed and working at home, not because they were househusbands. Those women who did paid work at home described daily routines that were closer to those of the home-working men than to those of other women. However, the women in Silva's sample did describe time in cyclical rather than linear terms, because they were more likely to be multi-tasking 'working mums', juggling the demands of paid and unpaid labour. They also seemed to experience time in relational terms, that is, time spent caring for others (partners and children), to whom they subordinated their needs, whereas the men in the sample experienced time instrumentally, in terms of activities and achievements. One exception to this trend was single fathers, who also spoke of relational time, reinforcing the notion that these are differences of lifestyle and circumstances rather than essential gender identities.

Sullivan (1997) also found that men and women experienced time differently. She conducted a secondary analysis of 408 couples' time-use diaries (see chapter 10) from the Economic and Social Research Council's Social and Economic Life Initiative survey, in which they had recorded what they did and when they did it each day, as well as the amount of time they spent upon different tasks. Traditional gender differences remained even in households with an egalitarian division of domestic labour, as, again, women revealed themselves to be skilled multi-taskers. Crompton (1999) concurs that, despite increasing numbers of women working, a basic gender difference persists whereby men commit more time to employment than women, who seek to reserve time for family responsibilities. In addition, it may be that men enjoy more 'pure' leisure time, whereas women tend to synchronize theirs with childcare responsibilities (Southerton 2006).

Social class may also mediate the gendered experience of time. Those in higher status, better paid jobs now work longer hours than their counterparts in lower skilled occupations, a reversal of the trend found in the nineteenth and early twentieth centuries (Gershuny 2000). Middle-class professionals increasingly work long and unsociable hours that eat into 'family time' at home, creating a parity of effect between the traditional working-class male breadwinner and the middle-class dual earner couples of late modernity. In Silva's (1999) study, there were clear differences in the households' divisions of labour along class lines. Marc and Diane, for example, were a middle-class couple who had reversed the stereotypical gender divide: Diane went out to work all day as a civil servant while Marc combined childcare and housework with working from home as an academic researcher. By contrast, Brenda was a working-class woman whose builder husband worked long hours and did no housework; she shared responsibility for this with her three children.

Consequently, Brannen (2005) observes that managing the work–family balance is becoming a more pertinent issue for middle-class women, as working hours in white-collar jobs are increasing. Working-time schedules are being restructured by the shift towards 'flexible' working hours, with service industry employees increasingly being asked to work part-time evenings, weekends and night shifts, which create time pressures for all members of the household (Fagan 2001). Social-class differences may determine the extent to which employees have the autonomy to negotiate these working patterns and their effects upon the temporal rhythms of the household, as well as the extent to which employers provide 'family-friendly' policies of maternity/paternity leave, flexi-time, and so on (ibid.). Clearly, gender and social class intersect as variables affecting the experience and use of domestic time.

Time and daily routines

Changing times, changing paces

The perception of not having enough time may be unique to modern societies. In pre-industrial times, we can imagine that days would have passed more slowly, with more physically arduous and tiring manual labour (both paid and domestic), less designated leisure time, no television, radio or other entertainment media, and little disposable income. Daily life would have centred on the rhythms and routines of work, family and religion, its pace limited by the cycles of nature and hours of daylight. By contrast, industrial or post-industrial (Bell 1973) society is characterized by a much faster pace of life. New information technologies, faster methods of transport, more sophisticated mass media and the rise of the 'digital age' have all changed the way we experience time in everyday life. Days are broken down into hours, minutes and seconds, each of which must be accounted for; we have more things to do, and less time in which to do each of them. Thus Robinson and Godbey (1997) noted that, although Americans actually had more leisure time in 1985 than in 1965, they felt more rushed and tired. Southerton (2003) agrees that the pressures of consumer society have created a 'time squeeze', whereby the demand to spend more time on some activities, particularly work, reduces the time available for others. Consequently, he suggests that 'feeling harried' is a common experience of time in contemporary Western societies.

Social theorists have traced the historical development of this accelerated pace of modern life. Writing in the early twentieth century, Simmel (1950a [1902–3]) was famously sceptical of the decline of traditional forms of sociation, such as close kinship ties, membership of town or village guilds, and the loyal dependency of feudal employment relations. Industrialization had created a 'nomadic' existence, as individuals moved between different social circles with no strong ties to any particular one. In his essay on 'The metropolis and mental life', Simmel (ibid.) pointed to the fast pace of modern city life: urbanites survived on fleeting, impersonal encounters and did not form deeper social bonds. Although life in the city could be exciting and dynamic, it was also lonely and impersonal, characterized by an affected 'blasé attitude'. Clock time had come to rule everyday life, as people rushed from one appointment to another, scheduling every moment and worrying about 'getting things done' in time. Simmel asks us to imagine what life would be like if there were no clocks or watches: would we know how to organize our daily lives, or would sociation grind to a halt? It is interesting to reflect on how relevant Simmel's ideas remain today, over a century later. If you have visited large cities such as London or New York, you will have noticed precisely this blasé yet harassed look of passers-by. Parallels can be also drawn with Gergen's (1991) critique of 'media-saturated' culture in modernity. Gergen observed a bombardment and overstimulation of the senses with fast-moving images and constantly changing social scenes, which leaves us feeling invaded, empty and emotionally impoverished.

Figure 5.2 *Have our lives been 'speeded up'? Some critics argue that the fast pace of modern life leaves us feeling stressed, harassed and unfulfilled.*

A similar argument was proposed by Anthony Giddens (1991) in relation to the late twentieth century. Giddens was writing at a time when many believed that there had been a cultural historical shift towards postmodernism, characterized by fragmentation, uncertainty and the dissolution of traditional forms of knowledge and power. However, Giddens contested these views, arguing that we had simply moved into a new phase of modernity, which he called 'high' or 'late' modernity. Thus many of the defining features of modernity remained but had changed in form, and so were experienced differently by individuals. One example of this was the social organization of time. In traditional, pre-modern societies, time and space were intrinsically linked, because social interaction tended to be direct and face to face, but, in late modern society, time and space have become separate, resulting in the 'disembedding' and 'distanciation' of social relationships. That is, we can move between temporal and social spaces that are far wider than has ever been possible before: air travel allows us to cross time zones, twenty-four-hour shops and businesses allow us to subvert conventional clock time, while the Internet enables us to communicate with people anywhere in the world at any time of day.

Giddens (1991) argues that this has created a new experience of time as something outside of physical, bounded space and independent of social relationships. Just as society as a whole has become self-reflective about its identity, risks and (hazy) boundaries, the individuals within it have adopted a similar attitude to their own lives. Time has suddenly become something we have the potential to control, as we can choose how to move between temporal zones and how to manage the passing of time – a double-edged sword that is at once empowering and stressful. In particular, Giddens suggests that we are increasingly concerned with the need to feel in control of the way in which our lives unfold over time: we create biographical narratives or 'stories of the self' (Plummer 2001) to account for how we became who we are in relation to key life events.

Empirical studies show the continued relevance of these theories to the contemporary experience of everyday life. Nowotny (1994) observes that being aware of the infinite number of ways in which we can manage our time more efficiently and cross time–space boundaries has led us to cram more and more activities into our daily schedules and expect more to be 'achieved' each day. Instead of simply going to work, coming home, eating a meal and going to bed, we might now try to go shopping before work, to the gym in our lunch break, out with friends in the evening, and on the Internet late at night. Nowotny suggests that we live in an 'extended present', whereby each day lasts longer and longer and we remain busily immersed in our immediate activities. Unlike Giddens, she does not perceive late modern individuals to be self-reflective about the past and the future, but rather suggests that we lose sight of the wider picture – we simply do not have time to think about it. Meanwhile, there is a constant feeling of being rushed and of not having enough time to do all that we want to do (Robinson and Godbey 1997). Southerton's (2006) interviews with twenty-seven householders in Bristol, England, revealed a common perception that society was more time-pressured than in the past. The rhythms of the day alternated between periods of rush and relative calm, which had to be carefully juggled: for example Cindy 'dashed' to the shops while her partner Bradley took their daughter for a 'leisurely' trip to the park (2006: 442).

Widerberg (2006) also identifies a sense of life being 'speeded up' that is quite exhausting to experience day after day. Her study in Norway combined a large-scale survey of living and working conditions with 100 qualitative interviews with employees in four different workplaces (a company, two schools, a restaurant and a community services bureau) and revealed widespread reports of tiredness pervading work and home life. Widerberg suggests that this 'life of doing' is the driving force of late modernity, but at the expense of individual emotional wellbeing. Manual and non-manual jobs alike have created a new form of tiredness, she argues, as increasing workloads, longer working hours and fewer scheduled breaks mean that the body must 'run at full speed' throughout the day. Her interviewees revealed how crucial it was to manage one's time efficiently and to discipline the body to meet the demands of the timetable, as, for example, the teachers would take ten-minute 'power naps' during school breaktimes, or regard even five minutes of unexpected free time as a luxury. Waiters felt that they had little control of their time and had to be constantly 'on the go' throughout their shifts, with no time to 'wind up' or 'wind down'. Thus the 'speeded-up' life involves not only doing more tasks each day but also doing them at a faster pace. This may spill over into home life, as one interviewee explained:

> I notice that I sometimes sit on the edge of the chair. I am aware of it. I walk fast, take the steps in three, I run. I notice it at home as well. I hurry and then I have forgotten something, so that I have to run down the stairs and then up again. I live in a house with a lot of stairs. 'Do not stress so much', my daughter tells me when I have not even noticed it. (female, 57; Widerberg 2006: 111)

Widerberg's study shows how such feelings of being rushed, tired and 'sped up' can become so embedded (and embodied) as to become normal and taken for granted: 'I have not even noticed it.' The structural reorganization of the workplace, with its ever-increasing demands for efficiency, flexibility and maximal output, means that, for most occupations, 'it has become normal to "have too much to do"' (2006: 114). She suggests that this creates feelings of restlessness and irritability in the 'emotional bodies' (Williams and Bendelow 1996) of late modernity. It is interesting to contrast this with the blasé attitude of Simmel's metropolitan man, who was able simply to retreat from social life when it became too stimulating. By opening up the boundaries between work and home, time on and time off, we have created a new way of experiencing time.

Making and using time

So far we have looked at the ways in which time and schedules structure individual lives through the rituals and routines that we unthinkingly follow. However, it is also important to consider how people respond to these perceived structures with active strategies of resistance. This reminds us of the interplay between everyday routines, social order and rule-breaking challenges. Thus in this section we examine the agentic ways in which we use and manipulate the time we have or our perception of it: we may plan time, save time, use time more efficiently or try to transcend it altogether.

Firstly, we can plan our time to make it stretch further and enable us to do more pleasurable things. In Foucauldian terms, the discipline provided by the daily schedule is not always repressive and controlling, but can instead be creative and empowering to its adherents (cf. Foucault 1977 [1975]). Zerubavel (1981) argues that self-imposed timetables help to make our lives flow more smoothly and predictably; they allow us to co-ordinate meetings with other people, divide our time between tasks and minimize uncertainty. Schedules keep us oriented in space and time; in Giddens's (1991) terms they act as re-embedding mechanisms that enable us to deal with the problem of time–space distanciation (see above). For example, a British woman, Lucy, might have an Australian friend, Rachel, who is separated from her both geographically and by oppositional time zones, but they can arrange to chat online on a given date and at a given time. The schedule therefore provides temporal symmetry (Zerubavel 1981) between social actors that contributes to micro-level social order.

Of course, this desire to maximize our time is itself a reflection of social values. As we saw above, it can be traced back to the Protestant work ethic described by Weber (1985 [1904–5]), which favoured rational, efficient, instrumental action based upon means–end calculation. Franklin's maxim 'time is money' expressed the idea that time was a precious and finite resource to be used carefully, an attitude that persists today. Consequently, we can feel 'time poor' as much as 'money poor' (Zerubavel 1981) and struggle to create more time in our daily lives. We feel triumphant about managing to save time by working faster, delegating tasks or multi-tasking, while in the home we may welcome convenience meals and labour-saving devices that promise to reduce the time spent on domestic chores. Conversely, we feel guilty about 'wasting' time by 'doing nothing', as if every moment of the day should be rationally accounted for (Southerton 2003). Zerubavel (1981) adds that there are moral values implicit in these judgements about more or less worthwhile uses of our time, again because of the idea that time is limited and not to be spent frivolously. Even weekends and holidays, which are designed to provide legitimate 'time off' (see chapter 9), are increasingly filled with activities, as if we feel that we must cram as much pleasure as possible into these designated periods.

Furthermore, in industrialized societies time is spent as efficiently on leisure and consumption as it is on work (Jäckel and Wollscheid 2007). The question 'What did you do at the weekend?', often asked in friendly conversation, carries with it the implicit assumption that one should always be doing something, making the most of one's time. We feel a certain amount of guilty pleasure about being 'lazy', by indulging in extra sleep, beach holidays and 'trashy' television, as if even our free time should be spent in morally enriching ways. There is a burgeoning industry of self-help books on how to avoid time short-age by using the resource more efficiently, and this is depicted as a 'life management strategy' to improve one's quality of life (Larsson and Sanne 2005).

Other strategies suggest more Machiavellian tendencies in the agentic use of time. Goffman's (1959) concept of 'make work' (see above), for example, shows how people can manipulate their behaviour to present the appearance of efficient time use, even when the reality is quite the opposite. He gives the example of the shipyard workers in Archibald's (1947) study, who would be idly chatting to each other until their supervisor appeared on the scene, at which point they stopped talking, picked up their tools and appeared immersed in work. Conversely, some members of the 'leisure classes' (Veblen 2005 [1899]) might wish to appear more idle than they really are. Goffman (1959) gives the example of the upper-class ladies of Victorian society who were expected not to 'tire' themselves with any intellectually demanding activities: they would 'make no work' when men came into the room by hiding their reading books and picking up embroi-dery. We also 'make work' when we account for our use of time retro-spectively: if asked how much time we have spent on work over the past week or month, the tendency is to exaggerate in order to sound more diligent than we really are, which of course brings into question the validity of data collected from time-use diaries (Tijdens 2003).

For many people, however, manipulating time has a positive and self-serving function of increasing the amount of pleasure that they gain from a given period of time. Whether an hour is spent at work or leisure, generally speaking, the greater number and diversity of activities we can fit into that hour, the more we feel we have achieved. Robinson and Godbey (1997) argued that a common response to the experience of feeling rushed was to engage in 'time deepening':

increasing the density of a given period of time by doing more within it and/or being more efficient at tasks, which creates a sense of satisfaction and value. They identified four ways of deepening time: doing a given task more quickly, replacing a slow activity with an equivalent, faster one, multi-tasking or doing more than one activity at once, and being more aware of time when performing a task.

Meanwhile, Southerton (2003) suggests that a common response to the 'time squeeze' to avert feelings of being harried is to 'squeeze' time ourselves and get more out of it. For example, his respondents reported multi-tasking, delegating tasks, co-ordinating schedules with other household members, planning and adhering to a daily schedule, and using time-saving devices such as microwave ovens and answerphones. Thus Southerton argues that the extent to which we feel rushed, tired and temporally squeezed depends on the extent to which we are able to schedule, allocate and co-ordinate our activities with others in our particular social network: it is a matter of power and agency.

Southerton (2003) also suggests that people's daily routines vary in their activity density hour by hour, in that they are punctuated by hot and cold spots. A 'hot' spot is characterized by intense bursts of activity, institutionally timed events (such as 'the school run' or household mealtimes) and a sense of urgency to complete one's tasks on time. A 'cold' spot, by contrast, is a period of relaxation and/or interaction with significant others, during which time does not feel squeezed or need to be deepened; this is often valued as 'quality time' for 'pottering' or 'chilling out'. Southerton argues that we try to compress our activities into hot spots in order to free up more time for meaningful activities in our cold spots.

Finally, on a cultural level, Adam (2004) suggests that we have devised various strategies to transcend the constraints that time structures impose on our lives. For example, we can attempt to deny the passing of time by 'modifying nature's rhythms': having cosmetic surgery, adopting diet and fitness regimes, and so on, may help to reduce our awareness of the ageing process. We may also 'make time stand still' by externalizing personal skills and knowledge: storytelling, writing, artwork and music take ideas out of the mind of the mortal individual and into the social world, where they may be passed on to future generations, giving their creators a form of symbolic immortality (cf. Giles 2000). A third practice involves 'knowing one's fate' by attempting to learn more about our past, present and future: tracing one's family tree, reading horoscopes, practising feng shui, and so on, are becoming increasingly popular practices insofar as they promise to tell us who we are and why we are here, and thus root us more firmly in the present. Adam suggests that these practices of time transcendence function to alleviate some of the anxieties we would otherwise feel about our inability to control the passing of time.

Challenging temporality

Unstructured time as anomie

Much of this chapter has focused on the rhythms of the working day, typically spent outside the home during daytime hours, and its contrast with time spent at home. However, for those who do not follow these conventions, the structure, timing and pace of daily life can be quite different. We have already seen how homemakers engaged in domestic labour throughout the day may feel as if the working day is never over, and that they never manage to 'come home' or 'switch off' (Oakley 1974). Similarly, unemployment has been identified as a factor that can contribute to poor psychological health, insofar as it deprives people of the temporal structure, routine and predictability that come from having a regular job (Waters and Moore 2002). While we may resent the drudgery of going out to work each day at designated hours, employment does provide a sense of purpose, identity and shared experiences, as well as temporal regularity, from which we create the meaningful order of our lives. When work ceases to be the focal point of a person's day, through unemployment or retirement, unstructured time stretches out before them and the comfort of the schedule may be sorely missed. In Durkheim's (1984 [1893]) terms, this can create feelings of anomie or normlessness, whereby the structures and routines on which one has relied are suddenly taken away – an experience that can be as frightening and depressing as it is liberating (Jahoda et al. 1972).

Similarly, students may have few scheduled classes, at irregular hours, and fit their private study around these times; they may also be working at a part-time job, raising a family or pursuing extracurricular activities. Work and home life become blurred, as student residences double as study areas, and those living on campus do not 'go to work' each day. The student lifestyle often invites criticism and moral indignation from those who follow more conventional work schedules, because it breaks some of the residual rules (Scheff 1984 [1966]) they have about these routines: by not following a conventional

9–5 schedule, and by not having a clear separation between work and non-work, the lives of students appear to be relaxed, unstructured and easy to manage. We often hear jokes about the stereotypical lazy student who gets up late and does little work, but the reality is often that they will work at evenings and weekends, sometimes through the night, and feel that they never have legitimate time off.

Relaxation and 'down time'

Meanwhile, alongside the chores, routines and drudgery of work, we make time for leisure, and this plays a significant role in most people's schedules. We often hear about the importance of maintaining an appropriate 'work–life balance', as if all of the meaningful aspects of 'life' are those which occur outside of work. We might then think of leisure time as something that subverts the rules of working life: it occurs in different spheres, at different times, and has different connotative meanings (see chapter 9). However, Ken Roberts (2002) suggests that there may be a discrepancy between the way we think about leisure (as being impoverished by longer working hours) and the ways in which we actually prioritize our leisure time and protect it at all costs. Roberts conducted a secondary analysis of British census data and a MORI survey in 1999, which asked respondents about the leisure time they spent outside the home. He found that every social group made concerted efforts to protect their leisure time, however many hours they worked, although there were some demographic variations. The youngest age group (eighteen to thirty-four) enjoyed the most leisure time, as did the middle classes; women spent more time on leisure than men and enjoyed a wider range of activities, but men spent more money on their pastimes. Interestingly, income level did not seem to limit participation: those with both the highest and the lowest incomes spent more time on leisure than those with medium levels. A similar pattern was found in terms of working hours: those with both the longest (forty-nine hours or more) and the shortest (under twenty-nine hours) working weeks spent the most time on leisure activities, and those who worked full time did not spend significantly less time on leisure than part-time workers. Even those who felt they worked 'odd' or 'unsocial' hours, such as night shifts, did not suffer undue deprivation of their leisure time: although they spent slightly less time on activities outside of the home, they did so with frequency. Roberts concludes from this that leisure time is an extremely important and highly valued part of our everyday lives that we protect at all costs. Thus although we may complain vociferously about our long working hours, we may be exaggerating!

Losing sense of time

More fundamental changes occur when time stands still or becomes irrelevant. Susan Hogben (2006) describes the experience of time for the family members of missing persons, for whom daily life is simply about waiting. The clutter of activities related to work, domestic chores and leisure time, which had once been so important in providing structure to the day, now seem trivial and meaningless, and there is a shift in these individuals' temporal perspective. Hogben argues that the unexplained and prolonged absence of a loved one disrupts the 'private calendar' (Sacks 1987) that we would normally use to structure our days around interaction with significant others, which results in a 'suspension of normal service' (Hogben 2006: 328). The waiting time involves feelings of worry, hope and despair, which stretch into the future: worrying about a person implies that they remain psychologically present despite their physical absence, and that they may eventually come back. The uncertainty about the individual's welfare is then compounded by further uncertainty about whether, how and to what extent the family members can continue with their normal daily lives.

Extravagant disposals

A final context in which the meaning of time can be subverted is on holiday. Vacationing, like retirement, can make people feel luxuriously 'time rich' (Shaw 1994; cf. Zerubavel 1981) rather than 'time poor', as the resource can finally be taken for granted and attended to less consciously. Thus Chaplin's (2002) study of British people who had second homes in rural France revealed how they liked to distinguish between 'holiday time' and normal, everyday life. When on holiday, they sought to act spontaneously by letting each day unfold without a plan: as one respondent, Richard, put it, 'you just go with the flow' (2002: 222). Schedules were abandoned, activities were chosen whimsically, and their timings were made flexible, which created a sense of luxurious, carefree living. A common strategy used to achieve this was to remove all wristwatches, alarm clocks, and so on: conventional clock time was replaced by the natural rhythms of sleeping, hunger, and so on. As Sandra said, 'the watch comes off, life is more spontaneous' (ibid.). Holiday time therefore represents an opportunity for the defiance of social conventions, paradoxically exercised by taking 'time off' from time itself.

Time is a phenomenon that we take for granted as real and external, but is it no more than a social construction? It is almost impossible to imagine our daily lives without a temporal dimension and outside of the categories suggested by calendars, schedules and routines. This is one of the most difficult social structures to resist, for it is so integral to the smooth operation of everyday life: what would happen if we stopped observing clock time? Why do we regard those with unconventional schedules as deviant individuals rather than join them in a critical mass? Like many reified structures, time is both constraining and enabling: schedules control our lives but also provide comfort, routine and predictability, which in turn create social order at the micro-level. Time uses us, but we use it too, as a currency to be managed, distributed, squeezed and subverted. In the next chapter we consider eating and drinking as another such aspect of individual life that is apparently private, subjective and even innate, yet still subject to social regulation: what exactly is a 'mealtime' and what social functions does it serve? We will continue to explore the relative balance of power between cultural norms and individual practices, and see what happens when these forces collide.

Summary points

- The ways in which we experience, measure and represent time are socially constructed or 'conventional', and serve social functions. Clock time helps us to co-ordinate our activities with others, while calendars mark significant events within a culture's history. Schedules regulate the behaviour of individuals throughout the day and create the rhythmic routines of everyday life.
- The temporal rhythms of the individuals within a household may vary according to their gender, social class, age, and so on.
- Historical changes can be observed in the social organization of time. (Late) modernity is characterized by a fast pace, longer working hours, a 'twenty-four-hour' culture, and feelings of being rushed or harried. Time is perceived as a commodity – a finite resource that we try to save, use more efficiently and avoid wasting.
- Various strategies enable us to use or manipulate time to our own advantage. These include using plans and schedules, making

work/making no work, time deepening, time squeezing, and time-saving technologies.

- The conventional use of time (epitomized by the 9–5 working day) reflects many residual rules and taken for granted assumptions. These can be challenged by those who experience time differently, such as students, the unemployed, homemakers and holiday-makers.

6 Eating and Drinking

Perhaps the most frequent and regularly performed of all rituals, eating and drinking are integral to everyday life. While of course we are driven by biological need, our decisions about when, what, where, how and with whom we eat are socially shaped. In this chapter, we explore these social and cultural aspects of food and drink in relation to our three key themes. After considering the symbolic significance of food, we look in detail at some of the rituals and routines associated with its consumption, such as the family meal. Just as with the timepieces, calendars and schedules discussed in chapter 5, we shall see how these apparently normal, natural events are socially constructed, driven by cultural norms and practices. The chapter goes on to look at the ways in which eating is structured by factors such as social class, age and gender, and how the organization of food practices serves to reproduce social order. Challenges to some of the norms and unspoken rules of eating can be found in such issues as obesity, vegetarianism and eating disorders. In the final section, we examine the rituals of drinking both alcoholic and non-alcoholic beverages, as well as some deviations from these norms. Throughout the chapter, we shall see how eating and drinking are rule-governed social practices which nevertheless allow room for individual agency.

Food rituals and routines

Eating as a meaningful practice

In contemporary Western societies, food choices and practices are becoming increasingly diverse, as we are exposed to more food production, more advertising, wider ranges of food and more ways of consuming it but, at the same time, more information about its possible risks or benefits to health. Deborah Lupton (1996) argues that this has made food a focus through which we address questions of self-identity, in dialogue with Western values of discipline, control, individualism, risk and consumerism. Eating – or not eating – is a matter of individual and social identity, embodiment and subjectivity.

However, the social dimensions of food and drink pre-date modernity and may even be seen as historically and culturally universal. Eating is often a social activity, performed in the company of friends and family for the purpose of pleasure as much as biological necessity. The act of 'breaking bread' together (the literal meaning of 'companionship') expresses a group's communality, and is used to form or consolidate social bonds. It is striking to consider the amount of social activities that revolve around food: dinner parties, family get-togethers, student house meals, Christmas and Thanksgiving, all function to bring people together. It is the very routine and regularity of eating that allows this to happen – we all need to eat, and if we are to be in the presence of others for more than a few hours, a 'mealtime' will occur. Meals act as punctuation marks in the day, separating it into recognizable sections, which lends structure to the everyday world.

The timing and composition of each meal vary between cultures and groups and are socially constructed according to local norms and values. 'Breakfast' for a Chinese person may mean hot noodles and vegetables, while for a Swede it may mean fruit and yoghurt. 'Lunch' for a Briton might mean a sandwich, but for the Japanese, a Bento box. A common convention is to eat three meals a day – breakfast, lunch and dinner – each composed of particular food types, but these combinations seem quite arbitrary: why do we follow the 'three meal' rule rather than having two meals or four? Why is it acceptable to eat apple sauce with pork but not custard with chips?

These ideas were explored by the structural anthropologists of the mid-twentieth century, who sought to find meaning in the 'coding' of food (Barthes 1972 [1957]). Lévi-Strauss (1963) argued that cultural practices such as eating reveal the underlying 'grammar' or 'syntax' of a society: they were the surface-level manifestations of deep structures that were culturally universal (see chapter 2). Although the rituals and routines of one culture might vary widely from those of another, he said, every society addressed certain binary pairs of oppositional values. In the case of food, a distinction between the 'raw' and the 'cooked' was important, as every culture has ways of transforming material from one form to the other. Mary Douglas (1975 [1972]) also suggested that we can decipher the meaning of any particular meal, insofar as food categories express social relations and cultural values. There may be rules about which foods can be combined with which others and the dangers of contamination that would otherwise be faced. For example, in Orthodox Judaism, it is taught that milk and meat should not be mixed, and separate cooking utensils are used for each; to keep a non-kosher kitchen is to disobey the word of God (Solomon 1996). However, Douglas suggested that the rules we impose upon food in this way really symbolize social concerns about drawing the boundaries between private and public, inner and outer, self and others. This reminds us again of the connections between our themes of rituals and routines and social order.

Family meals: a thing of the past?

One of the most common rituals of social eating is the family meal, a rule-governed event that appears to lie at the heart of domestic life. The traditional family meal was prepared by a housewife for her husband and children in a nuclear family; they would eat together in the evening, seated around a dining table, and make conversation about how they had each spent the day. While this may no longer be the case for younger generations of dual earner and single-person households, it remains a vivid ideal and one that shaped middle- and working-class culture for much of the twentieth century. Nickie Charles (1995) argues that the family meal shows how traditional gender ideologies are reflected in the material reality of everyday practices: it assumes the economic dependence of women upon male breadwinners and their primary role as caregivers. In the early 1980s, Charles interviewed 200 women in the north of England about their cooking and eating practices, and found that this patriarchal division of labour persisted in many family homes. In 88.5 per cent of the households, women did most of the cooking, even when they were also in paid employment, and accepted this as their responsibility. In planning meals, they often put their husband's and children's prefer- ences before their own, and found great satisfaction in providing for their families. The women in this study believed that having a regular family meal was an important part of their children's socialization, and maintained that the family should eat together, at least for the main meal of each day and especially on Sundays.

What should this meal consist of? Charles and Kerr (1988) discuss the notion of the 'proper meal', which often appears in popular par- lance, and suggest that each culture has its own 'dominant food ideol- ogy'. In Britain, this typically consists of meat, potatoes and vegetables;

Figure 6.1 *The family meal is a culturally valued ritual. It functions to bring people together to celebrate, perform and reproduce their collective identities.*

in Mexico, it might be rice, beans and tortillas, while in Bengali culture a fish curry is the norm. In her study of working-class households in South Wales, Anne Murcott (1982) found that the British trio of meat, potatoes and vegetables was regarded as an appropriate main meal, although its transformation into a 'proper meal' only occurred with the addition of gravy! She also noted that the 'proper meal' was to be consumed at home, with the family: the same foods eaten in other contexts did not hold the same emotional significance. The home-cooked, proper meal was regarded as inherently superior to cold meals, snacks and convenience foods, which had not been so carefully prepared. Like Charles (1995), Murcott found that the women she interviewed did not resent having to cook family meals; they saw it as a pleasure rather than a chore. DeVault (1991) agrees that 'feeding the family' in this way is an act of love: 'feeding' differs from the practical work of 'cooking' in that it involves emotional labour (Hochschild 1983). This includes planning a meal around family members' tastes and preferences, considering the nutritional composition and aesthetic appeal of different ingredients, serving and presenting meals as gifts, and engaging in conversation while eating.

Murcott (1982) argues that women perform the majority of the work of planning, shopping for and cooking household meals, and that this forms an integral part of their daily routines. The men in the households she studied did contribute something too, but this was defined as 'helping' rather than taking full responsibility. They cooked the family meal on special occasions, such as birthdays and anniversaries, or when their wives were ill. They might have a 'speciality' dish that they could cook well, but were not concerned with the regular, mundane meals of the average weekday. Men would also assume responsibility for certain cookery tasks that served as a performance of their masculine identities, such as carving a Christmas turkey or tending a barbecue. However, the routine, day-to-day work of providing family meals remained largely a female duty.

Moreover, this pattern is not confined to Western societies. Maclagan (1994) describes the elaborate rituals of the family meal in a small Yemeni community. Here, much of daily life revolved around an elaborate midday meal, the *ghada*, which was prepared by the women of the household for their husbands, children and guests. The *ghada* had a fixed sequence of dishes, each of which contained significant ingredients: a flaky pastry cake, a pancake soaked in buttermilk and served with onions and tomatoes, bread and milk, a rice dish, a meat dish, orange and apple quarters, and finally coffee. All of this was prepared by the women of the household throughout the morning and served ceremoniously to the men at midday. If guests were present, the men would serve the meal to them as a gift, enabling them to play the role of the 'good host'. Although their wives would have prepared the food, they were expected to remain out of sight in the kitchen and could eat only the leftovers; their role was to keep their husbands 'in face' (Goffman 1967a). At first glance, this may seem to embody deeply patriarchal values and to be exploitative of women's labour. However, Maclagan emphasizes that the gender dynamics of the Yemeni households were more complex, for the women yielded a certain amount of power too. They could refuse to cook the meal, or deliberately sabotage it by making 'mistakes' in its presentation, and this would reflect upon their husbands' social standing rather than their own. Knowing this, the men in the community were deferential to their wives and showed them great respect.

In recent years, it has been argued that the family meal is in decline in contemporary Western societies (Ryan 2006). A number of factors may have contributed to this change: the growing numbers of women working outside the home, dual earner households and people living alone; the increasingly fast pace of life (see chapter 5); the introduction of labour-saving devices such as the microwave oven and the popularity of convenience meals (Blaxter and Paterson 1983; Kemmer 2000). The 'TV dinner' has replaced the traditional family meal, as householders come home exhausted after a long day at work and lack the time and inclination to prepare a 'proper meal'. They may also eat separately in 'shifts', according to their different working hours and lifestyles (DeVault 1991).

Other theorists, however, suggest that the family meal has survived but simply changed form to meet the new demands of household members (see, for example, Murcott 1997). Post-feminist values may have changed the meaning of home-cooking from drudgery to pleasure, as glamorous celebrity chefs teach women that they can both work and be a 'domestic goddess' (Hollows 2003). Moreover, the idea of the communal meal may still appeal to many, insofar as it expresses important social values and is generally regarded as a positive, enjoyable experience. Thus, while the modern nuclear family may be unable to co-ordinate their schedules enough to eat together every night, they may make a special effort to have a family meal once a week, particularly on Sundays. Students living away from home often find themselves re-creating the family meal by having 'house meals' once a week or on special occasions. It seems that, while practical and lifestyle factors may have impeded the survival of the family meal in its original form, we remain committed to the values it represents.

Dining and social order

Table manners and etiquette

The ritual of the family meal can be seen as contributing to the social order of the household. By sitting down together, behaving in relatively predictable ways, and engaging in meaningful social interaction, the family symbolically reproduces itself and reaffirms its core values. One way in which this order is achieved is by the use of table manners, a set of rules about managing the body and handling objects. Norbert Elias (1994) showed how this set of rules could be traced back to the historical emergence of the 'civilizing process' in seventeenth- and eighteenth-century Renaissance Europe. In the wake of the mediaeval period, with its high rates of poverty, squalor, disease and early death, Renaissance individuals were able to look beyond the immediate concerns of physical survival and to enjoy better health. They then began to be concerned with matters of social status, particularly insofar as this was expressed through bodily deportment, fashion and public behaviour. Elias points to the many etiquette manuals that were published at this time which aimed to restrain individual appetites and impulses. In Foucauldian terms, such codes of behaviour exerted a form of disciplinary power over individuals by controlling their embodied behaviour (Foucault 1977 [1975]; Lupton 1996).

Table manners were central to this display of self-restraint, Elias said, symbolizing that not only did people understand the codes governing which knife to use, how to hold one's cup, and so on (signs of 'good breeding'), but also that they were able to put social norms before their raw appetites. Kate Fox shows how such rules of etiquette continue to shape our behaviour today, and how their (mis)interpretation can be read as an indicator of social class. For example, she discusses the 'small/slow is beautiful' rule: members of the upper and upper-middle classes learn to cut or break off small pieces of food and eat them one at a time, with painstaking slowness; vegetables and other soft foods must be squashed onto the back of the fork. The 'lower' classes, she says, adopt more inelegant strategies, such as buttering a whole bread roll or 'shovelling up the food with the fork alone' (Fox 2004: 317), which satisfy their appetites more efficiently but are regarded as less civilized. Fox comments that the 'small/slow is beautiful' rule and others like it are impractical and actually make eating more difficult, but that their real purpose is one of social display:

> What it all boils down to is not appearing to be greedy, and, more specifically, not appearing to give food too high a priority. Greed of any sort is a breach of the all important fair-play rule. Letting one's desire for food take priority over making conversation with one's companions involves giving physical pleasure or gratification a higher value than words. In polite society, this is frowned upon as un-English and highly embarrassing. Over-eagerness about anything is undignified; over-eagerness about food is disgusting and even somehow faintly obscene. (2004: 318–19)

Such rules about the finer points of dining etiquette may only be observed by some, but Fox argues that the basic principles behind table manners are those to which most people adhere – markers of civilized society that are relatively classless. These include being polite (saying 'please' and thank you' when asking to be passed dishes), not taking more than one's fair share, not talking with one's mouth full, and not dominating the conversation. The observance of such rules by all participants makes the meal, as a social event, flow more smoothly and facilitates its real purpose as a medium of harmonious interaction.

Class, taste and distinction

In terms of social class, food consumption practices differ noticeably. For example, Blaxter and Paterson (1983) found that working-class housewives regarded meat, potatoes, bread and milk as their staples, and prized foods that were 'simple', 'natural', 'plain' and 'nourishing', such as home-made soup. This was also mediated by age, as the younger generation of women in the sample placed less emphasis on meat and more upon fruit and vegetables. Warde (1997) agrees that income level is a very important factor affecting patterns of food consumption, and that, for those in poorer households, decisions are made on the basis of 'thrift' and 'economizing' as much as personal taste. Interestingly, however, he reports that those in lower income households spend a greater proportion of their weekly budget on food than those in more affluent households, perhaps because this is one of the cheapest ways in which to 'treat' oneself to luxury items in a consumer-oriented society. Warde conducted a content analysis of the articles and advertising used in a selection of food magazines in 1967–8 and 1991–2. He found that those magazines aimed at working- and lower-middle-class audiences, particularly in the 1960s, emphasized values of thrift and economy: recipes involving the use of leftovers were featured, as well as 'cost per portion' estimates for each dish. By contrast, magazines aimed at higher social classes would include more recipes for 'special occasion' catering, using extravagant ingredients such as oysters, truffles, champagne and lobster. The photographs emphasized the dishes' aesthetic attributes (nouvelle cuisine was popular in the early 1990s) rather than their economic value.

Other foodstuffs may be identified with particular social classes, in terms of either actual patterns of consumption or attitudes and stereotypes. For example, the consumption of organic and Fair Trade products remains a largely middle-class pursuit, because of their relatively high cost (Bunch 2006). Fox (2004) suggests that stereotypically working-class foods include prawn cocktail, pasta salad, tinned fruit and tinned fish. Conversely, olive oil, sun-dried tomatoes, home-made pasta and rocket leaves all signify a middle-class status (Paterson 2006). On the one hand, this suggests motives of self-presentation. Individuals may knowingly consume certain foods in order to associate themselves with a particular social class – Veblen's (2005 [1899]) 'conspicuous consumption' – or avoid certain foods to disassociate themselves from another class – Bourdieu's (1984) 'distinction'. On the other hand, food choices may simply unwittingly reflect personal habit, family tradition, or the class-based values into which we are socialized.

Fox (2004) suggests that even the way we talk about food is interesting in this regard: the linguistic terms used to refer to mealtimes, implements and foods themselves can be decoded as class indicators. Thus to call one's evening meal 'tea' suggests working-class origins, whereas to call it 'dinner' suggests a middle-class identity, and to call it 'supper' suggests upper-middle- or upper-class status. The latter may take 'afternoon tea', but this is a different meal, consisting of tea (the drink), sandwiches and cake. To make matters more confusing, the midday meal called 'lunch' by the middle and upper classes is often called 'dinner' by the working class, while the upper class use 'dinner' to refer to a formal, communal meal taken later in the evening (Fox 2004: 309–11). Each of these terms contains subtle but distinctive indicators of a person's class position and, as such, acts in Garfinkel's (1967) terms as an 'index' of underlying norms, values and shared background knowledge.

'Healthy eating' and nutritional advice

Another way in which eating practices reflect social order is in the shift towards 'healthy' eating that has occurred over the twentieth and into the twenty-first century. As public health, sanitation and living conditions have improved, along with levels of consumer spending power, relative affluence, advances in medical knowledge and increasing access to it (via the mass media and Internet), Western cultures have become more and more concerned with improving their health through dietary management. However, our ideas about how to do this, in terms of which foods to buy, how to compose a 'balanced' meal, how many calories to consume per day, and so on, are shaped by the cultural discourses of 'healthy eating'. This is an important way in which food is being increasingly subjected to processes of medicalization and politicization (Chamberlain 2004). Government guidelines on nutrition, such as the 'Five [portions of fruit and vegetables] a Day' campaign or the 'Pyramid' (showing the relative proportions of different food groups to be consumed), and the recommended intake of calories, fat, salt and sugar content, can be seen as another form of 'disciplinary power' (Foucault 1977 [1975]), shaping the embodied behaviour of individuals who believe that they are making free choices. Deborah Lupton (1995) suggests that this is one of many discourses of public health and health promotion that are disseminated as a subtle form of social control; the information embedded within them is presented as scientific, objective fact and therefore beyond question.

But how successful have these discourses been in changing social attitudes to food? On the one hand, there are discernible trends that have occurred in patterns of food consumption over the past two centuries that reflect the principles of 'healthy eating'. We are eating less red meat, more fish and poultry, and more wholegrain, higher fibre products (Fulcher and Scott 2007), lower fat milk (Lupton 1996) and more fruit and vegetables (Chamberlain 2004). On the other hand, we are also eating higher levels of fat, sugar, salt and overall calories (Fulcher and Scott 2007), more pre-packaged convenience foods (Murcott 2000) and more processed foods (Chamberlain 2004). Levels of obesity and coronary heart disease are rising as a result of our increased consumption of fat (Wiggins 2004).

Furthermore, adherence to nutritional guidelines may remain largely a pursuit of the (upper-)middle 'chattering classes' (Fox 2004) who have greater levels of disposable income: it is a privilege to be able to select foods on the basis of taste rather than budgetary constraints. A study by Charles and Kerr (1988) revealed that those on low incomes reported difficulty in eating 'properly' because they could not afford a sufficiently diverse diet; the nutritional guidelines provided by the government were not meaningful or relevant to their everyday lives. Wiggins (2004) concurs that healthy eating advice may be accepted as providing appropriate general guidelines, but this does not necessarily translate into the practical, situated lifeworlds of individuals. The participants in Wiggins's study (ten family households in the north and midlands of England) cited various reasons why they had rejected general nutritional advice: the guidelines did not apply to their age, gender or medical condition, they could not afford the 'healthiest' options, or the advice did not fit in with the practicalities of food provision in their households.

Eating around the norm

Eating out

Let us now consider some of the eating practices that challenge or subvert – and thereby elucidate – the norms of food consumption. Firstly, eating out in restaurants is a practice that is becoming increasingly common as a way of marking special occasions, or simply breaking the routine. By eating different types of food, in a different context, we symbolically demarcate that unit of time from others as exceptional, which in turn reminds us of the norms from which it is deviating. A birthday meal, for example, not only celebrates the individual's new age, but also stands in juxtaposition to all of the 364 ordinary days that have preceded it: we need *not* to celebrate these other days in order to make the birthday special. Rules and deviations therefore exist in tandem, each allowing the possibility of the other – or, to paraphrase Foucault (1980 [1976]), 'where there is power, there is always resistance' (see chapter 2). This in turn suggests a link between our themes of social order and challenges to the taken for granted.

Warde and Martens (2000) suggest that there are three main reasons why people go out to eat: for pleasure (e.g. birthdays, anniversaries and other celebrations), leisure (e.g. a sociable meal may be enjoyed by families or friends as a regular 'treat') or necessity (e.g. when away from home). Their UK survey of 1001 people in Bristol, London and Preston, combined with interviews with thirty householders in Preston, revealed that the restaurant meal serves certain social functions for its participants, such as an opportunity for contemplation (reflecting on the significance of the occasion), mutual gratification (seeing everybody else having a good time as well as oneself), instrumentalism (the satisfaction of organizing an event that runs smoothly), and of course sociality (enjoying each other's company). Thus although eating out represents a break from the norm, it ultimately serves to strengthen social solidarity.

Vegetarianism

A second challenge to cultural food norms comes from vegetarianism: the avoidance of meat, fish and, in some cases, all animal products. Since the establishment of the Vegetarian Society in 1847, this practice has become more and more common in Western countries, especially over the past fifty years (Beardsworth and Keil 1992). However, vegetarianism remains both statistically and socially deviant in relation to carnivorous diets. In 2007, only 4 million (6.7 per cent) of the British population were vegetarian (Vegetarian Society 2008), putting them in a small but significant minority. As Wilson, Weatherall and Butler (2004) argue, meat-eating remains the dominant discourse, generating a rhetoric against which others are compared. For example, party caterers work on the assumption that, by default, most guests will be carnivorous; those who are not will be requested to highlight their 'special' dietary requirements when replying to their invitation.

Figure 6.2 *One of the ways in which we may deviate from eating routines is to go out for a restaurant meal. We do out of the ordinary things like this to mark special occasions: the 'treat' is a reward for following the rules at other times.*

Nevertheless, vegetarianism is a practice replete with meanings of its own. Julia Twigg (1983) describes this as an explicit food ideology that suggests individual choice and agency rather than adherence to culturally prescribed norms and social conventions.

Twigg identifies an implicit hierarchy of foods in terms of their symbolic value and status within Western societies: red meat is at the top, followed by fish and poultry, eggs and cheese, fruit and vegetables, and finally cereals. The staples of a vegetarian or vegan diet therefore lie towards the bottom of this hierarchy, and are regarded as less desirable. This reflects cultural stereotypes about food, such as red meat's association with (male) power, strength, aggression and virility, compared to the association of root vegetables and pulses with poverty, physical weakness, hippie lifestyles, and so on. There are also gender stereotypes implicit in these judgements, Twigg argues, insofar as vegetarianism is often regarded as a feminine ideology, with connotations of purity, pacifism, intuition, spirituality and emotionality/irrationality. Eating foods of this nature presents a challenge to the assumptive world of many carnivores, and so is regarded as deviant: vegetarians often encounter scepticism and teasing, albeit light-hearted in intention. Veganism, the complete avoidance of all animal products, presents an even more extreme challenge to these norms, and vegan identities may be particularly stigmatized (Sneijder and Te Molder 2004).

'Disorderly' eating

The rules of eating behaviour can be challenged by the amount as well as the type of food that we consume. On the one hand, Western cultures are currently facing an alleged 'obesity epidemic', whereby 74.1 per cent of Americans and 63.8 per cent of Britons are classified as overweight, with a Body Mass Index (BMI) of 25 or more (US Temporal Trends 2007; WHO 2007), and between 22 and 25 per cent in each country are classified as obese, with a BMI of more than 30 (Government Office for Science 2007).

However, the mass-media coverage of this new trend can be read as something of a moral panic (Cohen 1972), insofar as deviant lifestyle practices ('junk food' consumption, lack of exercise, etc.) are blamed for the increased health risks associated with obesity (WHO 1998, 2007). According to Monaghan (2007), obesity has been constructed as a new public health problem for which disciplinary regimes are proposed as solutions. He suggests that, ironically, these follow the principles of the fast food industry, and as such are 'McDonaldized' responses (cf. Ritzer 2004). For example, extreme diet plans and exercise regimes carry the promise of success because they are devised in such a rational, calculated way. There is no element of luck or superstition here; the plans are standardized and impersonal, and individuals are taught that, if they work hard enough, adhere strictly to the plan and maintain a level of self-discipline, it will produce results. This reinforces the assumption that those who remain overweight are simply lazy, greedy, or both: cultural values and ideologies are inscribed upon the body.

On the other hand, we find equal levels of concern expressed about the risks of extreme dieting and underweight bodies, particularly among young women. It is estimated that 1 to 2 per cent of adolescent or college-age women are seeking help for anorexia, and 3 to 4 per cent for bulimia, in both the UK and USA (B-EAT 2007a; ANRED 2007), with many more remaining undiagnosed (B-EAT 2007a). In contemporary Western cultures, the slim body is depicted as an image of feminine beauty, but this judgement is historically and culturally relative. In contrast to the voluptuous bodies that were celebrated in Renaissance culture, since the Victorian era the 'ideal' female body has been getting smaller. Bordo (1993) argues that, as levels of affluence increased, the slender body came to be seen as an expression of restraint, self-control and appetites that were safely contained, a product of the civilizing process (Elias 1994). Managing the body served as a metaphor for contradictions in the wider culture, between the temptations of unrestrained consumption and the value of rational sobriety.

Insofar as these conflicts cannot be resolved in the wider society, Bordo argues, they are projected onto the body: women are taught to be ashamed of their appetites and desires, to feel as if they take up too much space in the world, to deny their needs, and to fear weakness, mess and disorder. Wolf (2007 [1990]) argues that the more social and political emancipation women achieved, the less they could be overtly controlled or discriminated against, and so the 'beauty myth' was created as the last remaining tool of patriarchal oppression. In this context, eating-disordered bodies present a challenge rather than a submission to conventional ideas about feminine beauty. In particular, the extremely thin anorexic body presents a grotesque parody of slenderness, showing what this value means if taken to its logical conclusion. However, these feminist theories cannot explain why increasing numbers of boys and men are becoming prone to eating disorders (B-EAT 2007b), a topic that remains under-researched.

Eating disorders also present a challenge to many unspoken rules, rituals and routines of everyday eating behaviour. The disorders are such that their incumbent behaviours involve regular and routinized breaches of the taken for granted assumptions (Garfinkel 1967) or residual rules (Scheff 1984 [1966]) that surround eating. Firstly, those with anorexia and bulimia will often eat alone, and in secret. Rather than enjoying mealtimes as social events, they are anxiously preoccupied with the food itself, feeling ashamed of what and how much (or little) they are eating. The anorexic may avoid eating with others for fear of being 'nagged' to eat more, while the bulimic would be mortified if anyone caught her in the throes of a bingeing episode. This in turn means that those with eating disorders may avoid social events that revolve around food – which, as we have seen, is most of them. Their avoidance may be misread by others as a sign of unfriendliness or aloofness, evoking reactions of moral indignation (cf. Garfinkel 1967).

Secondly, those with eating disorders challenge some of the symbolic meanings of food, for example, that it is given as a gesture of love (DeVault 1991). By using food as a means of bodily self-discipline, focusing on its nutritional or calorific content, and taking control of its preparation, anorexics in particular deny others the opportunity to make this symbolic gesture. Indeed, some psychoanalytic theorists argue that therein lies the real significance of the behaviour, as a symbolic rejection of a (m)other's love and thus a bid for individual autonomy (Orbach 1986).

Thirdly, those with eating disorders challenge many people's taken for granted assumptions about what a 'proper meal' is, when it should be eaten and how often. They may wish to avoid meals, eat at irregular times, or make unusual choices, which confound the expectations of others. Families of anorexics may have regular arguments about whether, for example, rice cakes and jelly constitutes a dinner (Hornbacher 1998), while those of bulimics wonder why food disappears from their cupboards every night. Although, as we have seen, the rules about food combinations, 'proper' meals and mealtimes are socially constructed, they are so embedded in the domestic cultures of everyday life that they come to be regarded as natural. As with all residual rules, we see them only when they are broken. This is illustrated in a scene from Mike Leigh's play *Life is Sweet* (1990), when the character of Nicola sits scowling and smoking as her family tuck into toasted sandwiches. When asked why she will not eat, she defiantly snaps, 'What's lunchtime anyway? It's only a convention!'

Remembering the mutuality of structure and agency (see chapter 2), it is important to think not only about what social environments do to bodies but also what embodied individuals do to themselves (Frank 1991). For example, Orbach (1986) interprets anorexia nervosa as a bid for autonomy within the family. She suggests that girls learn to have their needs denied, left unsatisfied, or subsumed beneath the needs of others. Anorexia serves as a metaphorical expression of this, but taken to extremes: it is a political 'hunger strike' that reveals what it ultimately means to deny one's needs, while at the same time demonstrating the individual's determination to control her own body absolutely.

We can also consider how some people with eating disorders seek to challenge the way in which their 'problems' are interpreted. As Rich (2006) explains, anorexia is a stigmatized social identity, which is often seen as selfish, irrational and self-indulgent, but the young women in her study demonstrated how they sought to manage this identity by finding different ways of thinking about their condition. They did not passively 'suffer' anorexia, but rather actively accomplished it as a performative identity. For example, in the residential eating disorders centre that she studied, patients confessed how they would strengthen each other's commitment to the goal of weight loss by sharing their resistant practices, such as 'skanking' (hiding food) or 'tanking' (drinking large volumes of water before a weighing). This message is also conveyed by the online communities of the pro-anorexia or pro-ana movement (Ferreday 2003), which argues that 'anorexia is a lifestyle, not a disease' (Atkins 2002). These websites typically contain 'tips and tricks' on self-starvation, 'thinspirational' pictures of celebrities, and a forum in which members can discuss their progress towards a (self-determined, medically dangerous) target weight. Fox et al. (2005a) suggest that pro-anorexia is an underground social movement that, while disturbing to many in its views, reminds us that the medical model is only one of several alternative discourses about the condition. Even the meaning of 'recovery' is contested as a value-laden assumption that to get better means to gain weight; for those in the midst of anorexia, self-improvement comes from losing weight. Thus eating rules, like other norms, are socially constructed and open to challenge.

Drinking rules and rituals

While the satiation of thirst is a matter of biological necessity, like eating, it also serves many social purposes. We drink when we are not thirsty, just as we eat when not hungry, because the situation demands it: a 'toast' in celebration of a newly wed couple, or an invitation to 'go for a drink' with a friend. If a visitor arrives unexpectedly at one's home, a polite custom is to offer them a drink as a display of hospitality. Drink, like food, serves the social function of bringing people together in a 'focused encounter' (Goffman 1961b), where there is a shared focus of attention but the real purpose is the interaction per se. Drinks can also serve as useful 'props', or 'side involvements' (Goffman 1963b), that distract the audience's attention from other aspects of one's behaviour. For example, at parties, they give shy people 'something to do with their hands' which disguises their self-consciousness (Scott 2007).

Tea and coffee breaks

Let us examine two examples of drinking rituals that are particularly salient in contemporary Western societies. Firstly, the tea (or coffee) break. Tea and coffee are caffeinated beverages that are consumed in huge quantities across the world. India and China remain the biggest exporters of tea and consume it in the largest total volumes, although the UK and Ireland have the highest per capita rates of tea consumption in the world: 3 kg per person, compared with 0.9 kg in Australia and 0.3 kg in the USA (World of Tea 2008). America is arguably more of a 'coffee culture', this being the drink of urban commuters and office workers, as well as the home of café chains such as Starbucks, which have become global corporations. Coffee consumption in the USA is 4.4 kg per capita; 54 per cent of the American adult population drinks coffee daily and in average quantities of 3.1 cups per day (NCA 2000). Meanwhile, tea remains stereotypically the drink of the English, with its origins in the colonies of the British Empire and its long tradition of cultural significance. In a tongue-in-cheek manner, Kate Fox writes,

> Tea is still believed, by English people of all classes, to have miraculous properties. A cup of tea can cure, or at least significantly alleviate, almost all minor physical ailments and indispositions, from a headache to a scraped knee. Tea is also an essential remedy for all social and psychological ills, from a bruised ego to the trauma of a divorce or bereavement. This magical drink can be used equally effectively as a sedative or stimulant, to calm and soothe or to revive and invigorate. Whatever your mental or physical state, what you need is 'a nice cup of tea'. (2004: 312)

The rituals of tea and coffee drinking are important too. Tea breaks punctuate the rhythms of the day for those engaged in some form of work, from the office clerk to the home decorator. We often find tea breaks written into the agendas of meetings or workshops, in recognition of their assumed necessity. They may also be taken as a reward or incentive for finishing a difficult task, such as writing an essay or revising for exams. When the nature of the work is mundane or boring, such breaks help to mark one's progress towards the end of a long shift. In his study of machine operators, Roy (1958) found that, at certain points mid-morning and mid-afternoon, someone would shout, 'Banana time!', and a cheer would go up as they all downed their tools. The phrase referred to a scheduled break in which the workers were allowed to have a drink, eat snacks (hence the bananas), smoke, and so on. This not only provided a short moment of relaxation but also reminded the workers that they had made it through a significant chunk of the day.

Going to the pub

A second type of drinking behaviour is the consumption of alcoholic drinks in bars and pubs, or public houses. This is one of the most common leisure pursuits in the Western countries, with an estimated 69 per cent of people in the UK engaging in it regularly (Mintel 2000). Indeed, for many people, the words 'drink' and 'drinking' are synonymous with this type of beverage: if we invite someone out 'for a drink', we generally mean an alcoholic one. Watson suggests that the pub is 'an icon of the everyday' (2002: 190), at least in British culture, where taverns and alehouses have existed since pre-industrial times as the focal points of local communities. Long before television, cinema and computer games were invented, people would congregate in their village pub and use it as a place for informal socializing.

In Turner's (1967) terms, the pub acts as a 'liminal zone' between work and home, which provides cultural remission from normal constraints upon interaction (Fox 2004). That is, people often drop in to bars on their way home from work and use this as an opportunity to unwind; because the bar is not part of either world, it provides a space in which one can feel free of social responsibilities and take some time for oneself. The pub is a backstage region (Goffman 1959), insofar as punters go there to relax, remove their 'work' personae and prepare themselves for their 'home' ones. Gusfield (1987) suggests that, by providing circumscribed periods of time for social drinking, bars reinforce the distinction between work and leisure, which in turn strengthens our commitment to the routines of daily life. More generally, alcohol is used to mark the transition from work to play: we 'break open a bottle' to celebrate success or good news in various contexts. Drinking together is a bonding activity which helps to dissolve social hierarchies: for example, colleagues may drink together after work, to erase the status barrier between the 'boss' and the 'juniors'.

The pub facilitates a certain form of social interaction, which is characterized by various rituals and routines. Fox (2004) points out that in this space there is an unspoken rule that one will engage only in light-hearted social banter, not in deep and meaningful talk (unless inebriated; see below). On the one hand, certain rules of privacy are suspended, so that at the bar it is acceptable to strike up a conversation with a stranger, but, on the other hand, an 'anti-earnestness' rule prevails, censoring the discussion of any emotive, controversial or, indeed, boring topic that would make the experience less pleasurable for others.

Furthermore, the kind of interaction to be found here is significant as an index of social relations. For example, Fox (2004) discusses the ritual of 'buying a round' of drinks for everyone in a group. She suggests that this apparently benign, pragmatic activity actually serves as a symbolic code of many underlying rules and values (cf. Lévi-Strauss 1963). It is a form of reciprocal gift-giving, whereby every member of the group provides for everybody else, dissolving any animosities and creating an egalitarian atmosphere. It is also a display of turn-taking, as every person in the group is expected to buy a round of drinks at some point over the course of the evening, and as such it expresses their commitment to the moral value of fairness. Fox observes that any hint of miserliness and reluctance to buy one's round is severely frowned upon, and people are so keen to avoid being regarded as deviant that they compete to 'get their round in' early on.

Figure 6.3 *Going for a drink with friends often involves the ritual of 'buying a round'. What are the rules of drinking?*

There are some exceptions to these rules, Fox continues: women are often politely overlooked in the search for the next round-buyer, as are those who are known to be less affluent, younger or more junior than their companions (for example, a professor might pay for his or her students' drinks). Even when we reach the bar, there are rules about how to order. The customers may be spread around the bar in an 'invisible queue', whereby each person is implicitly aware of the order in which they arrived, and thus whose turn it is to be served next. Any attempt at queue-jumping will be frowned upon, while any unintentional mistakes on behalf of the bartender in reading the order of the queue may be met by sympathetic glances from fellow customers (Fox 2004).

Deviant drinking

Drunkenness

It is an interesting paradox that drunkenness, perhaps the most commonsensical example of aberrant drinking, is actually not regarded as deviant unless it occurs with excessive frequency or in the wrong contexts. Within the liminal zone of the pub and its unique forms of interaction, drunkenness is condoned, even expected, as part of a 'good night out'. The ritual of getting drunk together is used, like the collective meal, to facilitate social bonding, particularly insofar as alcohol causes disinhibition and self-disclosure. In some contexts (such as flirting with a prospective partner) it successfully subverts the rule of sticking to light-hearted conversation and provides 'Dutch courage'. Drunkenness can also be worn as a badge of honour, allowing people to boast about 'mad' or 'stupid' things they did the night before: otherwise deviant behaviour is accounted for by the excuse that 'I was drunk', and thus condoned as harmless fun. This is an example of the normalization of a rule-breaking act.

There are even social events created specifically for this purpose, which are woven into the structure of social institutions. The office party, for example, is a notorious event deplored by all but attended by many who work in white-collar businesses and organizations. Its reputation goes before it as an occasion at which people will seduce one another, dance in an embarrassing way to 'cheesy' pop music, or photocopy their body parts – all activities at which we would cringe in the cold light of day, but which are tacitly accepted as signs of enjoyment. There is also an unspoken rule that any such misdemeanours will be politely 'forgotten' about and not mentioned in the office the next day, unless in jibes and banter. The office party, and other drinking events like it, is a site of licensed carnival (Bakhtin 1968), which allows us to suspend momentarily social conventions on the understanding that we will return to them with renewed vigour the next day. In this respect, drunkenness epitomizes the Durkheimian view of deviance as something that ultimately strengthens our commitment to the rules that have been broken (Durkheim 1984 [1893]).

Alcoholism

So where do we draw the line between harmless and problematic drinking? Sociological studies of alcohol addiction help us to see how the latter term is constructed in relation to social norms and values (May 2001). In some cases, a person's drinking behaviour becomes so excessive, frequent or inconsistent with the habits of those around them that it is perceived as a cause for concern. 'Problem' drinking is that which not only interferes with an individual's own lifestyle but also confounds the expectations of others. The drinking per se is not problematic, and each individual occasion could be normalized in isolation, but when viewed together the overall effect is one of aberration. The problem drinker has broken the residual rules (Scheff 1984 [1966]) of drunkenness outlined above, in that they have failed to restrict their drinking to a few, exceptional moments of licensed carnival. Denzin (1987) presents a Symbolic Interactionist model of the 'alcoholic' identity as being socially negotiated in this way: it is a role that is labelled as deviant in relation to the norms and values of a particular group. Rather than simply being alcoholic, one becomes this way through the patterns of interaction that occur as one is labelled, interprets and internalizes the meaning of this label, and responds by living up to it (cf. Becker 1963).

Abstinence

At the other end of the spectrum is the non-drinker. Again, this is a deviant identity that is constructed relative to situational norms and expectations: not drinking alcohol is perfectly normal and acceptable behaviour in all contexts except that of a group of people who are drinking it. Birenbaum and Sagarin (1973) present a fascinating account of the ways in which this identity is defined and negotiated, just like that of the alcoholic. The ritual of 'going for a drink' involves certain pieces of recipe knowledge (Schütz 1972) about what will happen, namely that everyone will have an alcoholic drink and keep pace with the others in the group in terms of whether and how much they get drunk. By not drinking, an individual confounds these taken for granted expectations and makes those around them feel uncomfortable: they are suddenly aware of the unspoken rule that has been broken. The non-drinker is challenging the drinkers' definition of the situation (Thomas and Thomas 1970 [1928]) as one of decadence and carnival, and may be perceived to be disapproving of it from a morally aloof standpoint.

This creates awkwardness and embarrassment on all parts, Birenbaum and Sagarin (1973) argue, as drinkers and non-drinkers alike suddenly become aware of how their behaviour might be viewed from the perspective of the other (cf. Mead 1934). However, as dramaturgical team-mates (Goffman 1959), they are also motivated to co-operate to restore the situation to its normal appearances by glossing over this embarrassment. Thus insofar as there is a degree of uncertainty over whether the non-drinker even has a right to be present, they will demonstrate that they do not hold a morally aloof attitude (by joining in enthusiastically with the conversation, laughing, and so on), while the drinkers will respond in kind to show that they accept the individual as an honorary member: 'The person who threatens the unstated norms of the group by refusing to do what is expected of him must show signs of recognition that others have the right to do what he does not choose to do' (Birenbaum and Sagarin 1973: 70).

Birenbaum and Sagarin go on to identify various types of non-drinker who use different strategies to account for their behaviour. When it comes to buying a round, the 'alcoholic' can say, 'No thanks, the doctor told me not to', or 'I'm on the wagon', which are generally accepted as beyond dispute. The 'occasional drinker' may decide to have a drink for the sake of keeping the peace, reasoning that they will be appreciated more for having aligned themselves with the drinkers' definition of the situation. Meanwhile, the person who has never drunk, does not enjoy it, and may indeed privately disapprove of it, may try to position themselves inconspicuously on the fringes of the group, or to 'pass' (Goffman 1963a) as a drinker by choosing something that could be mistaken for an alcoholic drink, such as ginger ale or lemonade. Another strategy is to assume the role of 'driver' in the group, so that the non-drinker identity can be normalized as a situational status. In each case, we see how rule-makers and rule-breakers alike work to uphold a common definition of their subjective world, and thus to maintain social order within it.

Both eating and drinking, therefore, are not simply responses to biological drives, but are social practices that are ritualistic, rule-governed and subject to the constant possibility of challenge. The collective consumption of food and drink can serve a number of social functions, including but not limited to communality, hospitality, liminality and the celebration of group identity. The practices involved help individuals to express and to perform identities of gender, class, ethnicity and age, as well as to distinguish and disassociate themselves from other such identities. Finally, as rule-governed practices, eating and drinking can be found in both conformist and deviant forms, the contrast reminding us of the interplay between our themes of social order, rituals and routines, and norm-breaking challenges.

This social shaping of an ostensibly personal, private experience raises interesting questions about what we define as 'natural' and 'normal', and where we perceive the boundary to lie between individual choice and social forces. This thorny issue cannot be reduced to a simple matter of 'nature versus nurture', for there are many and varied connections between the two. As phenomenologists argue (see chapter 2), we interpret private, subjective experiences within the framework of cultural discourses, social norms and shared stocks of background knowledge – but this knowledge is in turn shaped by our embodied experiences of being in the world. In the next chapter, we explore this duality further through the experience of health, illness and disability, which can be understood as both ontological states and social identities.

Summary points

- Eating and drinking are social practices, characterized by rituals, routines and culturally specific rules.
- The 'family meal', often synonymous with the notion of a 'proper meal', is one that is provided within households as a means of bringing people together for social interaction. It is questionably in decline, but may simply have changed form in line with changes in the domestic division of labour and household composition.
- Eating practices help to reproduce social order at a micro-level, insofar as they are rule-governed events. The 'disciplinary power' exerted by these rules can be seen in such conventions as mealtimes, table manners and discourses of healthy eating.

- The rules of food and eating can be challenged in various ways, for example by eating out in restaurants, vegetarianism and eating disorders.
- Drinking practices are also normative, conventional and governed by rituals, from the tea and coffee break to the rules for 'buying a round' in the pub.
- The rules of drinking similarly reproduce micro-level social order within a group, and accordingly can be challenged, for example by the 'alcoholic' and the non-drinker.

7 Health, Illness and Disability

This chapter considers how the experience of health, illness and disability both shape and is shaped by our relationships with others in the social world. Like the feelings of hunger and thirst explored in the previous chapter, states of ill health are at once private, embodied and personal, and public, discursive and social. We begin by looking at lay definitions of health and illness as local, subjective realities, and contrast this with the dominant medical model through which sick bodies are treated. We then examine some of the social processes involved in becoming ill and being a 'patient', focusing on the rituals and routines that occur at each stage. The third section addresses a number of challenges to common-sense notions of health, ab/normality and ways of thinking about differences between people: these include chronic, stigmatizing and otherwise contested conditions, and studies of disability. We shall concentrate on physical health, but readers may also be interested in exploring key texts on the sociology of mental illness (Busfield 2001; Pilgrim and Rogers 2005).

Defining health and illness

What do we mean when we say that somebody is healthy or sick? At the simplest level, health can merely mean the absence of disease, disorder or pathology: an individual is healthy if they are not ill. Alternatively, the terms can be defined in relation to statistical norms for a population: illness occurs when we feel significantly less well than most other people, while disability occurs when we are not able to perform tasks that most other people can. A third idea is that sickness interferes with everyday routines; it is defined by individuals in relation to their own perceived norms. Thus even those who are already suffering an illness may report that they feel relatively better or worse, day to day.

We also tend to think of health in positive terms, as a feeling of wellbeing, energy and motivation; it entails the ability to do things and get on with our lives as normal. Seedhouse (1986) offers four such positive definitions of health. It can be an ideal state: the World Health Organization referred to 'a state of complete, physical, mental and social wellbeing and not merely the absence of disease and infirmity' (WHO 1946). It can mean a physical and mental fitness to perform 'socialized' tasks – those an individual faces as part of their social roles, such as occupational or parental duties. Thirdly, health can be viewed as a commodity, something we can buy and enjoy in larger quantities or in an improved form, for example by paying for drugs or surgery. Finally, we can think of health as a reserve of strength and ability to fight off potential illnesses and adapt to life events; we are ill when we feel 'run down' and lack motivation.

Medical sociologists are interested in lay health beliefs, or those held by ordinary people and developed in the course of their everyday lives. Sarah Nettleton (1995) reviews a number of these studies, emphasizing how such beliefs are socially embedded and shaped by local cultural values. For example, the working-class British women in Blaxter and Paterson's (1983) study held quite functional conceptions of health as the ability to carry out their daily household tasks, whereas the middle-class French people in Herzlich's (1973) study emphasized the idea of health as both a reserve and a vacuum, or absence of disease. Calnan (1987) observed class differences in lay beliefs about maintaining health: working-class people stressed the benefits of physical exercise, a good night's sleep and a warm home, while middle-class respondents pointed more to having a balanced diet, mental stimulation and a general sense of happiness.

Similarly, we can observe cross-cultural differences in the ways in which particular illnesses are defined and understood. Medical anthropologists point to the folk classificatory systems, or culturally specific frameworks, that are used to make sense of different ailments. For example, Helman (2007) suggests that English people make a distinction between 'hot' diseases (such as fevers and infections) and 'cold' diseases (such as the common cold), which is reflected in the saying 'feed a cold; starve a fever'. Chrisman (1977) identifies four 'logics' used by lay people around the world to explain illness: logics of degeneration (the body ageing or being run down), mechanics (body parts in need of repair), invasion (germs and viruses) and balance (such as the ancient Chinese concept of yin and yang). These different frames of reference indicate the existence of culture-bound syndromes: those which exist only within the context of one society's norms and values. For example, the *mal ojo*, or evil eye, is a concept used in some Latin American cultures to explain why somebody might be struck down with disease (Helman 2007). Meanwhile, a national pathology for the French, according to Lynn Payer (1988) is the 'crise de foie', or liver crisis – damage to the liver caused by certain foods – which leaves the individual vulnerable to various minor ailments, such as headaches, skin problems, menstrual pain and general fatigue. Payer suggests that this syndrome emerged because the liver is symbolically to the French what the heart is to the British and Americans: the site from which health, and life itself, emanates. The liver creates a 'terrain', or constitution, that determines both the individual's temperament and their susceptibility to disease.

Biomedicine and social order

In contemporary Western cultures, the dominant model for understanding illness, often in contrast to lay perspectives, is called the 'medical model'. This is a term used to refer to the form of medicine practised in hospitals and by legally registered doctors to treat illness in physiological terms. Sociologists also use the terms 'biomedicine' (Mishler 1981), 'biomechanical model' (Hart 1985) or 'liberal-scientific model' (Busfield 1996), which are largely synonymous but emphasize certain features of the approach. The medical model is therefore a discourse (see chapter 2) – a powerful structure of ideas, values and representations which shape individuals' experiences of illness.

There are several characteristics of the medical model in its crudest form. Firstly, mind–body dualism: the body is treated as an organic, biological entity, and the patient's thoughts, feelings and social relationships are largely ignored. Secondly, a mechanical metaphor is employed: the body is viewed as a machine whose parts may become faulty and in need of repair. This relates to a third characteristic, the technological imperative (Rothman 1997), which describes the doctor's propensity to treat illness through surgery, drugs or other technical, physical means (as opposed to hypnosis or spiritual healing, for example). Finally, the doctrine of specific aetiology means that conditions are viewed as discrete biological entities (such as a cancerous tumour), each of which has an identifiable, specific biological cause (such as a virus or a hormone deficiency) and observable symptoms (such as shortness of breath or a skin rash). Hart's (1985) biomechanical model includes each of these features but adds that the doctor appears as a mechanic, disinterestedly tinkering with the patient's body parts in an impersonal manner: the doctor sees the patient away from his or her social environment and focuses on the disease as an autonomous entity, rather than the person in whom it resides. Hart observes that conventional medicine is 'heroic' and cure-oriented because of this: the doctor intervenes at a relatively late stage in the illness to cure it, rather than preventing its occurrence in the first place, and so 'rescues' the patient's health.

The medical model is important because it shapes every stage of an individual's encounter with the medical profession and experience of treatment. Medical power is invested in doctors insofar as they are professionals, with a claim to specialist knowledge and expertise, who enjoy exercising autonomy over their working procedures (Freidson 1970; Johnson 1972). To the extent that the medical model clashes with lay perspectives on health and illness, the individual may find themselves either complying with medical advice or resisting the doctor's authority. However, it is not only the sick who are affected by the medical model: we can identify a number of ways in which it also pervades the everyday world of the healthy.

Surveillance medicine

Firstly, Armstrong's (1995) idea of surveillance medicine explains how the dominant discourses of Western biomedicine are employed in the discourses of public health and health promotion to exert a form of disciplinary power (Foucault 1977 [1975]) over populations. We are taught how to include and exclude certain foods to maintain a 'healthy' diet, how much exercise to take, which screening tests to undergo for which diseases at which points in the life cycle, and so on (Lupton 1995; Hughes 2000). As Armstrong argues, this shifts the burden of responsibility for health away from society and onto the individual, through the modification of lifestyle practices. Consequently, we internalize these messages and learn to manage our own health, by obediently following the guidelines and 'disciplining' our own bodies (see chapter 6).

Medicalization

Related to this is the medicalization thesis – an argument that the discourses and technologies of medicine are expanding into more and more areas of everyday life that were previously not regarded as unhealthy (Zola 1972; Illich 1975). For example, in the twentieth century, pregnancy and childbirth moved from the home to the hospital as a new branch of medicine, obstetrics, developed and were turned into highly technical procedures through the use of drugs, surgical instruments and foetal monitoring equipment. Insofar as these measures reduced the rate of perinatal mortality, hospital births were deemed safer than home births. However, Graham and Oakley (1981) argued that this made the experience of childbirth less satisfying for women, because it took away their sense of control and comfort and the opportunity to make an immediate, intimate bond with their babies. In other cases, the picture is more complicated, because medicalization can be welcomed as a positive thing. For example, the identification of such 'new' conditions as attention deficit hyperactivity disorder (ADHD) has reduced the stigma attached to children who were previously regarded as simply deviant: their 'naughty' behaviour has been recast as a legitimate medical problem for which they should not be blamed (Rafalovich 2005).

Usually, however, medicalization is regarded as negative insofar as it extends the power of the medical profession and, arguably, disempowers lay people. Illich (1975) used the term iatrogenesis (literally, 'originating from doctors') to describe the negative effects he thought had resulted from this process. Clinical iatrogenesis referred to treatment risks, drug dependency and side effects; social iatrogenesis meant the way in which medical terms pervaded lay concepts of health and illness, as when, for example, we unthinkingly label people as 'pregnant', 'geriatrics' or 'addicts'. Cultural iatrogenesis was the ultimate effect of all this, in that people would become disempowered in their confidence and ability to heal themselves. However, in recent years, this assumption has been criticized for underestimating the autonomy of lay people. Lupton (1995) suggests that, as the availability of information, education and technical knowledge about medicine has grown, individuals have become relatively well-informed, reflexive consumers of medical services, who are able to make their own decisions about treatment. In particular, with the Internet giving increasing access to medical knowledge, they may become 'expert patients' who know as much as or more about their condition than some medical professionals (Fox et al. 2005b).

The sick role

A final effect of the medical model is what Parsons (1951) called the sick role. This is actually a set of social roles and expectations attributed to those who are ill, their doctors, and other people in their everyday lives. The sick role is so deeply embedded in the structure of Western societies that we rarely think to question it, but it is based on a number of normative assumptions. Parsons identified four components of the sick role: the individual is granted legitimate withdrawal from their usual social responsibilities (such as work) and exemption from moral blame for their condition, but only if they in turn are prepared to seek help from a medical practitioner and to show a desire to get better. The doctor is expected to treat the patient in a neutral, objective manner and assist his or her transition back into normal social life, while family and friends are expected to indulge the individual in their retreat from interaction, on the understanding that they will soon come back into play. We can find countless examples of these implicit moral bargains throughout everyday life: the rituals of calling in sick to work and being told to 'put your feet up' and relax when feeling ill at home, and, conversely, our resentment of 'malingerers' who appear not to be meeting their side of the bargain by 'refusing' to get better. The sick role is an institution of functional importance, contributing to social order at a micro-level. By providing a temporary outlet for those who are not able to perform their duties, together with the mechanisms necessary to bring them back into play (or to sanction them if they do not), this complex web of social relations shows how sickness is managed by lay people as well as medical professionals.

Routines of illness

Becoming sick: a social process

We may think of being ill as a state of physical or mental impairment, but it is important to consider the social context in which this takes place. Turner (1995 [1987]) suggests that we make a distinction between the terms disease (a physical pathology), illness (the subjective experience of discomfort) and sickness (the social consequences of being ill, such as the Parsonian sick role). Using the Symbolic Interactionist perspective (see chapter 2), we can think about the social process of becoming ill and managing one's symptoms in terms of the micro-level interactions we have with others at each stage. Armstrong (1989) suggests that we can trace a career trajectory for 'becoming a patient' like that of becoming deviant (Becker 1963); each step along this path is contingent upon both one's own actions and the reactions of others. We can then ask: How is access to the sick role negotiated, how do people decide that they (or others) are ill, and what constitutes 'feeling better'? How does being ill affect the rhythms and routines of everyday life, and what happens when this process is prolonged? Each of these questions implies social action and agency: as Turner said, 'sickness is something we do rather than simply something we have. Being sick involves interpretation, choice and action' (1995 [1987]: 205).

Illness behaviour

The term 'illness behaviour' is used to describe 'the way in which symptoms are perceived, evaluated and acted upon' (Mechanic and Volkart 1961: 52). These sociologists criticized the medical model for assuming that there was a simple correlation between feeling ill and seeking help: what about those people who do not visit the doctor, or whose complaints of illness are not taken seriously by those around them? Which factors affect the decision (not) to seek medical help for health problems? Gender may be a significant influence: women are statistically more likely to visit their general practitioners than men (Roberts 1985), although a large proportion of these consultations concern gynaecological issues or pregnancy (Nettleton 1995). Children are also more likely to be taken to the doctor by their mothers (Calnan 1983; Cunningham-Burley and MacLean 1991), while lay attitudes to health create different consultation patterns for working-class and middle-class people, insofar as the latter report feeling more vulnerable to illnesses caused by 'stress' and lifestyle factors (Calnan 1987). But how do we even get as far as the doctor's surgery?

The first hurdle is to define oneself as ill and recognize that one is feeling noticeably worse than usual (remember that health is a subjective and relative matter). Mechanic (1978) suggests that it is statistically normal to feel slightly unwell, but that most people do not interpret this as illness. We all have different thresholds of tolerance for pain and discomfort, and symptoms are often normalized, or explained away by reference to situational factors – a headache due to tiredness, or pain caused by menstruation (Scambler and Scambler 1992). Many people also self-medicate, for example by taking analgesic drugs for minor aches and pains. This results in a 'clinical iceberg' effect, whereby only a minority of cases reach the doctor and the majority remain unreported. So when does an affliction become serious enough to warrant attention, and when do bodily changes get redefined as symptoms?

Mechanic (1978) identified numerous factors that affect a person's response to illness, including the visibility or perceived salience of the symptoms, the extent to which they interfere with one's family, work and other activities, the individual's tolerance threshold, and the amount of knowledge and information that they have, as well as their cultural assumptions and understandings and the availability, proximity and cost of medical assistance. Similarly, Zola (1973) identified five social triggers that facilitate the decision to seek help: an interpersonal crisis (such as the loss of a partner who had been providing care at home), perceived interference with one's work activities, perceived interference with one's social or leisure activities, sanctioning by others who insist that help is sought, and the persistence of the symptom beyond a certain time limit or deadline ('I'll go to the doctor if I still feel bad on Monday'). For example, a respondent in Calnan et al.'s study of upper limb pain reported that he had adopted a 'wait and see' approach, reasoning that the pain he was experiencing might simply be a natural facet of the ageing process: 'I try to only go when I am bad. I usually wait a while and see if it wears off but you get aches and pains at my age. Basically I work with the rule that what can clear up by itself isn't serious so I wait but if it is something specific I don't go until I have tried simply waiting it out and treating myself' (A2954, Calnan et al. 2007: 328).

Related to this is the idea of the lay referral system proposed by Elliot Freidson (1970). This refers to the way in which, having decided that we feel ill, we seek out the advice of others as to whether or not to see a doctor. Family, housemates and colleagues may offer their suggestions as to what the ailment might be (lay diagnosis), how serious they think it is, whether (and how) it might be treated at home, and whether to seek medical help. Thus Kleinman agrees that 'It is the lay, non-professional, non-specialist popular culture arena in which illness is first defined and healthcare activities initiated' (1980: 50).

Doctor–patient interaction

The next stage in the process is to consult a doctor. In the UK, this normally means visiting one's general practitioner (GP), a service provided free on the National Health Service (NHS). Canada also has a largely government-funded health service, whereas in the USA access to health care depends more on private-sector funding, from personal or employer-funded health insurance. Visiting the doctor is what turns an illness into a sickness, as, in most cases, the doctor

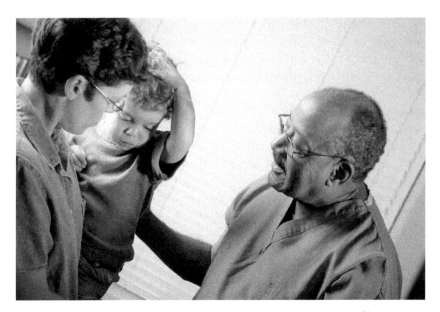

Figure 7.1 *Visiting the doctor is an important stage in the process of becoming sick. An individual may feel* ill, *but it is only when they receive a medical diagnosis that they become* sick, *a role with social consequences.*

makes a diagnosis and prescribes a treatment. 'Symptoms' reported by the individual are interpreted as 'signs' of disease by the doctor, who acts rather like a detective (Armstrong 1989). By virtue of the authority vested in their professional status, the doctor has the power to legitimate a patient's complaints by giving them a name, and thus the condition becomes 'real'. Armed with this official diagnosis, the individual can make a claim to enter the sick role, if they have not already done so. In this respect, visiting the doctor serves as a symbolic ritual: nothing actually changes in the patient's body at that time, but the fact that they have been examined and have received a diagnosis is usually enough to validate their claim to sickness. This is why we are often asked to provide a doctor's certificate to excuse absence from official duties on the grounds of illness. However, this is an unusual ritual in that it is conducted in private, not in public: maintaining patient confidentiality is a value of central importance to the medical profession (Helman 2007).

Byrne (1976) suggests that the ritual of going to the doctor involves six clearly distinguishable stages. The doctor seeks to establish rapport with the patient (by a friendly greeting and polite manner), asks what the perceived problem is, and conducts a physical and/or verbal examination; then both parties discuss the problem again in light of the evidence, the doctor makes a diagnosis and prescribes further treatment or tests, and the consultation is terminated by the doctor. Thus the doctor retains the position of authority in this interaction and the balance of power is firmly in their favour. The flow of private information is all one way; the patient has no control over what is kept on record, and must subject themselves to whatever examination and/or treatment the doctor deems necessary (Helman 2007). GP consultations on the NHS are also notoriously short and rushed, as doctors are under immense pressure to see more patients and reduce their waiting lists, and this can make the whole experience quite unsatisfying for the patient.

According to Helen Roberts (1985), this is a particular problem for women. Those that she interviewed were very aware of this power differential and felt that they inhabited different worlds from their doctors. These women defined a 'good doctor' as someone who listened and had time for them, but found that, in reality, many GPs were quite the opposite. They were sometimes reluctant to make an appointment for fear of 'bothering' the doctor, who was thought to be extremely busy; they also feared that the symptom would go away before they reached the surgery, leaving them looking like foolish time-wasters. Roberts describes how many of these women – the 'patient patients' – tried to treat themselves at home instead, waiting until symptoms became much worse before they sought help. More recently, of course, the Internet has emerged as an alternative source of information and resources, and so individuals can research their own symptoms and make a lay diagnosis before deciding whether or not to approach their doctor (Lupton 1995; Fox et al. 2005b). However, this is often related to the same concerns about 'bothering' busy doctors, as another respondent in Calnan et al.'s study demonstrated: 'I will go and look myself, knowing how busy doctors are. I would rather go and look on the internet; that's probably the primary source as far as I'm concerned rather than go and bother them' (A3033, Calnan et al. 2007: 329).

From the doctor's perspective, however, things look quite different. As Tuckett (1976) argues, the medical encounter can be read as a dramaturgical performance, involving roles, scripts, props and scenery (cf. Goffman 1959). The doctor is concerned not only with attending to the patient and the practical tasks at hand, but also with managing his or her own role performance to convey an impression of competent professionalism. For example, the doctor's surgery may be decorated with certificates, surgical instruments, technical equipment, and so on; they will often wear a white coat to symbolize their scientific expertise and authority, and carry props such as a stethoscope, thermometer, prescription pads, and so on (Helman 2007). Many of these objects do not actually need to be used in most consultations, but their presence in the background of this frontstage arena helps to support the doctor's claims to professionalism.

The balance of power in the doctor–patient relationship can vary enormously. Szasz and Hollander (1956) suggest three models that can shape the dynamics of the encounter. The activity–passivity model reflects the traditional idea of the doctor being in complete control of the compliant patient's treatment regimen. The guidance–co-operation model recognizes the importance of listening to patients' views of their own condition and their preferences for treatment. Finally, the mutual participation model allows for a much more egalitarian, frank discussion of the patient's condition and the risks and benefits of different treatments. Correspondingly, Veatch (1972) suggests that the doctor may assume four different roles, each of which suggests a different level of power within the encounter: they may play the role of an engineer (disinterested mechanical tinkering), a priest (offering enlightened advice), a colleague (egalitarian) or a contractual partner (with clearly defined rights and responsibilities) (cf. Young 2004). We can observe an historical shift since the late twentieth century, away from the tradition of the doctor yielding complete power, towards the ideological stances of patient-centredness, patient empowerment and patient satisfaction (May and Mead 1999).

The interaction dynamics of the doctor–patient encounter are therefore important in determining how far individuals move along the trajectory of sickness. The level of rapport between the two parties will affect how much information is relayed, how accurate a diagnosis can be made, and how appropriate a course of treatment can be offered. As Elder and Samuel (1987) suggest, patients will sometimes be so reticent and embarrassed about discussing a particular problem that they will present with a collection of vague, other symptoms; it is only as they rise to leave that they say, 'While I'm here, doctor …', and the real problem is revealed. Jack Novell (1987), himself a GP, identifies this as a problem for doctors, not patients, to address, by improving their 'bedside manner'. Novell compared doctors' and patients' perceptions of how a consultation had gone, and found a great discrepancy. Patients focused less on what was said than on how it was said, and how approachable the doctor had been, disclosing more or less accordingly.

Managing chronic illness

So far we have talked about 'illness' in rather commonsensical terms – as an acute, short-lived period of discomfort that marks a distinct break from the health norms of an individual. However, many forms of chronic (long-term) illness, such as rheumatoid arthritis or recurrent back pain, do not fit this model. One of the most widely cited critiques of Parsons's (1951) sick role is that it neglects these latter kinds of illnesses (Radley 1994); it assumes the possibility of making a complete recovery within a relatively short period of time, and implies that those who do not do so are simply deviant malingerers. Those who experience chronic illnesses may not be able to resume the social roles and activities that they enjoyed before becoming ill, and must adjust to making permanent changes to their everyday routines (Cockerham 2000). Furthermore, sufferers of chronic illnesses often find that they are regarded as socially deviant, insofar as they cannot fulfil these duties and obligations, yet are not exempt from them either. Many chronic conditions involving aches, pain or tissue damage are not immediately visible on the body, and so the individual is expected to participate as normal in routine social encounters. They cannot simply retreat from social life altogether, and so must find ways of managing the effects of the illness in the course of their everyday life.

Consequently, many studies of chronic illness focus on the ways in which symptoms threaten to interfere with normal, routine interaction and the development of social relationships. For example, Kelly's (1992) account of living with ulcerative colitis identified four different tasks that would not normally be encountered in the Parsonian sick role. These were the technical and practical management of symptoms (dealing with pain, learning to use a colostomy bag, difficulties with mobility at home and work), managing interpersonal relationships (dealing with embarrassment, trying to conceal the condition in romantic relationships, avoiding social situations in which there might not be toilet facilities nearby), managing thoughts and emotions (feeling different and excluded, embarrassment, shame and anxiety), and interpreting or making sense of the condition in relation to one's life as a whole ('why me?'). Barker's (2002) study of women suffering with fibromyalgia syndrome similarly showed how they tended to monitor social situations in terms of anticipated awkwardness, embarrassment and disruption.

It is not only the individuals themselves who are affected by these matters, but also family members, friends and colleagues. For example, Gregory (2005) discusses the effects that one family member's diagnosis of coronary heart disease (CHD) and coeliac disease (CD) had upon the dynamics of the household, in terms of adapting to the sufferer's change of diet. Those with CHD are instructed to follow a low-fat, high-fibre diet, while those with CD must avoid wheat and gluten products. Food and mealtimes are such a regular part of 'normal life' for many families that any challenges to the way in which food is prepared and eaten will disrupt their everyday routines (see also chapter 6). For example, insofar as women take responsibility for cooking the majority of household meals, and value sharing dishes as a symbol of love, the requirement to cook a special meal for one family member will disturb this ritual of 'doing family'. Meanwhile, carers may be concerned with protecting their family member from feelings of embarrassment that may result from their condition being disclosed to others. This can also be read as a form of Goffmanesque teamwork, designed to keep a fellow actor 'in face' before their audience (cf. Goffman 1959). Thus one of Gregory's respondents, Mr Garside (whose wife had CD), explained how he dealt with visitors to the family home: '… as far as I am concerned anyone who comes here I can sit anyone down at the table and I give them a meal which they would enjoy and which Maureen can eat and nobody will know the difference …' (Gregory 2005: 383).

Narratives and accounts

Those with chronic illnesses are forced to confront the longer-term implications of their condition for their social identities. Bury (1982) argued that the onset of such conditions creates a sense of biographical disruption: it challenges the individual's taken for granted reality, sense of self and relationships with others. Sufferers of chronic illnesses come to see themselves as different to those around them because their symptoms lead to unintended breaches of the 'normal rules of reciprocity and mutual support' underlying interaction (1982: 169). For example, a young woman, Amy, may have been enjoying carefree socializing with friends, buying her first car, making plans to go to university, and planning her career, when suddenly she becomes ill with cancer. The university plans are put on hold, her life revolves around hospital appointments, and she feels too tired to go out and meet her friends. Amy feels as if her life has been turned upside down and her priorities change as she contemplates the future: she begins to appreciate the little things in life more, to 'take each day as it comes' and to make shorter-term plans. She also begins to reflect on these very changes that have occurred in her life, and what she has learned from the experience of being ill.

In addition to managing the day-to-day symptomatology of the condition, then, chronic illness sufferers have to perform intense identity work to make sense of its impact on their lives. Arthur Kleinman (1988) coined the term 'illness narratives' to refer to the ways in which people construct such accounts of how and why they became ill, how the illness has affected them and what it means in the context of their life as a whole. They may imaginatively reconstruct points of 'genesis' in the past to account for their present situation (Williams 1984), for example by reflecting on a lifestyle of heavy drinking and smoking, or they may reflect upon the impact that managing symptoms has had upon their daily routines (Charmaz 1991). Kleinman (1988) also used the term explanatory models (EMs) to refer to the different narrative frameworks used by lay people to make sense of their own illness, which may contrast with those of biomedicine. For example, we saw in chapter 6 how the pro-anorexia movement has allowed some individuals to reclaim their 'disease' as a 'lifestyle choice' (Fox et al. 2005a; Rich 2006). The EM confronts such questions as 'What is the nature of this condition?', 'How do I feel about it?' and 'Why has it affected me?' (Kleinman 1988: 121; Fox et al. 2005a: 946), and we may think of illness narratives as the stories that are composed by individuals to answer these questions.

Ville (2005) describes how the question of returning to employment after a spinal cord injury presented a challenge of identity work to her sample of respondents in France. During the initial stage of rehabilitation, these patients spent some time simply taking stock of what had happened, assessing the damage to their bodies, finding out which activities they now could not do, and grieving for the loss of many future opportunities. It was only later that they began to think about the future and make plans either to pursue a new career path or to give up paid work altogether. As one respondent, Gérôme, explained, this was an empowering turning point in his life:

> You are so low after an accident, you're just shattered! Your only aim is to be like everyone else. I had to work, all my mates were working. … [but] I've changed since then [rehabilitation]! At B [vocational rehabilitation centre] I met a lot of different people who opened my eyes. Because, before that, I wasn't worth much. I was just a yob who just wanted to mess around, and they gave me a whole load of interesting ideas. But that's because in hospitals and centres you've got a lot of time, you know! … I've had two lives, one before and one after. (Ville 2005: 332–4)

By contrast, Fairclough et al. (2004) found different patterns in the way that stroke survivors in the USA sought to find meaning in their experiences, to maintain a sense of biographical flow. One respondent, Philip, reflected on the minimal impact that his stroke had had upon his life: 'It's not the first one I've had. The last one was a lot stronger, but what can you do? This one is just a hiccup. Not even as bad as the other ones. Just a hiccup' (2004: 255).

Both of these comments remind us of the resilience of the everyday world. It seems that, whatever challenges are thrown at us by life events, we strive to maintain a sense of order. We search for continuity and meaning, and where there is none we create it through retrospective narratives. Chronic illness serves as another reminder of a central paradox in everyday life: that, wherever we find breaches of the norm, we find responses that attempt to restore social order.

Challenging ab/normality

Contested conditions

Some of the illnesses outlined above are doubly challenging to the assumptive world of biomedicine, because as well as being chronic in duration they are also difficult to diagnose and treat. Medical sociologists have explored the ways in which these 'contested conditions' try the patience of some doctors insofar as they defy straightforward categorization within biomedical nosologies. Canadian sociologist Christopher Adamson (1997) suggests that, in these cases, the existential uncertainty of the patient is compounded by the clinical uncertainty of the doctor, making it impossible to achieve the 'ideal' medical encounter (in which the doctor is confident in their diagnosis and able to reassure the patient). He describes the long illness trajectory faced by those with the many and varied symptoms of inflammatory bowel disease. This contested condition may also be diagnosed as ulcerative colitis, Crohn's disease or avascular necrosis, each of which has different treatment implications. As a sufferer of this condition, Adamson was left feeling uncertain as to what was wrong with him, how the illness might progress, and whether and how it could be treated. As Glenton (2003) observes, until one receives a conclusive diagnosis, access to the sick role may be denied, leaving patients unable legitimately to claim the rights associated with it.

May et al. (2004) present a secondary analysis of data from a selection of qualitative studies of three very different chronic illnesses (menorrhagia, chronic back pain and depression) to show how, in each case, the contested nature of the conditions affects the relationship between doctor and patient in the medical encounter. In particular, the patient is morally evaluated in terms of the perceived legitimacy of the symptoms they report. Those complaining of back pain, for example, may not display any visible signs of tissue damage and can only report on the subjective experience of pain. There are also psycho-social dimensions of some chronic illnesses, which challenge the biomedical model of pathology. May et al. suggest that, when there is such incongruence between lay and medical definitions of illness, combined with uncertain possibilities of 'disposal' (referral for further treatment), doctors may show less empathic responses to the patient.

Perhaps one of the most well-known contested conditions is myalgic encephalomyelitis (ME), sometimes known as chronic fatigue syndrome (CFS). Lesley Cooper (1997) explains how this very issue of terminology reveals its uncertain nature, and how it can be interpreted as a physical or psychological disorder, respectively. Cooper shows how the very existence of ME is contested within biomedicine, where it is denied the legitimate status of an organic disease. Instead, it is conceptualized as a vague 'syndrome', whose symptoms include some combination of severe muscle fatigue and pain, weakness, depression, headaches and difficulty concentrating. These symptoms vary between sufferers, do not result in any visible abnormalities in the body, and cannot be diagnosed by standard medical tests. Consequently, Cooper suggests, ME is sceptically viewed as a 'non-disease' by many general practitioners, who dismiss sufferers as hypochondriacs, malingerers, school phobics or bored housewives (Cooper 1997: 198). This account from one of her interviewees, a sixty-year-old woman, is typical:

> I had an hour with this chap and he just insulted me the whole time … He was a consultant physician … it was obvious from the onset that he was trying to either break me down or I don't know what he was trying to do … make me come to my senses or something. But it was a bullying tirade … It started off with him bumping the table saying 'all right, cards on the table now, what's wrong with you? Something wrong with your marriage?'. (Cooper 1997: 198)

Disability and social attitudes

Some embodied conditions, then, challenge not only the individual's own perceptions of health but also those of other people. One of the ways in which we see this most clearly is in studies of the effects of disability upon social interaction. 'Disability' is a term used in everyday language to refer to physical or mental differences that are assumed to be inherently problematic. But is this really the case? It is important to distinguish between the effects of an embodied condition per se and the effects of social attitudes towards it.

Negotiating disability

Sociologists use the terms 'impairment' to refer to the physical reality of bodily damage, dysfunction or abnormality, 'disability' to refer to the limitations caused by the impairment to a person's functional ability, and 'handicap' to refer to the social disadvantages resulting from the disability (Bury 2004). For example, a person with cystic fibrosis (CF) may suffer inflammation and infection of the lungs (impairments), resulting in difficulties with breathing, mobility and tiredness (disabilities). They might then be unable to access some buildings or to work long hours (handicaps). However, it is worth noting that the term 'handicap' is now regarded as somewhat offensive, and so the term 'disability' is often used to refer to both the limitations of impairment and the social disadvantages resulting from this.

Definitions of impairment, disability and/or handicap reflect social judgements about ab/normality. While some impairments, such as CF, might be experienced by the individual as inherently undesirable, other conditions only become so through the way in which they are socially evaluated. For example, imagine a man, James, who is extremely short-sighted (a visual impairment), but is able to correct this with contact lenses. Not only does this mean that he can circumvent the functional disability he would otherwise have, but also, insofar as the impairment becomes invisible, he avoids discriminatory treatment by others. Furthermore, we think of myopia (short-sightedness) as a relatively common condition and so, even if James were to wear glasses that made his impairment visible, he would be unlikely to suffer any negative social effects: this disability is normalized. Conversely, imagine a young woman, Holly, who has the condition alopecia, which causes hair loss. She may not suffer any impairment or disability but, insofar as her baldness makes her visibly different from her peers, she may experience teasing, bullying, staring, and so on. So is disability something that exists inherently in the individual, externally in the eye of the beholder, or in the interaction between the two?

This question was addressed in a classic study by sociologist Fred Davis (1964), who was interested in the ways in which having a visible physical disability affected people's experiences of social interaction. He studied what happened in encounters between visibly disabled (wheelchair-using) and able-bodied individuals in the various stages of getting to know each other. His study reveals the ways in which the perception of difference challenges the rituals, rules and routines of interaction that most able-bodied people take for granted. Beginning with encounters between strangers, for example when the two actors are introduced by a mutual friend, Davis suggests that the interaction is rather strained, as both parties are aware of the potential for awkwardness. The able-bodied actor perceives the handicap as a sensitive issue and is concerned about whether, and how, to address it: they do not want to make the disabled person feel self-conscious or 'freakish' by saying the wrong thing. Davis identifies three potential threats to the smooth flow of interaction as experienced by the able-bodied person and responded to by the disabled person. Firstly, there are 'signs of stickiness': for example, an able-bodied man makes guarded references to a woman's disability, he avoids looking at her wheelchair and stares elsewhere, and he displays 'compulsive loquaciousness' and 'artificial levity' – that is, he talks too much and with a false jollity. Secondly, the able-bodied man may perceive a risk of 'expressive boundaries' being transgressed: he must carefully control his facial expression to avoid showing any inappropriate feelings of fear, pity, embarrassment or discomfort. Finally, the disability appears as an 'ambiguous predictor of joint activity': the able-bodied man may be unsure as to whether his friend's disabled friend will be able to join them in playing football or accessing their local pub, and so avoids suggesting such activities for fear of embarrassment.

In response to this, Davis points out that the disabled person intervenes to 'repair' the situation and rescue the other actor from embarrassment (cf. Goffman 1956). Experienced in dealing with such awkwardness in onlookers, the disabled woman in our example will have developed various strategies for helping to save face, keep the interaction flowing and building the potential for future relationships. She makes gestures to reassure the able-bodied man that she is not offended by his clumsiness, and together they engage in 'deviance disavowal'. Firstly, there may be a display of 'fictional acceptance', whereby both parties politely disattend to the disability and act as if it does not exist. Secondly, they may engage in 'reciprocal role-taking', whereby both actors work to close the social distance between them: the disabled person mentions 'normal' activities in which she can partake, while the able-bodied person downplays any activities in which he thinks she cannot. Finally, Davis talks of the 'institution-alization of the normalized relationship'. That is, if the two actors do become friends, they may explicitly address this initial awkwardness and establish routine ways of managing it. For example, the woman may tell her friend that she does not like him to push her wheelchair except when she is navigating steps, and so he knows not to intervene in most situations. In Goffman's (1959) terms, the two actors form a team who stage the presentation of their public selves: they devise a set of rules and strategies backstage, which can then be performed smoothly next time they are in a frontstage setting. The able-bodied person may even become an honorary 'wise' member of the disabled person's private world, granted a licence to make jokes and banter about the disability (cf. Goffman 1963a). Davis's study is significant not only in showing how the perception of visible difference can chal-lenge people's taken for granted assumptions about routine interac-tion, but also in showing how interactants work together to restore a harmonious definition of the situation. It supports the idea that dis-ability is a social rather than an individual 'problem', insofar as it can emerge or disappear according to the joint action of participants.

Stigmatizing conditions
Strained interaction can also result from conditions that are less visibly apparent: impairments may be hidden inside the body, only visible at certain times, or be of a mental rather than a physical variety. Of relevance here is Goffman's (1963a) notion of stigma – a discrep-ancy between one's virtual (presented) and actual (privately experi-enced) selves, which results in a 'spoiled identity'. By this Goffman did not mean that disabilities were inherently undesirable, but rather that we may perceive them as such and try to keep them hidden. Goffman distinguished between those stigmatizing conditions that were discrediting – already evident and impossible to disguise, such as facial disfigurements or the use of a wheelchair – and conditions that were discreditable – not immediately visible but vulnerable to exposure at any moment, for example, having a criminal record or a certain mental illnesses. The former type of attribute is illustrated by Davis's study, but it is also interesting to consider how the second type of discreditable attributes can affect routine interaction. Scambler and Hopkins (1986) show how Goffman's ideas can be applied to the experience of epilepsy, a condition which, although neurophysiologi-cal in origin, is not visibly apparent except during a seizure. Although epilepsy is not socially deviant, and does not interfere with daily life

most of the time, those with the condition often feel uncertain about when and where an attack will occur and embarrassed about the possible consequences. In this respect, it is a discreditable attribute which is normally concealed but may emerge at any time. Scambler and Hopkins identify two further subtypes that may result from this. Enacted stigma occurs when the individual experiences actual hostility, discrimination or ridicule. Felt stigma occurs when they simply anticipate this happening and fear the consequences of being seen as 'that type of person'; they experience 'hidden distress' (though see also Scambler's [2004] subsequent critique of his own concept). Epilepsy is more of a felt than an enacted stigma, Scambler and Hopkins argue, although this makes the discomfort no less real.

A second example of discreditable stigma comes from Acton and Hird's (2004) discussion of stammering, a speech impediment that occurs intermittently and can be controlled through carefully learned vocal techniques. Stammering is an interesting form of disability, as to an extent it can be seen to emerge from social interaction. Acton and Hird point out that we all speak ungrammatically and ineloquently in everyday conversation, and so whether or not a person is stammering depends as much upon the listener's interpretation as the speaker's verbal performance. Furthermore, many people who stammer in formal social situations can speak fluently when in a more relaxed setting, and so perhaps the impediment arises from concerns about performing in public. As we saw in chapter 3, the same applies to shyness (Scott 2007). Acton and Hird show how stammerers devise techniques of disguising their discreditable attribute and 'passing' (Goffman 1963a) as a non-stammerer. They may practise certain vocal sounds when alone 'backstage', or learn to avoid certain words that they know to be difficult to say. This reminds us again of the distinction between impairment and disability. Can we say that stammering is not a disability if it is successfully concealed?

A third variation of this conundrum comes in the form of autism, a developmental learning disorder that involves difficulties in understanding the perspective of others, together with impaired skills of communication and social interaction. Autism is sociologically interesting because it is often misperceived as social deviance: those affected do not look visibly different, and so their 'odd' behaviour cannot be accounted for by reference to an obvious disability. Gray (2002) explains how many autistic children regularly break the unspoken rules of interaction in various social situations and evoke reactions of moral disapproval: they are assumed simply to be 'naughty'.

Interestingly, Gray adds, this condition is not stigmatizing for the individual themselves (who may be unaware of how they are perceived), but rather it confers a kind of 'courtesy stigma' (Goffman 1963a) upon those who are associated with them. He gives the example of an autistic child behaving inappropriately in a supermarket: the disapproving looks that this evokes from others are directed at the parents, not the child, and it is these carers who feel humiliation on the child's behalf.

The social model
The idea that disabilities are socially defined and managed relates to a critical approach known as the social model of disability (Barnes 1991; Oliver 1996). Central to this is a conceptual distinction between impairment and disability, along the lines suggested above. Impairments are (usually) physically embodied, individual and privately experienced, whereas disabilities are socially imposed disadvantages that arise from cultural attitudes, the structural organization of institutions, and the design of public spaces (Shakespeare 2006). The social model was presented as a critique of conventional, medicalized understandings of disability as a deficit of the individual's body or mind – the 'personal tragedy' model (Oliver 1990, 1996, 2004; French and Swain 2004). Instead, it shifted the emphasis onto society as creating disabling barriers to participation for those with impairments, which can and should be removed. Thus a person who uses a wheelchair may be physically impaired but does not need to be disabled, because the social environment can be adapted to meet their needs: steps can be replaced by lifts or ramps; wider seating spaces can be provided on buses, and so on. The model also employs a relativist rhetoric: Oliver (1996) points out that a wheelchair is a mobility aid for those who cannot walk just as an aeroplane is a mobility aid to those who cannot fly; why do we think of one as an impairment but not the other? The social model is extremely powerful in challenging taken for granted assumptions about the nature of disability and about disabled people's political status: the responsibility for change is placed firmly on 'society' (social institutions, policy-makers and lay people) to be more tolerant, adaptive and inclusive, rather than on individuals to sacrifice their right to participation.

However, Shakespeare (2006) points out that there are a number of problems with this approach in terms of what it does not do. Most importantly, he says, it neglects the reality of physical impairment as something that does disable many people, regardless of their social environment, and that is experienced as inherently unpleasant. Chronic and degenerative diseases, for example, may cause great pain and difficulties with simple tasks such as eating, drinking and bathing, which significantly impedes the sufferer's quality of life (Williams 1999). By denying the reality of these lived experiences, Shakespeare says, the model is an 'over-socialized' one (cf. Wrong 1961) that risks silencing disabled voices. He adds that disability is not simply an issue of identity politics, akin to feminism or gay activism, because it is intrinsically limiting: removing prejudice, oppression and discrimination would not make disabled people able-bodied. We do not celebrate Disability Pride in the same way as we celebrate Gay Pride or women's rights, as identities that can be wholly positive to experience. Shakespeare also argues that the barrier-free society is utopian and idealistic, because some places remain inevitably inaccessible: beaches cannot be traversed by wheelchairs, sunsets cannot be made visible to blind people, and historic listed buildings cannot be structurally adapted for wheelchair access. In addition, he says, the model was presented by white, middle-class, heterosexual men, and is biased towards their experiences, as well as to certain disabilities that are physical, visible and static (such as spinal cord injuries resulting in wheelchair use). Is it equally easy to remove the barriers encountered by those with more hidden disabilities, such as epilepsy, autism or stammering, and those conditions which do not cause impairment but are subjected to cultural prejudice, such as achondroplasia (restricted growth, or dwarfism)? Overall, Shakespeare concludes, the social model of disability may become a barrier itself, in limiting our understanding of the complex interplay between individual biology and the social environment.

These challenging ideas lead us back to the ontological question: What exactly is the phenomenon we call illness? Is it a real, physical state of impairment caused by biomechanical dysfunction, or just a social label we impose upon experiences that are out of the ordinary? Is it a way of making sense of 'odd' behaviour in others, and thus asserting control over them? Or perhaps illness is not an object but a process, a transition from one social identity to another? Indeed, these are questions we might ask of any social role status, whether imposed or 'freely' chosen. Thus, in contrast to the generally negative experiences of ill health explored here, chapter 8 examines the significance of shopping, as an ostensibly pleasurable, agentic pastime that is perhaps equally subject to social control. How much choice do we actually have in the role of consumer, and what is the relative impact of social order, ritual and resistance in this practice?

Summary points

- Lay health beliefs are those held by 'ordinary' people about what it means to be healthy or sick. They vary according to class, gender and cultural background.
- The medical model is a dominant discourse that explains illness in terms of organic damage or dysfunction, and treats the observable symptoms of disease. It employs a mechanical metaphor, a technological imperative and the doctrine of specific aetiology.
- The 'sick role' (Parsons 1951) is an institutionalized set of rights and responsibilities associated with acute illness. The patient is permitted to withdraw from their social obligations and is not blamed for their illness, providing they seek medical help and show a wish to get better.
- Becoming sick is a social process as well as a physical/mental one. It involves illness behaviour, lay referral, clinical encounters and experiences of treatment.
- Many chronic illnesses do not fit the Parsonian sick role and involve managing the long-term effects of symptoms upon one's everyday life. Sufferers often construct illness narratives to account for how and why they became ill. Sometimes the existence of these conditions is contested by doctors and/or lay people.
- 'Disability' refers to the disadvantages, discrimination and social exclusion that may result from having physical or mental impairments. The social model of disability suggests that it is society's responsibility to make its built environments, institutions and spheres of activity more accessible to everyone.
- Stigmatizing conditions are those which are experienced as having a detrimental effect upon one's social identity. Stigma can be felt or enacted, actual or anticipated, and directly or vicariously experienced.

8   Shopping

For most people, shopping – the choice and acquisition of goods or services for a price – forms a significant part of everyday life. It is estimated that women spend twenty-two minutes a day, or two years of their lives, shopping, and men about half this amount of time (McCaffrey 2006). Shopping is one of our most popular leisure activities, after watching television, socializing and playing sports (Bureau of Labor Statistics 2006). Yet, despite this, there is something of a stigma attached to shopping: it is regarded as trivial, vacuous, a sign of moral weakness, and arguably a feminine activity that is not really important (Shaw 2009), and it is implicitly contrasted with the socially useful work performed in the 'male' sphere of production (Pringle 1983). However, viewed in its wider context as a form of consumption, we can see how the purchase of goods and services is vital to the capitalist economy, from the small pieces of costume jewellery bought by teenage girls to the takeover of huge multinational corporations. As Marx (1959 [1844]) argued, commodities have both a use value, which is their actual cost to produce, and an exchange value, which is the price they can fetch on the open market.

We might add that, at the micro-social level, things we shop for also have a symbolic value, which is their significance and meaning to us in the context of our everyday lives. Individuals choose products on the basis of not only their functional use but also their image, appearance and connotative meanings (Barthes 1972 [1957]), which are defined by cultural norms and values. Douglas and Isherwood (1996 [1979]) coined the term 'material culture' to refer to the relationships between people and objects. In other words, the 'stuff' we acquire, display, exchange and consume helps us to relate to one another and to reproduce the structure of society.

In this chapter, we examine the way in which shopping practices both reflect and constitute the social worlds in which they are embedded. We begin with a discussion of the various meanings that 'buying things' can have and of the rituals of interaction involved in 'going shopping' as a cultural practice. The next section looks at the orderly nature of (most) shopping, insofar as it is structured by factors such as class, gender, shop design and the psychology of buying and selling. We also examine the rise of consumer culture and its effects upon shopping practices: how does our choice and display of objects help us to perform social identities? In the final part of the chapter, we identify some instances of rule-breaking, from the supermarket to the gift exchange, which highlight the unspoken norms of shopping behaviour.

Meaningful rituals

Why do we shop?

Ostensibly, we consume instrumentally, to acquire something that we want or need. However, shopping is not just a means to an end, but also an end in itself: it is a meaningful process, which can be interpreted in different ways. Firstly, we may regard shopping as either a duty or a pleasure, a virtue or a vice (Shaw 2009). As Yue (2003) points out, there are different connotative meanings to the phrases 'doing the shopping' (as a dreary routine), 'going shopping' (enjoying the process as a recreational activity) and 'shopping around' (for a specific, desirable item). A homemaker's weekly trip to the supermarket to buy food for their household may feel like something of a chore, because it is repetitive, predictable, and involves the purchase of mundane goods. On the other hand, the same task might be understood as a means of 'feeding the family' (DeVault 1991), or an act of love (Miller 1998). One may make a special trip to spend birthday money or 'treat' oneself, enjoying the process of choosing as much as the products consumed. Even a routine shopping trip can be performed as a leisure activity, especially if it involves the purchase of non-essential items and interaction with familiar faces. Thus Sharon Zukin describes her experience of browsing the farmers' markets of downtown New York:

> I take weekly strolls to East Village Cheese, for pre-wrapped sections of Brie and H&H bagels at cut-rate prices … I am also a frequent customer at the small, storefront dairy where Joe makes the best smoked mozzarella in Manhattan and at the nearby pasta shop where the owner sits behind the cash register and occasionally shares her recipes with me … as

often as I can, I make a pilgrimage to the Greenmarket at Union Square, where Vincent D'Attolico, an electrician from Brooklyn who moved to the country to grow organic vegetables, taught me how to choose the deep-coloured squash for their sweetness, and Elizabeth sells blackberry jam and offers tastes of apple ... (Zukin 2004: 3–4)

Secondly, shopping can function as an escape from the norms of everyday life. Cohen and Taylor (1992) describe how we seek opportunities to pursue minor infractions of our own routines (see chapter 9). These 'escape attempts' remind us that we have some autonomy and are not at the mercy of (what appear to be) externally imposed schedules. Thus an office worker may walk into town during her lunch break to inject some pleasure into an otherwise boring day, or schoolchildren may 'bunk off' (play truant) to go shopping, demonstrating to each other that they are not at the mercy of teachers' rules. Langman (1992) suggests that, to most people, shopping represents freedom, fun and escape from the mundane reality of everyday life, and as such it is a strategy of resistance. As we saw in chapter 2, de Certeau (1984) used the term 'making do' to refer to such minor acts of rule-breaking that demonstrate human agency.

Thirdly, shopping can serve as a site of identity performance (Miller et al. 1998). By the products we consume and display, we demonstrate who we are, what we like, and with whom we identify. In dramaturgical terms (Goffman 1959), shopping provides us with items of identity equipment, which we use to present versions of ourselves to others. These objects include various commodities, such as clothing, home furnishings (see chapter 4) and food (see chapter 6). Moreover, it is not only the objects themselves that help us to perform these identities, but also the process of buying them: teenagers hanging out at the mall on a Saturday are demonstrating a group identity simply by being together, even if they do not buy anything (Langman 1992). In this respect, shopping is about social participation, or 'doing member' (Garfinkel 1967). We construct our allegiance to particular social groups through the rituals of how we shop, when, where and with whom. Garfinkel's ethnomethodological approach encourages us to read cultural practices such as shopping as methods employed by social actors to make sense of their world.

When do we shop?

Our reasons for shopping also affect the time at which we do so in relation to other activities. In chapter 5 we saw how socially constructed schedules govern our daily, weekly, monthly and annual routines, telling us what to do, when and for how long. Thus we may have a regular weekly shop for groceries at the supermarket, treat ourselves to a special purchase once a month after pay day, and shop for annual festivals such as Christmas according to their place in the calendar. Insofar as it represents a break from the routine, shopping has to be scheduled alongside other, less flexible timetabled activities: we may drop into the local store on the way home from work, or shop while the children are at school. Jenny Shaw (2009) argues that we structure our lives with patterns of rhythmic activity, which provide the scaffolding on which other things rest. Shopping becomes habitual, a regular, predictable task to be done, even when it is a source of pleasure. Shaw suggests that, however infrequently it is performed, shopping 'punctuates' temporal routines: it may be the high point (exclamation mark) at the end of a day, a chore (full stop) at the end of the week, or an interim activity (comma) throughout the year.

Our shopping activities are also constrained by the temporal structures imposed by other people's schedules, as well as those of social institutions. Household routines, work, and shop opening hours determine the times we can browse, and Sunday trading laws continue to limit our shopping on one day of the week (see chapter 9). Insofar as this affects buyers as well as sellers, does it mean that shopping is a form of work?

How do we shop?

Shopping practices are influenced not only by the individual's needs and preferences, but also by the ways in which other people manage their behaviour, socially and psychologically. First of all, we can examine consumer behaviour, or 'the psychological and social processes people undergo in the acquisition, use and disposal of products, services, ideas and practices' (Bagozzi et al. 2002: 1). This begins with marketing, advertising and promotional work: the product must be made to appeal to its target audience. Rachel Bowlby (1993) suggests that there are four stages of the buying process – attraction, interest, desire and sale – and it is only in the final stage that the customer takes action. Bowlby explains that advertising succeeds by combining a warning with a promise: audiences are told that they lack something or have a problem, to which the new product is offered as a solution. We see this most obviously in adverts for beauty products (to 'cure' ageing, spots, grey hair, and so on), but also in adverts for foods

Figure 8.1 *We fit shopping trips into our everyday routines and schedule them alongside other responsibilities. For some, visiting the local store is a treasured daily ritual, while for others the weekly supermarket trip is just a big chore.*

(chocolate is depicted as a seduction tool; low calorie meals are promoted at the peak of the post-Christmas dieting period) and travel (the need for a holiday is conveniently met by the offer of cheap flights).

Products are often targeted at niche markets, but Pitkin (1932) suggested that advertisers really think in terms of only two main types of consumer: the classical and the romantic. The classical consumer is sensible, rational, level-headed, and sees goods in terms of their practical use and cost-efficiency, whereas the romantic consumer is more emotional, hedonistic and easily seduced by enchanting images. Although Pitkin was writing in the 1930s, these discourses do still prevail today, often combined with gender stereotypes: think of the way in which male grooming products (shaving equipment, hair gel, and so on) are advertised in terms of their functionality, whereas equivalent beauty products for women are associated with images of luxury and indulgence. Thus the connotative meaning (Barthes 1972 [1957]) of a product is what sells it – the ideas, values and ideas evoked by the image of the object, rather than the actual properties of the object itself (see chapter 2). In semiotic terms, the images portrayed in advertising are floating signifiers (Baudrillard 1975; Williamson 1978), detached and relatively autonomous from the signified product (cf. de Saussure 1974 [1916]).

Once consumers have been attracted to a product, the action of the sale itself takes place. Bowlby (1993) suggests that there are four metaphorical forms of interaction that can occur during a sale. The religious conversion comes about when retailers adopt an 'evangelical' style of talking about the product as something that will effect miraculous changes in the consumer's life. The latter is regarded as a sceptic who can nevertheless be won over, and whose doubts are unfounded. We can observe this approach in the techniques used by television presenters on the Shopping Channel, or retailers demonstrating new gadgets at the Ideal Home Show. The second type of sale takes the form of the trial, whereby evidence is assessed 'for' and 'against' the value of the product; this is often targeted at Pitkin's classical consumer, as an appeal to reason. We find this in the way that schools market themselves to local parents (citing league table results, recognizing limitations that have been overcome) and in the way political parties canvass voters in the lead up to elections. The battle is an aggressive sales technique in which the buyer is regarded as an enemy who must be won over and forced into submission; this may be familiar to those who have ever worked in call centres or been on the receiving end of persistent calls about double glazing. Finally, seduction is a form of sale that appeals to Pitkin's romantic consumer: the object is so alluring that it cannot be resisted, and desire takes over reason. This technique is often used to advertise foodstuffs that are nominally 'unhealthy' (high in fat, sugar and salt): cakes are 'naughty but nice', chocolate is 'wicked' and 'indulgent', but the implicit message is that the pleasure is worth the pain.

For Bowlby, the ritual practices of buying and selling are highly dramatic. Everyone is acting, the lines are scripted, and the scene progresses to a climactic point, at which the sale is clinched. She talks of 'the moment', when desire takes over from will and the individual loses the power to think rationally about the purchase. This creates the thrill of the impulse buy and converts shoppers into buyers (Underhill 1999). Bowlby also talks of 'the close', or the point at which negotiation ends and the sale is complete. By this point, the buyer is so psychologically involved in the product that backing out is unlikely, and so they feel a renewed enthusiasm for the product. This makes (some) shopping a win–win experience: the consumer thinks that they have skilfully negotiated a bargain, while the seller thinks they have successfully 'seduced' them. When both parties walk away feeling satisfied, the customer is more likely to return for a future purchase (Bowlby 1993).

Secondly, we can consider the ways in which shop design and layout affect people's experiences of shopping, whether intentionally or otherwise. For example, Underhill (1999) suggests that shop entrances are ignored by most customers: they stride purposefully in and head for the aisles, not wanting to appear hesitant. For this reason, there is a 'twilight zone' just inside the door of any shop in which it is pointless to display any goods. Underhill suggests that shoppers like to be given a 'landing strip' on which to collect themselves and make the transition from outside to inside unselfconsciously. Next, he considers the casual browser, who arrives looking for one item but finds herself collecting two or three others: her hands are full, and she is in danger of abandoning some of the potential purchases. Managers may then strategically place shopping baskets around the store (rather than just at the entrance), to encourage customers to buy more and allow hands-free browsing. Underhill also observes the tendency to leave merchandise out on the shelves for customers to pick up, touch, see, smell, and sometimes taste. Shopping is a sensory experience, he says, and so the longer we spend handling products, the greater 'involvement' we feel with them, and the more likely we are to buy them:

> Supermarkets are wisely trying to become more conducive to sensual shopping. Most good ones now feature on-premises bakeries, which fill the air with warm, homey scents. You may be in the vitamin section when that aroma hits you, and before you know it you've followed the olfactory trail right up to the counter. Suddenly you're thinking, I need bread! Stores have taken a tip from Starbucks and begun brewing and selling by the cup the expensive coffee beans they sell loose, another way of putting a product's sensory assets to work. In a perfect world we'd enjoy lots more scents in stores. The laundry aisle would smell of soap and fabric softener. In the meat section there'd be steak on the grill or bacon on the griddle ... some infant apparel stores now pipe in baby powder through the air ducts, to put shoppers in mind of the sweet-sour smell of newborns, which is perhaps the most powerfully evocative scent of all. (Underhill 1999: 164)

Thirdly, it is interesting to explore the forms of interaction that take place within a shop. From a dramaturgical perspective (Goffman 1959), a shop has both a frontstage area (the publicly visible shopfloor, where encounters between shop assistants and customers take place) and a backstage region (the stock room, back office and any other areas into which only staff are allowed access). Here, employees can drop the polite masks they have been carrying and indulge in bickering, complaining and clowning behaviours that enable them to 'let off steam'. Shop staff also form teams of actors who co-operate in staging a routine (Goffman 1959: 85) and in upholding a particular definition of the situation (Thomas 1923). While, individually, they may dislike their job and feel disdain for the products they are selling, collectively they tacitly agree to put on a show to give the opposite impression. They may exercise dramaturgical loyalty by supporting each other's performances (for example, echoing a colleague's praise of an item to help them sell it to a customer), dramaturgical discipline, by appearing to be immersed in their work but simultaneously keeping an eye on how successfully the show is running, and dramaturgical circumspection, by observing any audience members (customers) who appear on the scene and detecting their weak spots; the script they follow can be adapted accordingly. Used car salespersons and estate agents are notorious for doing this!

Goffman was particularly fascinated by what happens when the boundaries between frontstage and backstage are transgressed. A customer may catch a glimpse of employees misbehaving in the back room, or hear anecdotes about 'what really goes on' in restaurant kitchens, and change their own performances accordingly (for instance, not complaining in case the waiter spits on their meal). At other times, elements of backstage behaviour are carried into the frontstage region to enable actors to talk about the audience and discuss the performance while it is still going on. Goffman (1959) used the term 'communication out of character' to refer to these exchanges between team-mates or between actors and audience members in which information is conveyed that contradicts the official definition of the situation. In Garfinkel's (1967) ethnomethodological terms, the explicit dialogue serves as an index of the situation's contrived nature. Thus while the shop assistant maintains their sales patter, they may hint to the customer that 'this is only a performance' to be taken with a pinch of salt. An estate agent negotiating a house price, for example, might hint to the prospective buyer that the vendor will accept a certain offer, even though their job is to hold out for the highest price.

Another type of communication out of character was called team collusion, which involved performers talking about the audience in front of them, using coded language. For example, Goffman describes a system of manoeuvres used by workers in a shoe store observed by David Geller (1959 [1934]: 285). If a customer asked to try a shoe in a larger size that was out of stock, the shop assistant would call out to his colleague in the back room to 'stretch the shoes on the thirty-four last' – a code term for 'wrap them up as they are and leave them under the counter for a while' (cited in Goffman 1959: 176). Later on, the first salesman could get the shoes out and pretend they had been stretched into a larger size. On another occasion, a customer asked for size 'B', which was not available, so the salesman called to his colleague, 'Benny, what size are these?'. The colleague, whose name was not Benny, would then know that he was required to answer, 'B', which successfully fooled the customer. In each of these cases, the shop staff communicated by making meta-statements about the performance and how it was to be staged, while simultaneously following the script that they were meant to be following.

Orderly patterns

Structuring shopping

As well as helping actors to perform their self-identities, shopping involves rule-following behaviour that helps to maintain social order. The shopping list, for example, is a tool of self-discipline, designed to regulate our behaviour in the face of distraction. It keeps us focused on what we need for the household, what we intend to buy, and what we think we should be buying, according to cultural norms and values. Although we may think that we construct our own shopping lists according to individual whims and preferences, these choices are constrained by wider discourses and ideologies. Thus a supermarket shopping list often begins with items that we know to be 'healthy' or 'sensible' choices, such as fruit and vegetables, or store cupboard staples such as bread and milk; we rarely include sweets and chocolate, crisps and impulse buys, though we may buy them just as regularly. This suggests that the shopping list acts as something more than just a practical *aide-mémoire*: it is also a reminder of the rules that we are trying to observe. Miller (1998) explores this through the notion of the 'treat': items that we do not plan to buy and that are definitely not on the shopping list, but that we find ourselves slipping into the basket as we browse around. The treat represents a departure from the rules, an act of defiance of these social structures that remind us of our individual agency.

A second structural factor is gender. We have already seen how everyday life in general tends to be regarded as a feminine realm (Felski 1999), and the same applies to shopping in particular. Cultural stereotypes abound that represent shopping as an activity for women, and men have traditionally been excluded from this sphere (Reekie 1993). Nevertheless, sociological studies have shown that shopping is a leisure activity on which women spend more time than men (McCaffrey 2006; ONS 2006) and enjoy as a social activity. Pairs or groups of female friends may meet for a day's shopping as a pleasurable way of spending time together: talking as they browse, taking turns to try on clothes or decide which store to visit, and stopping for lunch halfway through are all ritualized practices or 'authoritative performances' though which women reinforce the social bonds of friendship (Arnould and Price 2000).

Meanwhile, we can observe a rise in the number of men's fashion outlets and high-street stores that aim to attract the young, image-conscious male. Sean Nixon (1996) explains that menswear emerged as a new niche market in the 1980s, resulting in an explosion of new shops, such as Top Man and Next for Men. He explored how the design and layout of these shops in the UK created 'shopping spectacles' for male shoppers that encouraged narcissistic acts of looking – that is, individuals were drawn into gazing at images of masculinity with which they identified or to which they aspired, and thus were seduced into buying the clothes associated with these values. For example, Next for Men was designed with a minimalist décor of black and white paint, dark wooden shelves and open spaces for younger men to browse comfortably, whereas Top Man was aimed at a slightly older market, decorated with solid wood and smarter furnishings, and filled with a greater quantity of goods out on display. Each of these shops promised different versions of masculinity, to be achieved through the consumption of goods.

Underhill (1999) suggests that, traditionally, men and women have displayed different styles of shopping behaviour. Whereas men tend to decide in advance exactly what they want, head straight for the shelf and select the first one that comes to hand, women like to research the array of products available and take their time to select the 'perfect' item. Is this gender difference a matter of nature or nurture? On the one hand, Underhill observes, it does fit with archetypal images of the pre-modern hunter-gatherer division of labour, which is assumed to be a matter of biological destiny. On the other hand, as social scientists, we should question where these beliefs come from: are men and women socialized into different shopping roles by the cultural context in which this activity is given meaning? For example, Underhill describes a male supermarket shopper who disinterestedly approaches the fresh produce system and 'breezes through, picks up the head of lettuce on top of the pile and wheels away, failing to notice the brown spots and limpid leaves' (1999: 116). Is he really oblivious and bored, or does he feel as if he has to display this attitude? If shopping is typically regarded as a feminine activity, then some men may defensively perform role distance (Goffman 1959) from it. Furthermore, Underhill observes that these gender roles can be reversed in the context of certain kinds of shopping that do not have such a feminine 'stigma'. In computer software stores, for example, Underhill suggests that male shoppers are happy to browse, taking pleasure in the idea that gaining knowledge about these products is compatible with their masculine identities. By contrast, women shoppers display a much more pragmatic, instrumental attitude to technology:

> they were in the store with some practical mission to carry out, not just to daydream over a new Zip drive or a scanner. Most women would rather just learn what they need to know to use the damn thing. Everywhere in the world of hardware and software, the sexes swap places: Men love to browse and wander while women are purposeful, impossible to distract while they look for what they need. (Underhill 1999: 126)

Insofar as these gender roles are socially constructed, they are, of course, fluid and open to change. The very presence of women in hardware and computer stores, Underhill points out, is testament to the blurring of the boundaries between supposedly male and female shopping behaviour. As more and more women work in paid employment and/or live alone, they consume DIY (home improvement) tools, computers, gardening equipment and other artefacts traditionally associated with 'men's shops'; meanwhile, men are becoming increasingly notable consumers of fashion and beauty products (Black 2004). The rise of the male 'metrosexual' (Simpson 2002), who takes pride in his appearance without being teased or stigmatized by his peers, suggests that cultural attitudes towards shopping are changing, and that retailers must adapt to make their goods appeal to a more gender-neutral market (Reekie 1993).

A third structural factor is social class. Perhaps the most obvious way in which this affects consumer behaviour is in terms of economic inequalities: income differentials mean that many of the goods advertised are not equally accessible to all, and so social class determines the type, quantity and quality of the products we consume (Zukin 2004). As we saw in chapter 4, Kate Fox (2004) suggested that the kinds of furniture and decorative artefacts we display in the home can be read as indices of social class, and she makes a similar point about food choices (see chapter 6). This may even extend to the shops we visit: Hoggart (1994) suggested that different UK supermarkets could be associated with different groups of clientele: Waitrose was the grocery store of choice for the upper-middle 'executive' class, Sainsbury's was frequented by the 'respectable working class', while Safeway and Tesco targeted the lowest income groups. Since then, many of these supermarket chains have undergone radical image overhauls, with Sainsbury's becoming a very middle-class establishment and Tesco now the largest retail company in the UK. Asda, the contemporary 'budget' supermarket, is owned by American giant Walmart, and is aimed at a similar client group.

The goods we consume can be used more actively to display class identities. Shopping is therefore another realm of everyday life in which Bourdieu's (1984) theory of 'taste', distinction and social class is relevant. Bourdieu argued that social order is maintained by the ways in which individual members of social classes symbolically reproduce themselves through the goods and services they consume (which include forms of education, health care, art and music as well as more simple material goods). Taste is embodied in the form of habitus, a system of lasting, transposable dispositions that reflect a person's class background – body size, posture, speech patterns, gait, and so on. It is also implicated in the way that people choose some products over others, whether consciously or otherwise: our preferences reflect either the social class to which we belong or that to which we wish to belong. This results in what Lury calls positional consumption: 'the way in which people seek to display their individuality and their sense of style through the choice of a particular range of goods and their subsequent customizing or personalizing of these goods' (Lury 1996: 80). For example, one might choose to read *The Guardian* or the *New York Times* (newspapers with educated middle-class readerships) instead of *The Sun* or *Daily Mail* (traditionally working-class tabloids), or to buy organic Fair Trade coffee (again, very middle class) rather than economy-sized 'value' brands. This is not to suggest that such purchases are only about display and posturing, but merely to emphasize that consumption choices are not made in a cultural vacuum.

Consumer culture

These trends in shopping behaviour are a relatively new phenomenon, shaped by the rise of consumer culture. This term refers to a pattern of increased spending on consumer goods for the purposes of pleasure, relaxation and entertainment, which has occurred since the mid-twentieth century as a result of greater levels of disposable income, leisure time, consumer credit and instalment buying (Featherstone 1982). For example, whereas in bygone eras torn clothes would have been washed, mended and reused until they wore out, the modern consumer simply disposes of and replaces clothes as soon as they become unfashionable. We can also observe a culture of mass consumerism (Lury 1996), in that patterns of consumption tend to follow social trends and fashions. Featherstone (1982: 19) observes that the advertisement of modern consumer goods emphasizes core values of youth, beauty, luxury and opulence, which simultaneously promise to awaken suppressed desires and offer opportunities for self-improvement. As we have seen, these meanings act as floating signifiers (Baudrillard 1975; Williamson 1978) that can be attached to any objects to increase their symbolic value.

Consumer culture is an individualistic culture. We purchase non-essential but seductive artefacts, such as fashionable clothes, fast cars, expensive jewellery and luxury holidays. Helga Dittmar (1992) suggests that the maxim of this culture is that 'to have is to be': possessions are regarded as extensions of the self, and used accordingly to perform identity. We have already seen how this occurs in the case of social class through the display of taste and distinction, but consumer goods can also be used to perform identities of gender, age, ethnicity, political standpoints, and so on. In the words of Featherstone (1982), we are 'performing selves'. Yet, paradoxically, these leisurely practices can become something of a chore: they have been incorporated into the reflexive project of the self in late modernity (Giddens 1991). Goods are selected no longer on the basis of their intrinsic value or aesthetic appeal to the individual, but on the basis of their legibility as cultural codes – that is, what your possessions say about you and how easily these meanings can be read. Bourdieu (1984) wrote of the 'calculated hedonism' displayed by the new middle classes in particular, who saw pleasure as a duty: under cultural pressures, we feel that we must have fun, go shopping, treat ourselves and decorate our homes with tasteful artefacts.

Some theorists have gone as far as to argue that it is not even self-identities we are shopping for, but whole lifestyles, with their incumbent value systems. Rob Shields (1992a) coined the term 'lifestyle shopping' to describe the new modes of consumption we can find in (post)modern Western societies. He argues that, when shopping for material goods, we are effectively trying on different social lifestyles, like outfits, and imagining ourselves in these positions. The identities associated with each lifestyle are transient and non-binding: in the space of one shopping trip we can put on and take off several different masks and play with multiple identities. Shields suggests that new spaces, or consumption sites, have been devised for the purposes of lifestyle shopping, such as shopping centres, retail parks, markets, museums and heritage sites.

One of the most familiar consumption sites (and indeed sights) is the shopping mall. Malls originated from the arcades that were frequented by the European bourgeoisie of the nineteenth century, but only became large-scale commercial ventures in the twentieth century, with the rise of mass produced goods and consumer capitalism (Shields 1992b). This was bolstered by the advent of department stores, such as Bloomingdale's and Macy's in the USA and Selfridges and John Lewis in the UK, from the late nineteenth century to the 1930s (Lancaster 1995). Just as department stores embodied rationalist principles of efficiency, convenience and affordability, shopping malls were designed to encourage people to spend more time and money on each trip. A multitude of popular high-street stores are brought together under one roof, their proximity being ostensibly convenient for the shopper, but of course also lucrative for retailers. Ritzer (1999; cf. Crossik and Gaumain 1999) refers to shopping malls as 'cathedrals of consumption', for they are used as places in which we worship (through its rituals and routines) the art of shopping. They often have a 'monumental' look, with sculptures, statues, skylights, fountains and marble features (Shields 1992b), which creates the impression of luxurious relaxation.

Shields (1992b) goes on to consider how the architectural design of malls creates a visual spectacle: they are built in multi-storey centres that allow shoppers to scan the whole array of storefronts. Malls are typically built around two major department stores ('anchor stores') at each end, with rows of smaller boutiques along the sides and a food hall at one end; this maintains a steady flow of customers in both directions across the mall, and forces them to notice shops they might otherwise have overlooked (Morris 1988). Like the urban *flâneur* of nineteenth-century Paris (Baudelaire 1986 [1863]), the shopper is invited to stroll at leisure past the many storefront windows, browsing the various images and lifestyles on display (cf. Featherstone 1982; Bauman 1996). There will often also be a food hall, a crèche and, in some larger centres, a cinema or other forms of entertainment, all of

Figure 8.2 *Modern shopping malls are designed with order, efficiency and discipline in mind. Shoppers are directed along paths, and there will often be an 'anchor store' at each end.*

which add to the length of time that people spend there. Whole days can be consumed by a visit to the mall, and in cities such as New York and London there is a growing trend in shopping holidays, devoted to a tour of nothing but the major malls.

Collective practices

Meanwhile, what kind of meanings do such trips hold for individual consumers? Miller et al. (1998) argue that shopping is an embodied, temporal and performative activity, much more than the mere act of paying for goods; it is about performing one's identity and relations to others. This reminds us of Durkheim's (1976 [1912]) understanding of collective ritual practices as functioning to reinforce social solidarity (shopping with or for someone) – but, of course, asserting one's allegiance to one group can often mean distancing oneself from another. For example, we may buy gifts for family members as an act of love but, equally, we may go to the mall to escape these same people. Fiske (1989) suggests that, for the traditional suburban housewife, the shopping trip represented a high point of the day insofar as it meant escaping the dreary routines of domestic life; even shopping for groceries allowed for a few moments of casual browsing, daydreaming and buying the occasional treat. In this way, Fiske argues that shopping can be used as a subversive act of resistance, a way of asserting one's own individual identity against social norms. We find this not only in the case of traditional gender roles but also with age ('hanging out' at the mall is a common teenage activity) and social class (shopping malls are designed to accommodate different niche markets and to be accessible to all). As a collective ritual, going shopping with people, especially friends, illustrates what ethnomethodologists call 'doing member' (Garfinkel 1967), or performing a group identity.

Furthermore, the position of these sites is significant in representing an escape from the familiar. Zukin (1995) describes shopping malls as liminal zones (cf. Turner 1967) that are spatially bounded, displaced and positioned between other realms of everyday life, such as work and home. We have to make a trip to the mall, or to out-of-town retail parks, as islands unto themselves. Zukin suggests that this is what gives these places their appeal: they represent safely controlled, bounded spaces in which we can escape from our daily routines, and which are entirely devoted to leisure and relaxation. As we saw in chapter 6, similar arguments have been made about the pub (Fox 2004), and in chapter 9 we examine the meaning of liminal zones in more detail.

The meaning of shopping rituals and routines in relation to ethnicity, class and family life was explored in Miller et al.'s ethnographic study of two shopping centres in the UK (1998). Brent Cross, the first of its kind to be built in the UK, was situated in a more middle-class, affluent area of London than the Wood Green centre, which served a large working-class, immigrant and ethnic minority community. The authors conducted a questionnaire survey of shoppers in each mall over twelve weeks, held focus groups with the residents of each neighbourhood, and observed a sample of the households' shopping practices by shadowing them when they went to the mall; the shoppers were also interviewed afterwards. Miller et al. found that, in both communities, the shopping centre played a significant role in shaping the rhythms and routines of everyday life, and that visiting the mall was often a social, family-centred activity. Family members would either shop together or buy things for each other and, insofar as this shopping was regarded as a feminine activity, mothers and older daughters would make trips together. However, the meaning of this

changed according to women's position in the life cycle and the age
of any children that they had. For example, the focus groups in both
neighbourhoods discussed the chore-like experience of 'dragging the
children shopping' and having to 'struggle with buggies' (Miller et al.
1998: 97) in shopping malls, but reflected wistfully on the days when
they had been childless and independent. Then, shopping had meant
leisure, relaxation and self-indulgent spending:

- Ooh, I loved shopping.
- I loved it.
- There was so much money to spend.
- It was the bestest thing.
- It was the most relaxing thing to do.
- We'd go out every weekend and spend all the money.
- It didn't matter, you didn't have to worry about what the kids was gonna
  have next week. When you're on your own that's best.
- As soon as you have kids, it changes all of that 'cos you've always got to
  worry are they going to need something by the end of next week. Are you
  spending money you're going to need by the end of next week?
  (Devon Close Mother and Toddler Group, cited in Miller et al. 1998: 98)

The shops themselves were viewed differently by the local residents
according to their age and social class. The middle class of Brent Cross
resented the way in which malls and supermarkets were 'taking over
everything' (Miller et al. 1998: 89) and forcing local shops to close,
while elderly residents in the Wood Green neighbourhood were nos-
talgic for 'the good old days' of friendly local shopkeepers and personalized service: 'you used to get the service. I mean, they used to cut you
the size of cheese you wanted, you know, or the butter' (ibid.: 80).

Other residents viewed the shopping centres more positively, as
an opportunity for identity performance. In terms of social class,
department stores such as John Lewis or Marks & Spencer were seen
to have given Brent Cross a more 'sophisticated', 'respectable' appeal
to the middle class, who regarded Wood Green as a hotbed of petty
crime and run-down stores (Miller et al. 1998: 140). For the immigrant
communities of both neighbourhoods, meanwhile, many of their
local shops seemed archetypically English and rather quaint, which
left them feeling excluded. However, they would also use the shopping areas as sites in which ritualistically to perform their own ethnic
identities. Greek Cypriot youths would congregate outside certain
shops in Wood Green and were disdainful of the local supermarkets
that stocked 'inauthentic' Greek foods. Meanwhile, in Brent Cross,
residents spoke about the importance of this being 'a Jewish area

and a lot of people go there and being Jewish we notice other Jewish people' (ibid.: 167). At the same time, they joked about the perils of over-identifying with this place and becoming a 'Brent Cross shopper'; they sought to distance themselves from the image of 'everybody's worst nightmare of stereotypical Jews' by showing disdain for those who bought ostentatious clothes and jewellery: 'Fenwicks targets the rhinestones' (ibid.). Thus, in both neighbourhoods, identities of gender, age, class and ethnicity were self-consciously performed through attitudes to and practices of shopping.

Shopping and rule-breaking

Finally, let us consider some of the ways in which the various rules, routines and rituals of shopping may be challenged. Deviant consumer behaviour may be trivial or serious, intentional or unintentional, but, as with any realm of everyday life, these instances serve to highlight the very rules that they are breaking. Perhaps the most obvious example is shoplifting: there is an explicit, formal rule (a law) that states that goods must be paid for, and so to ignore this is a deliberate act of defiance. Most other forms of deviance in shopping, however, are non-criminal and subtle, breaking more implicit rules and norms.

Textual poaching

We can challenge the rules of shopping through the goods we buy. As we have seen, there are unspoken rules governing the products associated with different social classes, age groups, genders, and so on; people's tastes tend to reflect their social positions. However, the notions of distinction (Bourdieu 1984) or positional consumption (Lury 1996) remind us that people can choose to buy certain items specifically because they are associated with other social groups to which they desire to belong. Here, the purchaser buys not only the object itself but also the status associated with it, which is conferred on them by proxy. This has been described as textual poaching (de Certeau 1984; Jenkins 1992) – effectively stealing the meanings associated with the cultural artefacts of a social group and making use of them oneself. This is similar to Shields's (1992a) notion of lifestyle shopping, but whereas the latter suggests pursuing the symbols of an identity with which one 'authentically' identifies, textual poaching suggests more cynical, aspirational motives. One famous example of this is Burberry, a check pattern once produced by a luxury fashion house and granted a royal warrant, but then popularized by football firms, supermodels and celebrities; it is now mass produced and consumed by people of all class backgrounds. Veblen (2005 [1899]) coined the term 'conspicuous consumption' to describe the way in which members of the aspiring middle classes would intentionally choose goods they saw as being associated with the upper classes, regardless of their aesthetic appeal: all that mattered was the impression they would create. Conspicuous consumption involves buying goods for the purpose of display to others, rather than to reflect one's actual lifestyle.

Making do

A second way of subverting shopping rules, albeit unintentionally, relates to what de Certeau (1984) called 'making do': using social spaces for purposes other than those for which they were intended, or navigating new paths through them. We have seen how stores are designed to manipulate consumer behaviour: supermarkets display their fresh produce near the entrance, entice shoppers inside with special offers, and use coin-operated trolleys that make us feel committed to spending time there. You may also have noticed that, from time to time, supermarkets change the layout of the goods in each aisle, so that shoppers have to hunt around for the things they want. This strategy was cunningly devised because managers realized that many people do a routine weekly shop, in which they rush around, picking up the same goods every time without thinking about it; they use their 'recipe knowledge' (Schütz 1972), almost literally, to shop more efficiently. By changing the store layout, managers can jolt their shoppers out of this daze and make them look at products they would not otherwise have considered: in searching for the tinned tomatoes that used to be in aisle 4, we find ourselves walking down aisle 5 and noticing a new range of pasta sauces. We are afforded a different view of the supermarket's landscape, and thus discover new ways of using its products. Shopkeepers who deploy this technique are making do with the constraints of their environment, but shoppers who recognize this and defiantly stick to their lists are also making do by resisting the manipulation.

Meanwhile, the rise of Internet shopping has enabled customers to browse at leisure, select the specific goods they want, and avoid pushy salespersons and seductive store layouts. Online shopping is becoming increasingly popular as more women are entering full-time employment rather than performing the role of the traditional house-wife, and it is central to consumer culture more generally. The 2005 Time Use Survey reported that, in the UK,

> A slightly higher proportion of men than women used the Internet to purchase goods or services associated with leisure, such as travel, accommodation or holidays (53 per cent of men compared with 48 per cent of women) and videos or DVDs (45 per cent compared with 39 per cent). Conversely a higher proportion of women than men used the Internet to purchase clothing or sports goods (42 per cent of women and 34 per cent of men), and food and groceries (25 per cent of women and 16 per cent of men). (ONS 2006)

Gift exchanges

A third set of rules that can be broken relate to buying for others in the form of gifts. Anthropologists, such as Mauss (1990 [1925]), have explored the role of gift exchanges in cementing social relations. A gift is an object or service given to another person without any expectation of payment or immediate return; it is an altruistic gesture aimed at bringing pleasure to others. However, Mauss pointed out that, in the longer term, there is an implicit expectation that the gift will be reciprocated: for example, a dinner party guest will one day host his or her own event, to which the original host is invited. In this way, objects given as gifts have a power embedded in them: they obligate the recipient to return the favour, and his or her honour is at stake. If we fail to reciprocate a gift within a reasonable time period, unless we have a good excuse, we risk offending the gift-giver. For example, a person who fails to 'buy their round' at the pub evokes reactions of moral indignation from their peers (see chapter 6), and a person who neglects to send a Christmas card back may find that they do not receive one from that sender the following year. Even failing to reply to an email can be read as something of a personal snub, as it implies ingratitude for a gift (Knight 2005). Defaulting on a gift exchange is like one of Garfinkel's breaching experiments: it confounds a set of 'seen but unnoticed' rules of social behaviour that are normally taken for granted.

Other breaches of gift etiquette occur in giving a present that is inappropriate or unappealing to the recipient, or by refusing to show gratitude for such an object. Mauss (1990 [1925]) argued that the gift is symbolically tied to the giver's identity, as if they are imparting a piece of themselves: to reject this is effectively to reject the person behind it. For this reason, we will often pretend that we like a gift we cannot stand in order to protect the feelings of the sender. However, the recipients of such gifts may also feel that they have been offended: the sender has failed to understand their tastes and misread their character, which challenges the tacit rule that a gift should be 'personal'. Mauss pointed out that, in contemporary Western societies, the things we give as gifts are typically mass-produced commodities, which carry just this risk: they are alienated from both the giver and the recipient. In shopping for a gift, we struggle to avoid these pitfalls by finding something with a personal touch, which ironically turns a pleasurable, spontaneous activity into a complex, rule-bound chore.

The various rituals, rules and deviations involved in consumerism raise interesting questions about the social functions of this practice. When we go shopping, what are we ultimately searching for? Alongside the goods and services themselves, there may be the pleasure of acquiring pieces of material culture that win admiration from our peers. There may be the satisfaction of providing for others, affirming a social bond and performing a group identity. Alternatively, the pleasure of the act may lie in its connotations of hedonism, frivolity and escapism. Like many social practices, shopping involves both the comfort of rule-following and the thrill of rule-breaking – the recurrent dialectic of structure and agency. In the next chapter, we delve further into this puzzle: how and why do we create opportunities for leisure in our everyday lives, and is it really a coincidence that these 'escape attempts' ultimately strengthen our commitment to social structures and routines?

Summary points

- Shopping serves many purposes beyond the instrumental acquisition of goods. It may be experienced as a duty or a pleasure, as an escape from everyday routines, or as a site of identity performance.
- Consumer behaviour is shaped by the psychological and social processes involved in buying and selling. These include techniques of advertising, shop design and layout, and the forms of interaction involved in a sale.
- Although enjoyed as a form of individual agency, shopping practices are also structured and rule-bound and contribute to the maintenance of social order. Gender and social class, in particular, create differences in the process and products of shopping.

- Consumer culture describes a recent trend of increased spending on non-essential items for the purposes of recreation, leisure and entertainment. This has been perpetuated by concurrent trends of mass production, mass consumption and advertising in the mass media.
- Lifestyle shopping involves the acquisition of commodities that represent a particular lifestyle or identity. Shopping malls were designed with this in mind, and encourage certain forms of consumer behaviour. However, the rituals of going to the mall with family and friends also play an important part in everyday life.
- The tacit rules of shopping can be challenged by various norm-breaking acts, such as textual poaching, 'making do' with shop designs, and defaulting on the obligations of a gift exchange.

9 Leisure

In this chapter we look at some of the ways in which leisure time is used to inject moments of freedom, pleasure and escapism into our daily lives, from the small breaks we schedule into chores, through the hobbies that carve out hedonistic enclaves, to the vacations we take to new landscapes. At the same time, we should remain critically aware of the limits to these practices: to what extent does leisure actually enable us to escape the everyday world? Do we find order, pattern and routine in even our most rebellious escape attempts? This reminds us of the interplay between agency and structure, freedom and restraint, rule-breaking and social order. We shall look firstly at recreation in relation to the themes of social order, rituals and routines, and norm-breaking challenges, before focusing on vacations as a particularly salient context in which these themes are played out.

Structured freedom?

Work and leisure

The most noticeable thing about leisure is that is implicitly contrasted with work. It is negatively defined as 'time off' from doing what we should be doing, a break from the routine that allows us to indulge in non-essential tasks: 'work represents the everyday routine; rest is a temporary interruption' (Rybczynski 1991: 51). Nobody lives a life of unmitigated pleasure, and our free time is usually limited to spatially and temporally bound zones; we remain aware that at some point we will have to return to our duties, though, as we shall see, this may evoke feelings of relief. The word 'leisure' itself originates from the Latin *licere*, meaning 'to be allowed' or 'lawful' (Williams 1958; cf. Parry and Coalter 1982), indicating that we experience leisure as something to be enjoyed only in moderation.

For Marx (1959 [1844]), leisure had to be seen within the context of the alienating effects of industrial capitalism. The demands of labour were such that workers were permitted only to take short breaks, never experiencing true freedom. Moreover, this ultimately served the interests of capitalist employers, by keeping the work-force in good spirits, fit and energized so that they could sustain a steady pace. Veblen (2005 [1899]), too, argued that the 'leisure classes' had emerged out of capitalism, with its emphasis on consumer goods as symbols of prestige. He was critical of the way in which the American middle classes emulated the lifestyles of the wealthy through their 'conspicuous consumption' of expensive goods, such as cars, holidays and household gadgets, which were proudly displayed but wastefully squandered (see chapter 8). Considering this literature, Parry and Coalter (1982) observe that leisure seems to mediate between the individual and society, or freedom and constraint.

Work and leisure may be mutually constitutive, but do we 'live to work' or 'work to live'? On the one hand, the classic theories outlined above suggest that the organization of leisure time ultimately serves a social purpose in keeping employees fit for work. Marx's (1959 [1844]) notion of false consciousness explains why we feel we have no choice but to work and accept the inevitability of returning to work after a holiday. This is strengthened by Weber's (1985 [1904–5]) theory of the Protestant work ethic as a driving force for capitalism: leisure breaks must be earned through hard work. Moreover, although we have a biological need for rest and relaxation, many people enjoy their jobs and would happily work longer hours, were it not for hunger and fatigue necessitating taking a break. On the other hand, work can be consciously experienced as drudgery, and is often regarded as a necessary evil: employment provides money, which enables us to buy things and participate in leisure activities. Even (or especially?) those performing unpaid domestic labour may look forward to a holiday, a coffee break or a luxurious bath at the end of a hard day. Leisure time is often understood as 'me-time', or a chance to perform identity work: we create and reinforce a sense of who we are by what we choose to do rather than what we have to do. Perhaps, then, we both live to work and work to live, maintaining a balance between the two. Excessive labour can induce 'burnout', while unstructured, open-ended leisure time can be surprisingly depressing (Jahoda et al. 1972). As Parry and Coalter (1982) argue, leisure is not the same as pleasure, and is best enjoyed in small doses.

Escapism

Leisure also represents freedom: it is the way in which we exercise choice over our everyday lives. Even when they are not enjoyable, leisure activities provide a break from the routine, reminding us that this is possible, that we are not doggedly committed to incessant work. Here again we meet the dialogue between social structure and human agency, or the 'transformative capacity' of individuals to make a difference to the worlds in which they live (Giddens 1984; see chapter 2). It seems that we have a social and an emotional as well as a biological need to take time out from everyday life.

This idea was explored in a famous study by Cohen and Taylor (1992) of the 'escape attempts' that people make in the context of mundane, day-to-day living. These might include daydreaming and fantasies, shopping, sex, or retreating to certain designated 'free areas', of which there were three types. These were activity enclaves, such as hobbies, sports and games; new landscapes, such as holiday resorts, art galleries, fashion and subcultures; and mindscapes, which take the escapist into altered states of consciousness, such as drinking, drugs and – intriguingly – psychotherapy. Interestingly, Cohen and Taylor suggest that each of these opportunities for escape is built into the institutional structures of everyday life – the very rules that we are trying to break. For example, daydreaming takes place while one is engaged in a boring activity, and vacations have to be negotiated with employers or co-ordinated with school timetables. In this way, acts of apparent resistance feed back into the fabric of the everyday world and reproduce social order:

> ... our life scripts will not always make room for our fantasies. We look elsewhere to cope with routine, boredom, lack of individuality, frustration. We want a genuine escape, a flight to an area in which we can temporarily absent ourselves from paramount reality, find ourselves out of play, and assemble our identity in peace or with new and more powerful symbolic resources. Society creates just such areas and signposts them. (Cohen and Taylor 1992: 112)

Leisure rituals and routines

The rhythms of recreation

The contrast between leisure and work (or other duties) reveals another important dimension of the former: free time has to be scheduled into the routines from which it provides an escape, and as such we can observe rhythmic patterns of what Rybczynski (1991) calls 'time on' and 'time off'. We divide our days, weeks and months into these two categories in order to make sense of the passing of time. For example, bored office workers find themselves counting the hours until 5.00 p.m. when they can go home, and 'waiting for the weekend' from as early as Monday morning. In Britain, there is an implicit custom that little serious work is done on Fridays, and colleagues often leave early to go for a celebratory drink. Indeed, as we saw in chapter 6, going to the pub is an important ritual in marking the transition between work and home, or time on and time off.

Crucially, however, Rybczynski emphasizes that these temporal categories are completely arbitrary, reflecting social customs, norms and values (see chapter 5). For example, the division of the week into five working days and two weekend days is specific to modern capitalist societies. In Roman times, a market was held on every eighth day, the nundine, whereas in ancient Greece and Egypt relaxation was seen as an important indulgence for all. Even within contemporary European societies, there is widespread variation in working hours and leisure time (Fagan 2002). Rybczynski suggests that every society recognizes the need for rest and recuperation, but that they interpret this in various ways.

Similarly, the religious origins of the word 'holiday'– holy day – reveal that time off is defined in contrast to the profane world of workaday life. Nowadays, we tend to think of holidays (or vacations) as pleasurable rewards, but in Judaeo-Christian history 'holy days' were ones of moral prohibition: it was forbidden to work, and the time was to be spent in spiritual contemplation. Traditionally, the Sabbath, or weekly day of rest, is one in which no work must be done, and this continues to be observed by many practising Christians, Jews and Muslims. In orthodox Jewish lore, 'work' is taken to mean not only paid employment but any expenditure of energy, from cooking to switching on lights; Shabbat, which lasts from sundown on Friday to Saturday night, is a time for worship and family interaction.

However, for many, as modern Western societies become increasingly secular, the religious meaning of the Sabbath has become somewhat obscured. For example, Sunday trading laws, which forbade shops from opening to customers on this 'day of rest', were repealed in England and Wales in 1994 (there was never any legislation in Scotland preventing Sunday trading), with similar patterns apparent in the USA and Australia. Now Sundays can be as busy as other days for shopping, trade and commerce, especially since Internet shopping has obviated the necessity of visiting store premises (see chapter 8).

Nevertheless, in other ways, the rhythm of 'six days working, one day resting' continues to beat. Sundays may no longer be spent in religious contemplation, but they do tend to be when we visit family and friends, have morning lie-ins, potter in the garden or go to the beach. Work performed on Sundays will often be the least stressful jobs, such as gardening, letter writing or home improvements (see chapter 4; cf. Fox 2004). In academia, faculty are entitled to regular periods of sabbatical study leave, during which they do fieldwork, writing or other research activities. Although these are all hard work, there is an implicit assumption that research is more enjoyable, autonomous and self-serving than teaching or administration, and so the sabbatical leave has to be earned by a certain number of semesters spent in dutiful service.

We also find rhythm in the pace of the months that comprise each calendar year, and their various associations with time on or time off. For example, the tradition of the long summer holiday, taken in July–August or December–January (depending on which side of the world you live), was designed to fit around the rhythm of the academic year as much as the warmer weather. Family holidays are often taken during this period, and parents, children, teachers and students find themselves looking forward to the summer as a rewarding break after a long period of work. Meanwhile, there are festivals such as Christmas, Thanksgiving, May Day and Hallowe'en, which break the year up into manageable chunks, each punctuated by a celebratory holiday. As soon as one festivity is over, we find ourselves back in the rhythm of the annual cycle, working towards the next timetabled break.

It is also worth noting that many of these festivals involve social activities that bring people together, such as family meals (see chapter 6). In structural functionalist terms, these events generate a sense of solidarity that reaffirms each person's commitment to the values of the group (Durkheim 1976 [1912]). For example, the Thanksgiving holiday in the USA and Canada typically involves the reunion of extended family units: students come home from college, grandparents come to stay, and everyone sits down to a large celebratory meal. Durkheim would argue that what they are celebrating is not Thanksgiving per se, but rather the very fact of their togetherness and their collective identity as a family. By performing such familiar rituals together, the group strengthens their commitment to each other and to the values they share. This would suggest that leisure serves a wider function of social integration (cf. Parsons and Bales 1956; see chapter 2).

Leisure time is scheduled to occur in the space between other duties and responsibilities. In chapter 6, we encountered Turner's (1967) concept of liminality – a transitional period in which one is suspended between two social identities. Liminal zones are those in which such changes occur, when one has severed the connection to a previous activity or role but not yet embraced a new one. Thus we could think of free time as that which occurs 'betwixt and between' periods of work. It is a time of relative freedom and autonomy, when rules can be transgressed and actors can relax out of role. For example, a clerk leaves the office on the last day before her holiday begins, and feels an enormous sense of relief as she is now free of alarm clocks, smart clothes and the daily routine of work for a few precious days, even though she knows that she will have to return to it soon. Leisure time provides us with carefully designed, temporally bound windows of opportunity that ultimately keep us committed to the wider social order. In Bakhtin's (1968) terms, leisure represents a time of 'licensed carnival', which stands in contrast to the mundane, everyday world. Carnivalesque activities are those which are joyful, exuberant, spectacular and celebratory; they allow us to 'let off steam' by indulging in playful, non-serious behaviour that transgresses the rules we would normally observe.

Hobbies, games and masks

The everyday world is replete with not only leisure times but also leisure places – sites specially designed for the purposes of recreation and enjoyment. Perhaps the oldest of these is the theatre and its related genres of performance art. Hinton (1987) argues that the theatre serves an important role in social life by strengthening the bonds between the individual and their community. This is because performance art generates myths, or timeless stories about a culture, which teach the audience about its history, politics, values and contemporary condition. Theatre is a form of living memory, Hinton argues, which uses archetypal characters to tell these stories in a meaningful way. We might empathize with the dilemmas faced by Hamlet, Scrooge or Bridget Jones, and use the time out we spend watching them to deal vicariously with our own concerns. At the same time, performance art belongs to another world, into which we escape for some time out. The tradition of going to the theatre is ancient and culturally dispersed: it can be traced back as far as the Confucian ancestor worship of China, Japan and Korea and the philosophical debates enacted in the public meeting places of ancient Greece and Rome (Wickham 1992). In the Middle Ages, theatres came to be used more explicitly for entertainment: poetry, song and dance displays were common, while the work of William Shakespeare was extremely influential in bringing dramatizations of the dilemmas faced by 'ordinary' people to the Elizabethan masses.

In more recent historical eras, we can trace the continued role of the theatre in cementing social ties. For example, the austere moral climate of Victorian Britain in the nineteenth century was given light relief by the introduction of variety shows, Vaudeville houses and music halls, in which local singers, dancers, magicians, and so on, would each take a turn to give a short performance. These shows quickly became a popular form of regular, inexpensive entertainment, for the working classes in particular: these were family outings, and punctuated the end of the working week (Wickham 1992). However, these small, local theatres began to lose business in the early twentieth century with the rise of the showbusiness industry, Hollywood and the emergence of cinema. Going to the pictures became a new favourite pastime in the Western world, and served the same social functions of giving individuals and families time out from their workaday concerns. Hollywood stars in particular were presented as the fodder of escapist fantasies, evoking feelings of desire and longing in their audiences (Stacey 1993).

Teams and collectivity

Other leisure activities reveal a similarly collective aspect, which may be their ultimate function. Vernon Bartlett (1969) points to the increasing seriousness with which sports and pastimes are regarded, but argues that the origins of many contemporary games can be traced back several centuries. Thus golf and hockey stem from the ball games of ancient Egypt and Greece, while lawn tennis was invented in the nineteenth century; its spin-off games badminton and ping-pong began as children's games, which were appropriated by adults. Card games emerged from the courts of Louis XVI, and quickly became popular across Europe; some, such as whist, were then created in England and spread back to France. Modern board games such as snakes and ladders can be traced back to the 'knuckle-bone' dice of

Figure 9.1 *Beach volleyball in Brighton: leisure activities provide a break from the routine – though, ironically, they can become routine practices themselves.*

ancient Greece, just as chess has its origins in ancient Egypt and Rome. Bartlett suggests that the persistence and continuity of such leisure pursuits demonstrates their social importance. All games can be reduced to four categories, he says, which serve social functions: they help people to 'let off steam' that might otherwise be channelled into aggression; they allow us to display physical skills in competitive hierarchies; they stimulate the brain to prevent boredom; and they pass the time pleasantly in the company of others.

In chapter 6, we saw how the ritual of going to the pub has remained an important feature of everyday life in local communities, wherein drinking together provides an opportunity for talk and social bonding (Fox 2004). In the late 1930s, researchers for the Mass Observation archive (Madge and Harrisson 1939) observed how this site had been infused with the styles of vaudeville and music hall by the introduction of a new dance craze, 'The Lambeth Walk'. This was a song and dance routine, popularized by the British comedian Lupino Lane, which parodied but also celebrated elements of cockney working-class culture in the East End of London. The routine soon caught on, and was often performed in pubs by local people during the 'summer dance madness' of 1938:

> Lambeth you've never seen
> The skies ain't blue and the grass ain't green
> It hasn't got the Mayfair touch
> But that don't matter very much
> We play the Lambeth way
> Not like you but a bit more gay ...
>
> (Madge and Harrisson 1939: 140–1)

Here, again, we might say that the ultimate purpose of this leisure activity was its ability to bring people together to participate in a collective ritual. In Durkheimian terms, the Lambeth Walkers were expressing their commitment to the working-class values that they shared, celebrating this group membership through their worship of its symbols. We can find numerous other examples of song and dance 'crazes' that have been popularized since this time and which tend to be enjoyed collectively – karaoke, line dancing, 'Riverdance' and salsa, to name but a few.

Leisure practices can also be used as a way of performing the collective identity of a subculture or minority group. Dick Hebdige (1979) showed how successive generations of post-war UK youth subcultures adopted distinctive fashion styles and their encumbent lifestyles to display an attitude of resistance to what they perceived as the dominant values of mainstream, middle-class British society. The 1950s Teddy Boys wore their hair in quiffs and hung out in milk bars, the 1960s Mods and Rockers dressed respectively in smart suits or biker gear and congregated on the streets, while the 1970s Punks sported ripped jeans, piercings and Mohican haircuts, adorned with an attitude of boredom and derision. Each of these, Hebdige argued, was a way of winning symbolic space for an alternative set of values, in resistance to dominant ideologies. In semiotic terms, they could be read as a symbolic violation of the social order through the performative enactment of conflicting values.

At the time of Hebdige's writing, social class was the most salient and provocative source of conflict in this regard, but more recently Andy Bennett (1999) has suggested that the class-based concept of subculture has become rather outdated as an analytical tool for understanding young people's involvement in music and related lifestyle practices. In the late modern culture of contemporary Western societies (Giddens 1991), identities have become fragmented, pluralistic and experimental. Young people move between different subcultures that are seemingly classless, based upon more aesthetic markers of 'taste' and distinction (cf. Bourdieu 1984). Bennett calls these new formations 'neo-tribes', emphasizing that they are still sources of collective identity, performed through ritual practices. For example, Sarah Thornton (1995) adapts Bourdieu's concept of cultural capital to describe the *subcultural* capital sought by the young people who visited nightclubs, dances and raves in the 1990s. They valued an abstract ideal of authenticity, which, paradoxically, they demonstrated through a taste for all things fashionable, 'cool' and 'hip'. Interestingly, however, Thornton points out that many of these so-called subcultures were formed organically, through word of mouth, fly posting, and so on, and acquired the appearance of collective entities only when their ritualistic leisure practices were defined as such by the music press.

Challenging leisure

Football hooliganism

In some contexts of leisure, the collective activities used to promote social solidarity can become a source of overt conflict and inter-group hostility. Perhaps the clearest example of this, in the UK at least, is football hooliganism. In the UK, football (soccer) is regarded as the nation's favourite sport and has a huge fanbase – like basketball or ice hockey in the USA, or cricket in Australia. Watching football matches at weekends is one of the most popular leisure activities, cutting across age, class and gender divides. Williams and Neatrour (2001) explain how many Britons are socialized into their fandom of a particular team, as, for example, children accompany their parents to football matches or support the team from their local area. However, in some cases, football fandom can become obsessive to the point of open conflict and violence. The term 'football hooliganism' is used to describe scenes of rowdy behaviour aimed at supporters of the opposite team during a match; this may include taunting, name-calling and chanting, or more serious acts of physical aggression.

Interestingly, however, even these apparently deviant, rule-breaking acts can be read as ultimately promoting solidarity and cohesiveness. Walter (1991) points to the quasi-religious practices of 'worshipping' a team or player, chanting in unison, and observing superstitious rituals, such as carrying a lucky mascot, and it is difficult to know where to draw the line between this 'normal' fandom and the 'hooligan' variety. Intriguingly, Marsh et al. (1994) argue that even the most violent, aggressive acts of football hooliganism can be seen as organized, ritualized and, above all, rule-governed. Chants of derision must be rehearsed and beliefs and sentiments reiterated, and acts of group violence can appear as efficiently performed as if they had been choreographed. Marsh et al. therefore point to the 'rules of disorder', and their research shows how the collective activities of hooliganism actually strengthen the ties between fellow team supporters. Furthermore, in a Durkheimian sense, such deviance promotes social solidarity in the non-hooligan majority: reactions of moral indignation and outrage directed at the offenders help to unite 'us' against 'them', the common enemy (cf. Durkheim 1984 [1893]).

'Chavs', class and moral panic

The pathologization of football hooliganism demonstrates the concept of moral panic, whereby the mass-media coverage of a small number of deviant acts is disproportionately large and targeted at a distinct group of 'folk devils' (Cohen 1972). Working-class young men, in particular, seem prone to being depicted as such, and in recent years this has been channelled into the lampooning of a new cultural stereotype, the 'chav'. This is a character who typically wears tracksuits, 'hoodies' and baseballs caps, lives on a council estate and has a materialist consumer lifestyle; the chav is presumed to be unintelligent, unsophisticated and lacking in the 'taste' and values of middle-class culture (cf. Bourdieu 1984). In the UK, hooded tops were infamously banned from the Bluewater shopping mall in Kent in 2004, shortly after police officers in Leicester had supported the decision of two pubs to ban certain clothing brands because of their association with the 'dress code' of chavvish football hooligans (BBC 2004). But is the chav an object of fact or fiction?

   Nayak (2006) suggests that the chav may represent a real figurehead of working-class culture, with a distinctive set of leisure practices. With the twentieth-century decline of traditional industrial labouring jobs and their replacement with temporary, contracted and part-time work in the service economy, many working-class families experienced intergenerational unemployment and unstable, fragmented labour biographies. This created a demarcation between the 'rough' and the 'respectable' working classes, reflected in the ways in which the young men used leisure to perform their masculine identities. In the latter group's case, the 'drinking culture' that had once meant fathers and sons going to the local pub together now involved groups of young men going out 'circuit drinking' around the town. Nayak argues that, although regarded as a deviant activity (there is another moral panic about 'binge drinking'), this leisure pursuit is highly ritualized and orderly, a regulated social routine, and functions to reinforce traditional working-class cultural values. The 'Real Geordies' he interviewed took pleasure in relating humorous anecdotes about things that had happened on nights out, involving 'drinking, swearing and physical horseplay' (Nayak 2006: 819), which gave them a sense of collective history and shared experience.

On the other hand, there was a distinct set of long-term unemployed youth in the city, whose working-class identities were more fragmented and marginalized. Priced out of the mainstream drinking venues, these young men took refuge in the 'Charver' identity by hanging out on the streets, drinking beer, smoking and taking illegal drugs. They wore regulation tracksuit and 'gangsta'-style gold chains, danced to techno music at illegal raves, and developed a characteristic gait, the 'monkey-walk'. Like the Real Geordies, the Charver lads earned a certain amount of subcultural capital (Thornton 1995) from each other by displaying these embodied practices, but they were regarded with disdain by other young people, who associated their lifestyle with crime and violence. Nayak argues that the Charver lads were using their bodies to respond to their structural position in society, as 'economically disenfranchised, socially excluded and culturally despised'; by appearing 'ruff, tough and streetwise', they expressed the symbolic violence of class inequalities (Nayak 2006: 826).

Normalization

In cases of moral panic, the 'folk devils' (Cohen 1972) in question tend to know that they are being scapegoated, but in other cases deviant leisure activities may not appear as such to those who are engaged in them. For example, Parker et al. (2002) point to the way in which certain patterns of illegal drug use are normalized within the culture of relatively affluent, middle-class young adults. Normalization is a process through which actors make sense of rule-breaking behaviour by emphasizing its place within conventional, everyday life: the deviant act is but a temporary aberration from an otherwise conformist personality (Fulcher and Scott 2007). Thus cannabis, cocaine and ecstasy may be consumed not as a rebellious act of resistance against mainstream culture but as a routine, unremarkable activity within it. The participants in Parker et al.'s study perceived their own drug use as a recreational leisure activity, pursued as a matter of personal choice and moderated by self-control. Their accounts sought to rationalize any mention of 'serious' drug use by pointing out its pervasiveness in youth culture. This reminds us of Cohen and Taylor's (1992) assertion that escape routes are built into the same realms of everyday life from which we seek to escape.

Similar arguments can be made about gambling, a practice that was for many years regarded as a sign of psychological disturbance, a pathological addiction (Neal 1998). This view was challenged by Erving Goffman (1967b), who argued that gambling was regarded by most of its adherents as a pleasurable leisure activity, in which they indulged as a matter of choice (though it is worth remembering that Goffman was himself a keen gambler and may have been seeking to normalize his own behaviour!). Neal suggests that gambling has become increasingly popular with the introduction of off-course betting shops, which attract a steady flow of punters. While some of these customers are 'compulsive' or 'professional' betters, putting in the hours as if this were a job (for they do occasionally make a big win), many more are recreational 'regulars' or 'uncommitted' occasional visitors to the shops (cf. Saunders and Turner 1987). Neal's ethnographic study of four UK betting shops in Surrey and Cheshire involved long periods of participant observation, through which he uncovered a number of rites and rituals. For example, the conversation between punters was important not only as a means of exchanging information on which horse they thought most likely to win but also as a form of social interaction: 'going to the bookies' was a significant and pleasurable activity, akin to 'going to the pub'. In placing their bets, they automatically dismissed the first and second favourites, for whom the odds of winning were too short, and held out for the 'big win'. This meant that they lost a lot of money but gained a great deal of excitement, which added to the 'effervescent' atmosphere of a collective activity (cf. Durkheim 1976 [1912]).

Neal observed demographic differences in terms of when and how the punters incorporated gambling into their everyday routines: for example, male pensioners would often come in for a 'morning flutter' that lent structure to their days, while those who worked would visit during their lunch breaks. Putting a bet on at lunchtime helped such customers to deal with the drudgery of returning to the office, for they could spend the afternoon dreaming about what they would do if they won (indeed, this is a slogan used to advertise the National Lottery in the UK). Meanwhile, non-routine workers such as bar staff would visit during the afternoon, seeking companionship and light-hearted banter after a tiring shift. In each of these cases, visiting the betting shop functioned as an escape attempt (Cohen and Taylor 1992): it provided solace from the routines of home or work, an opportunity for daydreaming and fantasies, and a source of social interaction that could not be found either at home or in the workplace. Like other apparently deviant leisure activities, therefore, gambling can actually be seen to be an orderly, rule-governed practice that is woven into the fabric of everyday life.

Vacations

One of the most important ways in which we spend our leisure time is by going on holiday, or vacation. Just as short-term escape attempts are built into our daily routines, we also set aside longer periods of designated free time within the rhythm of the calendar year. Indeed, the very word 'vacation' stems from the verb 'to vacate', or to leave empty – we abandon our homes and seek to forget their incumbent concerns. Vacations have an appeal in that they promise to provide a radical and prolonged escape to a site that is physically as well as mentally removed from the sphere of everyday life. As we shall see, this involves aspects of social order, rituals and routines, and norm-breaking challenges.

Historicizing holidays

In Britain, the seaside holiday is an important cultural tradition, and one that is relatively classless in its appeal. However, as James Walvin (1978) explains, this was not always the case. Until the mid-nineteenth century, holidaying by the sea was the preserve of the wealthy upper classes, who extolled the supposed medicinal benefits of bathing in salt water. The practice of seabathing was endorsed by Dr Richard Russell, and coastal resorts such as Brighton and Scarborough replaced the spa towns of Bath, Buxton and Harrogate as the most popular destinations for a leisurely retreat. Brighton in particular became a fashionable resort for the upper classes, as it was patronized by the Prince Regent in the late eighteenth century. It boasted a plethora of leisure activities such as billiards, bowling, tea dancing and theatre, and the town soon gained a reputation for fun, frivolity and escapism. By the mid-nineteenth century, seaside resorts of this nature had spread around the coast of Britain and, with the introduction of affordable public

Figure 9.2 *The traditional British seaside holiday developed over the nineteenth and twentieth centuries. Today it remains popular, but is often regarded with a wry nostalgia.*

transport through the building of the steam railways in the 1830s and 1840s, the practice of vacationing trickled down the class hierarchy. However, these visits could only be made as day trips until 1937, when a parliamentary committee ruled that paid annual holidays should be written into all employment contracts. This meant that working-class and middle-class people could take breaks of a week or fortnight, and thus the traditional summer holiday was born.

This new trend was bolstered by the rise of the mass entertainment industry in the early twentieth century, with cinema, radio and television creating an increased appreciation of leisure time. Holiday camps provided such entertainments alongside more traditional forms of recreation (ball games, dancing, outdoor sports) and soon became a popular source of 'cheap and cheerful', ready-made holidays for the working and middle classes alike (Ward and Hardy 1986). Nevertheless, the employment of Redcoat workers in these camps suggests that amidst the revelry lay a concern for order: the Redcoats were employed to shepherd guests from one activity to the next, remind them of the rules and generally keep order within the camps.

These camps attracted a regular clientele who would return year after year, indicating that the holidaymakers as much as the staff strove for order and predictability. Walvin echoes Cohen and Taylor when he observes: 'it seems ironic that holidays, which were a break from the sameness of everyday life, themselves became part of a wider annual routine' (Walvin 1978: 135).

Hedonistic escapes or irrepressible routines?

Indeed, more generally we find that, despite longing for a holiday as an escape from our domestic lives, we actually end up re-creating our homely routines on holiday: we schedule activities, plan meals and have an itinerary of 'things to do, places to see'. Perhaps we are really creatures of habit, who, in seeking to escape the routine, immediately seek ways to reinstate it? This is parodied by the character of Keith in Mike Leigh's film *Nuts in May* (1976), which depicts a middle-class 'hippie' couple on a camping holiday. Having marched wife Candice-Marie around Corfe Castle according to the strict numeric order of the guidebook, Keith is exasperated to discover that the road he was planning to take to the next attraction is closed:

Candice-Marie: Well, let's go somewhere else, Keith.
Keith: We can't go somewhere else. We're going to Lulworth Cove today; it's on the schedule.
Candice-Marie: Let's go to Lulworth Cove tomorrow.
Keith: We can't go tomorrow; we're going to a quarry tomorrow! Now look at the map …
Candice-Marie: We don't always have to stick to the schedule, you know, Keith.
Keith: There's no point in having a schedule if you're not going to stick to it.

This raises the interesting question of whether vacations, though designed as a means of escapism, actually contribute to the maintenance of social order. John Urry (2002) argues that hedonistic activity is only defined as such in relation to norms and rules of behaviour. Though socially acceptable, holidaying is a 'deviant' activity in that it departs from the routine practices of everyday life. In particular, it transgresses the rules of the workplace, with its structures of time-keeping, schedules and hierarchies of responsibility. Urry suggests that, by keeping the two spheres separate, we confine any potentially disruptive, rule-breaking activities to a carefully controlled time and place: we go away on holiday with the knowledge that we are obliged to come back and return to our workaday duties. Here again we see the idea of licensed carnival (Bakhtin 1968). Paradoxically, therefore, this strengthens our commitment to social order during the times when we are not on holiday; in Durkheimian terms, the deviance is ultimately functional. Urry observes that this rigid compartmentalization of time off and time on is a rational strategy that bears the hallmarks of modernity:

> Tourism is a leisure activity which presupposes its opposite, namely regulated and organised work. It is one manifestation of how work and leisure are organised as separate and regulated spheres of social practice in 'modern' societies. Indeed, acting as a tourist is one of the defining characteristics of being 'modern' and is bound up with major transformations in paid work. (Urry 2002: 2–3)

Breaking the rules

Holiday romances

Empirical studies lend support to the idea of holidaymaking as a source of carefully contained deviant behaviour. For example, Michelle Thomas (2000, 2005) conducted in-depth interviews and focus groups with thirty-five women who had experienced a holiday romance during a trip abroad. These women explained how they were much more likely to have sexual intercourse with a new partner whom they met on holiday than they were with one at home, despite (or perhaps because of) knowing that it would not lead on to the development of a serious relationship. Thomas suggests that this is because holidays represent a period of liminality (Turner 1967), when actors are between social roles and norms of behaviour are temporarily abandoned. As one of her respondents, Kirsty, put it, 'Everyone throws caution to the wind a bit really and just has a good time and doesn't worry about the consequences, 'cos you're not going to see that person next week' (Thomas 2005: 575).

The women in Thomas's study experienced holiday time as 'compressed': they would try to cram as much activity as possible into their short period of freedom, to 'make the most of it', whether this meant visiting more historic ruins or having more sexual encounters. Their holiday romances would progress much more rapidly than relationships back home, and sex was regarded as the pinnacle of this achievement. Nevertheless, Thomas emphasizes that the women were quite realistic about the limited viability of these new relationships, suspecting that they would not survive beyond the duration of the trip. Holiday time was therefore seen as inhabiting a separate world from that of normal, everyday life, and represented an escape from it. Another respondent, Lucy, said, 'it is something certainly that niggles you a little bit, you're just thinking well it's slightly different and I only really met him abroad on holiday, I don't really know what he's like in reality, sort of coming down to stay with me' (Thomas 2005: 578). Indeed, perhaps the whole appeal of such transient romances was precisely this: that they could be safely contained within that alternate reality, leaving the actors free to resume their workaday routines. As two focus group participants, Jodie and Tanya, reported, there was an unwritten rule that friends would not mention each other's sexual misdemeanours once they were back home: 'What happens in Tenerife stays in Tenerife' (Thomas 2005: 576).

Emigration

What would happen, then, if these boundaries were removed? Karen O'Reilly (2007) presents an interesting study of transnational migrants, or 'ex-pats' (ex-patriots), in three Spanish coastal areas, who had extended their holiday into a permanent lifestyle. In some respects, migration is the ultimate escape attempt: the individual manages to go away and not come back. O'Reilly writes of her respondents' initial hopes of 'starting a new life in a new place', and how they dreamed of escaping from the drudgery of workaday routines back home. Many of them were working in low-paid jobs in the UK or were struggling entrepreneurs; they emphasized the value of leaving the old country as much as joining the new one.

However, O'Reilly questions what happens when this novelty wears off and the reality of living abroad takes hold. Ironically, the ex-pats found themselves re-creating the very routines they had sought to escape: seeking an income from work, maintaining a new home, going shopping and running errands. Moreover, O'Reilly reports on her respondents' experiences of social exclusion as they struggled to settle into their new homes. They were not able to participate fully in the Spanish labour market, pay national insurance contributions and benefit from the nation's health and welfare services; many failed to learn to speak Spanish well enough to form friendships with the locals, and many of the children experienced racial bullying at school. O'Reilly refers to the tensions inherent in this 'mobility-enclosure dialectic': the ex-pats had physically escaped their old country but remained legally, administratively and, to some extent, socially members of its nation-state. They held an ambiguous status between the two countries and felt neither permanently on holiday nor permanently at home.

Mobility and the 'tourist gaze'

Going on vacation usually means travelling to a different geographical location, and this process is as sociologically interesting as what happens when we reach it. Urry (2006) points to the importance of space and place to holidaymaking and argues that one of the defining features of tourists is their mobility, which enables them to span different spatial and temporal zones outside of conventional clock time. In Urry's view, this reflects the increasing fluidity of social relations and their dispersal across time and space (cf. Giddens 1991). There is a constant flow of people, objects and information across physical boundaries, which challenges the traditional distinction between private and public as static regions (Sheller and Urry 2003). For example, contemporary patterns of tourism allow us to make regular trips to see friends and family in other countries from whom we might otherwise be estranged.

By theorizing mobility, then, we can explore the potential for individual actors to subvert the structures of time, space and place that would otherwise constrain their routines. The traveller is someone with agency, choosing when, where and how they move between places. For example, the (late) modern citizen has become adept at managing the passing of time while in transit, with retail outlets dedicated to the sale of travel items (games, crossword puzzle books and mp3 players) at airports and railway stations. These sites may be understood as 'non-places' (Augé 1995), where nobody belongs and everybody is in transit. They represent an odd kind of freedom that is at once empowering and immensely lonely. It is therefore interesting to consider the experience of travelling and the ontological status of the traveller, who is betwixt and between social spaces (cf. Turner 1967). When I am moving from one place to another, to which culture do I belong to and whose rules should I obey?

Both travelling and tourism while on vacation involve what Urry (2002) calls the 'tourist gaze'. That is, the modern traveller is not so much intent on being in a different culture and doing different things as they are on looking at visual scenes that differ from those they encounter in everyday life. We choose to visit places that represent something out of the ordinary when we go on holiday, and focus on its most striking contrasts to our own cultural background: we photograph breathtaking landscapes rather than our hotel room or local shop! It seems that holidaymakers have a fascination with the exotic, the 'other', and its relation to the self. Urry's idea of the tourist gaze draws upon the more general Foucauldian notion of gaze and surveillance (Foucault 1977 [1975]); the traveller yields a certain amount of power in their position of detached observation. Nevertheless, Urry also emphasizes how the direction of the tourist gaze is socially shaped and controlled as much as it is controlling. For example, we can identify trends in holiday type and destination, such as the eighteen to thirty group trip, student gap years spent travelling in Australia or Thailand, and the popularity of Disneyworld in the 1990s (Bryman 1995).

Urry describes how we take pleasure from gazing at landscapes we move around, vicariously consuming them. For example, Baudrillard's (1989) postmodernist text *America* contains little more than a series of images of different regional landscapes, his argument being that this is all we now seem to want to know about a place. Urry suggests that the tourist gaze is constructed by the collection of signs – iconic, meaningful images that appear to capture the essence of place. Thus we might photograph a romantic couple kissing in Paris, a mud hut in Samoa, or tranquil waters in the Lake District. Tourism often involves 'seeing the sights', consuming and capturing them for posterity in this way. Many resorts have a culturally recognized set of images that one 'must see' when visiting the place. This in turn becomes something of an identity performance, as we display our photographs like trophies. But what are we actually consuming through these practices? Postmodernist theorists such as Baudrillard would argue that the tourist gaze captures only the hyper-real, or representations of reality: the images we collect are empty signifiers that are all style and no substance. As tourists, we may never really get to understand a place from the inside, because we are always gazing at it hungrily from the outside. Similarly, Daniel Boorstin (1992 [1962]) wrote of pseudo-events, or scenes that we think we experience but that we can really only observe. As Urry puts it, 'Isolated from the host environment and the local people, the mass tourist travels in guided groups and finds pleasure in inauthentic contrived attractions, gullibly enjoying the 'pseudo-events' and disregarding the 'real world outside' (Urry 2002: 7).

Figure 9.3 *Increasingly cheap and accessible international travel has led to the rise of the postmodern tourist – an actor who roams through landscapes, gazing and collecting 'signs' such as this iconic San Francisco cable car.*

Staged authenticity?

On the other hand, patterns of contemporary tourism closer to home reveal a rather different character. Urry (2002) points out that, along-side the frenetic consumption of the exotic, we can observe a new trend of 'heritage tourism', through which people explore their own countries in order to gain a deeper understanding of their cultural heritage. He suggests that this is a response to the fragmentation and uncertainty of identities in contemporary Western societies: going 'back to your roots' or rediscovering a more 'authentic' way of life holds an appeal to the lonely, anxious, alienated self of late modernity. This might involve visiting locally or nationally designated sites of beauty, architectural design or historical significance, such as the Lake District national park, York Minster or Stonehenge (Hetherington 1992). However, it might just as easily involve an 'ironic' trip to visit places that are regarded with wry scepticism within one's own culture: a 'dirty weekend' in Brighton, a 'country retreat' to Devon or a 'glitzy' break in Las Vegas. Feifer (1985) argues that this 'post-tourist' attitude is one of relativity: we recognize various ways of 'doing tourism' that are equally valid, and so there is no greater kudos to be found in visiting one place rather than another.

Dean MacCannell (1976) writes of a quest for authenticity that is morally informed and critical. He suggests that, no longer content with package tours, we now seek to be unique and individual with our tastes, and select locations that signify authenticity. However, he submits that this can become something of a staged authenticity, one of posing and posturing. For example, comedians Steve Punt and Hugh Dennis, in *The Mary Whitehouse Experience*, speak of the 'travel bore', who revels in his display of photographs of obscure, 'unspoiled' locations (series 1, episode 5, 1991). This is the kind of person who protests that 'other people are tourists but I am a *traveller*'. The tourist and heritage industries are also complicit in staging authenticity. For example, we can witness the growing popularity of living museums in which actors re-create the 'traditional way of life' of a marginal or historically obsolete community: Wigan Pier in Lancashire and St Fagan's Museum of Welsh Life near Cardiff are two examples. Here, visitors take pleasure in seeing 'the way things were', despite knowing rationally that these are just staged performances. MacCannell (1976) observes that what is most intriguing about such places is that they appeal to tourists precisely because of their portrayal of routine, everyday situations. It is ironic that, in seeking to escape the mundanity of our own everyday lives, we feel drawn towards observing the same aspects of other people's lives! MacCannell calls this a 'fetishism of the mundane' that demonstrates our need for comfort, routine and familiarity in the face of postmodern ontological insecurity (cf. Giddens 1991).

This brings us back to the central paradox of holidays, leisure and recreation: they are designed to provide an escape from the routines of everyday life, yet leave us eager to return to these very same routines. We enjoy 'getting away from it all' for a short break, but perceive this in terms of recharging our batteries in order to resume workaday activities with renewed vigour. Additionally, we find ourselves re-creating similar routines in the sites of escape: vacations follow daily schedules, hobbies often involve systematically collecting things or going to classes, and sports activities demand regular practice to discipline the body (cf. Foucault 1977 [1975]). Even those who manage permanently to escape, as in O'Reilly's study, find that things are not that simple, and transport many of their old routines into the new context. Leisure practices remind us that apparently deviant challenges to the norms of everyday life are in fact orderly, predictable and safely contained within certain spheres of activity. Beneath the illusion of control and autonomy, the overall pattern is one of routine and stability.

Summary points

- Leisure is often negatively defined as an absence, escape or freedom from work.
- Social time is organized into rhythmic schedules of time on and time off, such as the division of the working week into weekdays and weekends, or the religious observance of 'holy days'.
- Holidays represent periods of carefully contained, temporally bounded escapism, during which norms of social behaviour are relaxed. They provide an opportunity for licensed carnival within liminal zones.
- Vacationing is a social ritual, although its form has changed in line with cultural shifts. For example, the traditional seaside holiday has been replaced by the mobile tourist gaze.
- Leisure time often involves deviant activities that break formal or informal social rules, such as football hooliganism or holiday romances.
- However, this apparent deviance is actually functional in keeping us ultimately committed to social order. Vacation time is enjoyed in the knowledge that it is time-limited, and workaday routines are resumed without question.

10 Researching Everyday Life

How can we study everyday life? Which research methods are most appropriate and why? The answers to these questions depend on which aspect of everyday life we are interested in and what kind of data we want to collect. The researcher's choice of method will reflect their ontological position (what they think the social world consists of) and epistemological stance (what they believe counts as valid knowledge). Do we seek to uncover the meanings that people give to their actions, the way they construct their own social worlds and account for them (interpretivist epistemology), or to map out patterns and trends in social behaviour on the basis of objective numerical measurements (positivist epistemology)? Is the aim to gather qualitative data (words and text) or quantitative data (numbers and statistics)?

In this chapter we examine some of the methods social scientists have used to study our three dimensions of everyday life: social order, rituals and routines, and challenges to the taken for granted. These methods correspond to the theories outlined in chapter 2 and are illustrated with examples from the empirical studies discussed in chapters 3 to 9. However, it is important to remember that these are not simply three discrete, separate categories of research methods; there is a great deal of overlap between them, and, in practice, researchers will select the most appropriate method(s) for their given topic. As such, this chapter presents a methodological 'toolkit' to complement the theoretical toolkit outlined in chapter 2, and may be of use when designing your own research projects. In the final section of the chapter, we consider some of the ethical and political issues involved in representing other people's lives and the researcher's responsibilities toward their participants.

Documenting social order

In some cases, we want to find out about a social context that is out of reach, either historically or geographically. The most appropriate strategy in these cases is to use documentary sources – written, pictorial or otherwise textual accounts created by or about the people under study. These might take the form of primary data, produced at the request of the researcher and devised with their research agenda in mind, or secondary data, which already exist, having been created for another purpose.

Official statistics

Although many researchers of everyday life tend not to use quantitative measures extensively (preferring to focus on words, texts and meanings), statistical sources can be extremely helpful as secondary data, by providing background information to map out the terrain of a topic. For example, a sociologist may seek to understand what it is like to experience divorce and how people manage the effects of this on their everyday lives, but they would first of all need to examine the wider patterns of marriage, divorce and family structure in that society.

Throughout the chapters of this book we have made similar use of statistical data on such topics as household structure (chapter 4), gendered employment patterns (chapters 4, 5 and 8) and leisure time (chapter 9). Many of the sources on which I have drawn are national social surveys conducted by governments, such as the Time Use Survey, Labour Force Survey, General Household Survey, and Social Trends. These are publicly accessible sources, which can be consulted either online or in university libraries; the Office of National Statistics (http://www.statistics.gov.uk/) in the UK has a website, as does the United States Federal Government (http://www.fedstats.gov/) and the Australian Bureau of Statistics (http://www.abs.gov.au/). You may also write to more specialist organizations to request copies of statistical reports that are intended to have a more limited circulation, or 'closed access' (Bryman 2008).

This method fits most comfortably with the Structural Functionalist perspective outlined in chapter 2: statistical data allow us to identify patterns, regularities and trends in human behaviour, which can be understood as representing the underlying structure of a society. Accordingly, the method can be helpful in generating evidence of social order: we can observe that, most of the time, most people follow certain normative conventions, for example of eating or shopping (see chapters 5 and 8). This in turn suggests routine behaviour at the micro-level, which could then be observed by a different method. Meanwhile, statistical data can also inform challenges to such theories: there may be anomalous or unexpected results that lead us to rethink an explanation.

The use of official statistics has been heavily criticized by some social researchers, particularly those working in the interpretivist tradition. Critics such as Cicourel (1964) and Douglas (1967) emphasized the socially constructed nature of statistical data: rather than standing as objective, factual records of events (such as the number of crimes committed or the actual prevalence of an illness), statistics represent the end point of a long process of interaction, negotiation and decision-making between various parties. For example, crime rates reflect not simply the number of crimes actually committed, but rather those that are witnessed, reported, taken seriously by the police, investigated and end in a prosecution. At each of these stages along the way, different people's actions determine which cases make it to the next stage and which fall by the wayside, and this depends on their various interests and values. Thus, when using any statistical data, it is important to ask yourself how and why they were created: Who devised the survey and what for? How were the key concepts defined and measured? Who were the respondents and was this a biased sample?

Personal documents

The term 'personal documents' (Bryman 2008) refers to items such as letters, diaries and autobiographies that were written by individuals for themselves or those close to them, rather than for the researcher, and thus constitute a form of secondary data. As first-person accounts, these types of documents provide very rich, detailed insights into the local, subjective lifeworlds (Schütz 1972) of the groups studied, and so are 'adequate at the level of meaning' (Weber 1949 [1904]). They reveal how people make sense of their everyday worlds and create their own semblance of order. This in turn can inform theoretical explanations from phenomenology, interpretivist sociology and, occasionally, psychoanalysis. Insofar as these data have not been contrived for the purposes of the research, they may be seen to be more valid than primary sources such as Mass Observation. On the other hand, research projects based upon personal documents tend to be limited in size and scope, such as case studies, and so the researcher cannot make any claims to representativeness.

Letters can be analysed in terms of both their content and their style, as windows onto the social worlds in which they were created. For example, in the Chicago School, Thomas and Znaniecki (1958 [1918–20]) studied an exchange of letters between Polish immigrants to the city in order to understand more about what it felt like to experience poverty, stress and social isolation in such circumstances. The letters were sent between family members, and so gave additional insights into how these various experiences affected the everyday life of domestic households.

Diaries are perhaps more often used in social research, particularly that which aims to bring to light aspects of the daily routines of a previous historical era that might otherwise be overlooked. For example, Liz Stanley's (1984) edited collection of the diaries of Hannah Cullwick, a Victorian maidservant (see chapter 4), reveals how the experience of everyday life within even the same household would vary according to social class; her accounts emphasize the drudgery of her labour in contrast to the leisurely lifestyles of her middle-class employers. Cullwick's diaries also reveal how, throughout her years of service, she conducted a love affair with an upper-class gentleman, Arthur Munby, whom she later married. Her diaries refer to the master–slave relationship that they played out erotically, which poses a challenge to stereotypical assumptions about the repression of sexuality in Victorian times (cf. Foucault 1980 [1976]).

In other cases, diaries can be used as a form of primary data, whereby the researcher asks participants to start keeping a record about certain types of experience that are of interest to him or her. These researcher-driven diaries (Elliott 1997) may be structured or free-text in form (Corti 1993), depending on whether the researcher seeks to collect quantitative or qualitative data. In the former case, participants are given a pre-printed diary in which they record the number of times they engage in an activity or the amount of time spent on it. Oriel Sullivan (1997) used this to great effect in her quantitative study of gendered time use (see chapter 5), which revealed the subtle forms of household structure and organization found at the micro-level.

Meanwhile, Heather Elliott (1997; see chapter 7) describes how free-text diaries can be used to enhance qualitative research by revealing more about people's daily rituals and routines. The diary acts as a proxy observer, she argues, in that it provides a window onto the minutiae of everyday events that might not be amenable to direct observation. In her study of people with musculoskeletal problems, Elliott asked a subset of eight participants from her sample of eighty to complete a free-text diary about the experience of illness, a sensitive issue that cannot easily be studied by an external observer. The diarists were asked to record daily their perceptions of any symptoms, the effects of these on their everyday lives, any action they had taken to seek treatment (from self-care to biomedical interventions and alternative therapies) and the reactions of family members. Elliott collected the diaries each week, and at the end of the third week conducted an in-depth interview with each person about what they had written. Thus diaries can be used in conjunction with interviews to form the diary-interview method.

Another variation on the diary method was suggested by Hislop et al. (2005), who asked thirty-five women aged forty or over to record audio diaries of their sleeping patterns over a period of seven days, complementing data they had already provided in focus groups, in-depth interviews and a questionnaire. These participants taperecorded a short oral account within twenty minutes of waking each day, remarking on such things as the time they had gone to bed, the quality of their sleep (rated 1 to 5), any disturbances, the influence of a partner on their sleeping that night, and so on. Hislop et al. argue that this adaptation of the diary method was appropriate for the topic of sleep as it was relatively unobtrusive, simple and practical for the participants to incorporate into their daily routines. In addition, the recording of the events shortly after they had happened served to reduce any errors of recall or interviewer bias, thus improving the validity of the findings.

Mass Observation

A particularly unique data source, on which I have drawn throughout the book, is the Mass Observation archive, housed at the University of Sussex. This holds the findings of an ongoing study of the everyday lives of 'ordinary people' around the UK, in the form of first-person written accounts, photographs and other documentary evidence. Ostensibly, these data reveal most about the rituals and routines of everyday life, but, as with other personal documents, this in turn can also be of relevance to questions of social order at the micro-level. For example, accounts of daily schedules, habits and household routines not only tell us what people do, but also suggest how and ultimately

Figure 10.1 *Visitors to the Mass Observation reading room*

why: we gain insights into the way people impose meaning and order upon social reality by constructing their own subjective lifeworlds (cf. Schütz 1972).

The project began in 1937 and was set up by an anthropologist, Tom Harrisson, a journalist, Charles Madge, and a documentary film-maker, Humphrey Jennings. It was particularly active before and during the Second World War, when, based in a central office in London, the research team recruited a panel of lay people to write regular short pieces in response to directives – open-ended questions about particular aspects of everyday life, such as shopping or gardening. In addition, the research team collected official reports, opinion polls, scraps of overheard conversation and general ephemera, such as adverts, posters, tickets, leaflets, and so on (Sheridan et al. 2000). These secondary data served to complement the primary data generated by the directives.

The results of these studies were published in a series of twenty-five paperback books, each of which focused on a different selection of topics, such as leisure time, food rationing and wartime employment. One of the most famous of the respondents was Nella Last, a

Figure 10.2 *Materials stored in the Mass Observation archive*

working-class housewife who wrote a series of diary entries about her domestic life between 1939 and 1963. These were later collated and published as a book, *Nella Last's War* (Broad and Fleming 2006) and as a televised drama, *Housewife, 49* (Granada Television 2006). During the pre-war period, the researchers also conducted their own social surveys and ethnographies, such as the study of the local pub in 'Worktown', Lancashire (Mass Observation 1987 [1943]), while during the war they gathered secondary data in the form of newspaper and radio propaganda, product advertisements and air-raid precautions (ARPs). In 1970, the archive was moved to the University of Sussex, where it remains open for browsing. Additional funding meant that more staff could be recruited as well as new panel members; more recent directives have been launched on such issues as dating, the death of Princess Diana, and the meaning of private and public space.

The value of the Mass Observation data, of course, lies in their authenticity: these are rich, detailed accounts of events as they happened, from the perspective of those who experienced them directly. For qualitative researchers, this suggests a high level of validity, insofar as the data provide insights into the meanings held by actors in local social worlds and situated settings. Sheridan et al. (2000) suggest that for the respondents, too, the experience of writing their accounts was enjoyable, even therapeutic, and gave them a sense of symbolic immortality (Giles 2000) in that their memories would live on through the words left behind. For example, in the descriptions of the home presented in chapter 4, we saw how these vivid narratives can bring theoretical points to life. If interpreting the social world means understanding it from the perspective of individual actors in local contexts, then first-person accounts in the actors' own words are an invaluable resource.

However, the project has invited some criticism from those who question its epistemological assumptions. Evans (1997) argues that Madge and Harrisson were operating from a privileged, male, middle-class standpoint, and as such exerted a 'colonial gaze' in their depiction of working-class life as 'other'. Picton (1978) made a similar point about the somewhat voyeuristic and perhaps condescending nature of the data, such as photographic scenes of pubs and residential streets as emblematic of 'working-class culture'. However, Highmore (2002) counters this by pointing out that the Mass Observation directives were much more diverse than this, particularly in the latter years. He does recognize a problem in the rather fragmented view of social life that is suggested by the amalgamation of varied data, but adds that this disadvantage is outweighed by the unique contributions of the data. In particular, he argues that the Mass Observation project was politically significant in presenting realistic, lay accounts of everyday life alongside the official, dominant ideologies depicted in mass-media sources. This juxtaposition of divergent data sets is, he argues, a powerful reminder of how we should always question the values, interests and bias behind apparently objective depictions of reality.

Evaluating documentary evidence

Indeed, similar caution should be exercised when appraising any secondary source of documentary data. While it is exciting to come across such sources, particularly first-person accounts of a previous historical era, we should not simply accept them at face value as 'true' depictions of reality. Scott (1990) suggests four criteria with which we can evaluate the quality of documentary sources and thus establish whether they constitute social scientific evidence. Authenticity refers to soundness of authorship: Is this a genuine document rather than a forgery? Was it really written by the author who is credited, or could it have been 'ghost-written' by someone else? Is it a complete record, or are there any missing sections? These are indicators of the source's validity: whether it really represents what it claims. For example, Mayhew's observations of the 'London poor' seem to be highly authentic by virtue of their attention to detail, and, even though they were collected in the days before tape-recorders, a researcher would be able to verify that his fieldnotes were detailed and extensive.

Scott's second criterion is credibility – the extent to which the data show a true and accurate version of events, rather than one that is biased towards the interests of the reporter. An edited diary, for example, may reveal as much about the researcher's values in selecting excerpts as it does about the subject's everyday life. Thus credibility is a measure of the reliability of the data, or its consistency across different measures: can we identify an underlying reality that would be the same even if someone else had recorded it or different aspects had been examined?

Thirdly, we can assess the representativeness of the documentary source: Why has this text survived over time, and is it typical of other, similar data that might have been produced in the same context? This criterion also helps us to evaluate official statistics, as outlined above: we need to be aware of how the process of producing such data sets means that some events will be selected for inclusion while others are rejected, which may bias the overall appearance of the findings.

Finally, we can evaluate the meaning of a document in interpretivist terms. If a source is 'adequate at the level of meaning' (Weber 1949 [1904]), this means that the researcher has really understood his or her participants' view of the social world, and reported it in terms that would be meaningful to them. For example, Elliott's (1997) account of the material she gathered from her diary-interview technique suggests that she successfully captured the lived experience of dealing with illness symptoms day to day, because she was able to quote her participants' own words and lay concepts. Conversely, Katherine Borland (1991) warns against the dangers of over-analysing a participant's remarks. She conducted a life history interview with her grandmother, who recounted an anecdote about going to the races and betting on a horse, independently of her father. Borland interpreted this as a gesture of defiance that was symbolic of her grandmother's rising feminist consciousness. However, when she showed the analysis to her grandmother, the latter looked perplexed and exclaimed, 'That's not what I said!'. This reminds us of Schütz's (1972) distinction between first-order constructs (the ways in which social actors themselves view the world) and second-order constructs (the researcher's interpretation of this): a meaningful document is one that achieves congruence between these two phenomena.

Researching rituals and routines

Ethnography

Perhaps the most obvious way of understanding somebody else's everyday life is to go to their locale and experience it directly. This technique of immersing oneself in the field has its roots in anthropology, where researchers sought to interpret the significance of the rules, rituals and routines found in 'other' cultures (Malinowski 1984 [1922]). In sociology, the same technique is used to study different enclaves within one's own culture, each of which is seen to have a unique view of the social world. The everyday life of one subculture, neighbourhood or occupational group may be quite different from that of another. Thus we see the potential to explore both the surface-level rituals and routines of a culture and the social order that underpins them, through a deep structure of grammar-like rules (Lévi-Strauss 1963; see chapter 2). This interplay between agency and structure was also what inspired Giddens (1984) towards his theory of structuration (see chapter 2).

Ethnography – literally 'depicting people' – was developed through the work of the Chicago School of the 1920s and 1930s. The Symbolic Interactionists who worked here (see chapter 2) were interested in the meanings people gave to their action, and advocated doing empirical research in the field. Robert Park famously told his students, 'Go get the seat of your pants dirty in real research!'. The city of Chicago formed the perfect setting for ethnographic research, because it was undergoing a process of rapid demographic transition and displayed high levels of migration, poverty and crime. Well-known studies of this period included Thrasher's (1927) ethnography of a criminal gang and Thomas and Znaniecki's (1958 [1918–20]) study of Polish immigrants to Chicago.

Ethnography is not, strictly speaking, a method in itself, but rather an approach or strategy. Its aim is to reach an in-depth, interpretive understanding of the way of life found in a particular cultural or subcultural context from the perspective of the people within it (Hammersley and Atkinson 1995; Bryman 2008). The ethnographer immerses themselves in the field for a relatively long period of time – typically several weeks or months – and tries to live as if they were a member of the group. This may mean researching under cover, or covertly, but always involves the researcher living alongside the people they are studying and participating to a greater or lesser extent in their daily activities. This enables them to develop an insider's view of what is going on in that setting, in terms of the meanings people give to their actions and interactions. Consequently, the ethnographer may claim to be in a stronger position to write about the group than other types of researcher, by virtue of their privileged standpoint; ethnographic writing is often regarded as being high in face validity (Bryman 2008) because it is full of 'authentic' illustrations and descriptions.

As a methodological approach, then, ethnography can involve several different research methods, the combination of which is designed to give a more complete, well-rounded and in-depth understanding of the field. The most commonly used methods in this regard are participant observation, in-depth interviewing and documentary analysis. The last was discussed in the previous section, so let us now consider the role of the first two techniques in ethnography.

Participant observation
Participant observation, as the name suggests, means participating in the activities of a group while observing them. As Gold (1958) famously argued, the relative balance between these two aspects of the process can vary: some researchers present themselves primarily as group members – perhaps covertly – and observe only as a secondary activity (participant-as-observer), while others present themselves overtly as observers and remain quite detached from the group (observer-as-participant). Often, the researcher will not literally participate in the activities of the group but rather interact with them while they are doing so (Delamont 2004). They may first have to negotiate access to the setting through a 'gatekeeper' or 'key informant'. For example, when Whyte (1955) conducted his notable study of a street gang, he first sought out the confidence of one member, Doc, who then introduced Whyte to the other men in the gang; the researcher was then able to 'hang around' and see what was going on.

Being thus immersed in the social setting, the ethnographer aims to observe everything they can and to provide a thick description (Geertz 1975) of the people in question. However, there is the incumbent risk of 'going native', whereby the researcher loses their position of detachment and comes to adopt the participants' views. They may neglect to convey the 'strangeness' of the scene (or what makes it distinctive) because the strange has become so familiar. This of course contradicts our aim to 'make the familiar strange' when studying everyday life. With these ideas in mind, some qualitative researchers have argued for a greater degree of reflexivity in participant observation: for example, Coffey (1999) advocates the cultivation of an 'ethnographic self'. Others, such as Reed-Danahay (1997), go further in suggesting that we can use our own experiences as a source of data, through the technique of auto-ethnography.

Another pertinent issue for participant observers is that of how, when and where to record one's observations. When used in ethnographic studies, such data tend to be qualitative (detailed, descriptive and analytical fieldnotes) rather than quantitative (frequency counts or checklists), and the production of these can be a very time-consuming process. Many ethnographers scribble brief memos to themselves throughout the day and write them up afterwards, which results in an extensive data set but does make the findings susceptible to errors of memory (Bryman 2008). Another strategy, often employed by covert participant observers, is to retire to a private space at intervals throughout the day, to record fragments of dialogue or observations as they happen. This makes for even more vivid illustrative data, of course, but does carry the risk of the researcher's cover being blown. Ditton (1977) reported how his research participants became suspicious when he kept sneaking off to the toilet after every meaningful exchange they made!

In-depth interviews
Interviews have been described as the 'favoured digging tool' of sociologists (Benney and Hughes 1956). This is because they provide the researcher with detailed, personal accounts by the participants of how they see the social world, composed and told in their own vernacular language. Such rich, qualitative data are regarded as highly authentic and valid as a source of knowledge, though there is a risk of reconstructive bias in the way that participants recall events (Bryman 2008). Interpretivist interview questions tend to be open-ended and semi- or unstructured, following a topic guide (known as an interview schedule) rather than a rigid script (Fielding 1993). This gives the interviewee both more of an opportunity to elaborate upon their answers and greater power to direct the course of the discussion.

These interviewing techniques were used long before the Chicago School was established. In 1861 on the streets of Victorian London,

Henry Mayhew famously conducted a series of face-to-face, informal interviews with working-class traders in various occupations, his aim being to depict the reality of everyday life for the urban poor 'in their own unvarnished language' (1950 [1861]: xv). Mayhew collected oral testimonies from an impressively large and varied sample of street traders and labourers, ranging from the costermongers, who sold fruit and vegetables from wooden carts, to street sellers of cutlery, pipes and walking sticks, to rat killers, jugglers and, most intriguingly of all, the 'pure-finders' – whose job it was to collect dogs' dung to sell for its cleansing and purifying properties!

Symbolic Interactionists view the qualitative interview as a social encounter in which ideas are explored and meanings negotiated (Kvale 1996). That is, the interviewer is not simply a neutral receptacle, soaking up the words that their respondents impart; rather, they are present as social actors too and, through their own words, gestures and expressions given off (Goffman 1959), help to shape the final narrative account that is produced. Holstein and Gubrium (1995) refer to the collaborative process of meaning-making work that goes on within the research interview and emphasize the importance of 'active listening'. This might involve asking open-ended, non-directive questions that encourage free response, attending carefully to the participants' answers and improvising appropriate follow-on questions, and sometimes simply remaining silent (Fetterman 1998). Feminist researchers have advocated the idea of building an egalitarian relationship with one's participants, based upon trust and reciprocity: self-disclosure on the part of the interviewee should be matched by that on the part of the interviewer, in order to develop rapport (Oakley 1981).

Semi- and unstructured interviews help to reveal how participants make sense of the everyday world, which in turn can inform different levels of theorizing. Firstly, the method lends itself well to phenomenology, by providing an insight into the subjective realities, or lifeworlds (Schütz 1972), of individuals. It is important to consider not only the manifest content of these – the concepts and categories people use – but also the motivations behind them. What is it about a person's social circumstances that leads them to interpret the world in this particular way? For example, in chapter 7, we examined research into illness narratives – the stories people tell themselves to account for the biographical disruption to their lives caused by periods of chronic sickness (Kleinman 1988; Bury 1982). This was exemplified by Ville's (2005) study of the experience of adapting to spinal cord injuries.

Secondly, in-depth interviews may give an insight into how social groups interact from the perspective of a significant member. For example, Thomas's (2000, 2005) study of young women's sexual activities on holiday (chapter 9) not only documented the behavioural rituals and norms of this group, but also allowed the researcher a fascinating glimpse into how this world operated and how the women made sense of their experiences. The rich, qualitative data provided by verbatim quotations captured dimensions of the setting that other methods would have missed, as for example vernacular phrases such as 'throwing caution to the wind' (Thomas 2005: 575) gave clues to the contextual meaning of this apparently deviant behaviour and showed how it was normalized by the women themselves. Meanwhile, interviews with non-members of a group can be equally revealing of its interactional norms. Scott's (2007) discussions with self-defined 'shy' people (see chapter 3) showed how these actors perceived themselves to be outsiders to the seemingly confident, extroverted majority, yet, by positioning themselves on the margins as detached observers, enjoyed a unique insight into what they saw as the non-shy world. They observed dramaturgical techniques that the 'Competent Other' seemed to take for granted, but that they, as shy actors, had consciously to learn.

Qualitative interviews can be used simply to record a snapshot picture of the respondent's lifestyle at that time, but they can also be used to generate a deeper understanding of how such patterns came about, in terms of the individual's biographical experiences. The life history interview is a technique that was developed in the Chicago School, where for example Clifford Shaw (1930) recounted the experiences of Stanley, a delinquent boy, in order to explain how and why he drifted into a career of crime. The approach has continued to be used in interpretivist research, from Thompson's (1975) oral testimonies of the Edwardian period to Squire's (2000) collection of narratives from people living with HIV (Plummer 2001). It also lends itself well to psychoanalytic theorizing, most famously in the clinical interviews Freud (1975a [1901]) used to inform his ideas about the psychopathology of everyday life, but also in the psycho-biographies of the late twentieth century. McAdams (1993), for example, points to the mythical elements to be found in the way people account for themselves in interviews: we tell stories both to and about ourselves, to make sense of our life experiences, and these typically involve heroes and villains, archetypes, narrative devices and linear plotlines. Thus although the reality of everyday life may be messy, unstructured and meaningless, we seek to impose order upon it.

This brings us to an important trend in qualitative methodology since the late twentieth century, called the narrative turn (Lincoln and Guba 1985). This involved a recognition, shaped by the Symbolic Interactionist ideas outlined above, that it was not only the content of an interview that was worth studying, but also the manner of its telling and the social context of its production (Samuel and Thompson 1990). That is, interviews do not simply uncover objective, factual data; rather, they are situated social events that involve the (re)construction of meaning, both by the individual as they try to recall and make sense of past events, and by the researcher, as they rewrite this account into a coherent narrative to make a theoretical argument. Writing does not merely capture, but rather constructs the reality it claims to represent (Plummer 2001). The result is at best a multivocal, polyphonic text (Denzin 1989) and at worst a work of fiction. When reading any sociological report of everyday life in a different context, therefore, it is important to consider how it was produced, for whom, and according to which political interests. We return to this point later in the chapter.

Challenging alternatives

Ethnomethodology and conversation analysis

Although more often regarded as a theory (Garfinkel 1967; see chapter 2), ethnomethodology involves practices of observing, analysing and sometimes testing out (through breaching experiments) the taken for granted assumptions on which a particular group of individuals rely. These sets of shared background knowledge, tacit ideas and normative conventions are what allow interaction to flow smoothly, maintaining the everyday world of that group. Participants may not reflect consciously on these rules unless they are broken, which renders them visible; we have seen how, in various contexts of everyday life, individuals can commit rule-breaking acts that confound the expectations of others and evoke morally indignant responses.

Ethnomethodology is also associated with the method of conversation analysis (Sacks 1992), in which short extracts of dialogue are scrutinized in order to identify the underlying patterns, rules and conventions of talk-in-interaction. These might include turn-taking and contingency pairs – utterances that convey a tacit expectation of a certain kind of response, such as apologies and acceptances. Such extracts therefore serve as documentary indices, pointing to stocks of shared background knowledge; it is, as ever, most interesting to see what happens when one of these assumptions is breached. A related approach of discourse analysis (Potter and Wetherell 1987) is often used in linguistics, psychology and cultural studies to interpret the narrative devices and meanings conveyed in texts.

Visual and virtual data

Another innovative source of information about everyday life is visual data – those that take the form of pictorial or moving images and graphics rather than text. This might include photographs; drawings, diagrams and illustrations; computerized graphics; and so on. Researchers may also be interested in collecting artwork, commodities and other items of 'material culture' (Mukerji 2002; cf. Douglas and Isherwood 1996 [1979]). Using such alternative methods can help to elucidate features of a culture or group that might otherwise have gone unnoticed or reveal different perspectives on a problem. As such, they can be used not only to document but also to critically unpack the meaning of rituals and routines in different social landscapes.

Visual data can be subjected to the method of content analysis, whereby the researcher explores either the number of times certain features appear (quantitative content analysis) or the meanings behind the images that are presented (qualitative content analysis). The latter is more common in the study of everyday life, insofar as visual documents can be scrutinized by the interpretivist researcher to enhance their understanding of a particular social setting (Pink 2001).

Photographs can be incredibly valuable in this respect. Bryman (2008) makes a distinction between extant photographs – those that already exist – and researcher-generated photographs that are created for the purpose of the study. Extant photographs can serve as useful documents of a previous historical era or social setting to which the researcher lacks direct access. For example, the diaries of Hannah Cullwick (Stanley 1984) contain some photographic images of the subject going about her daily work, which contrast with others taken by her lover Munby, in which she poses as a slave. This echoes a distinction Scott (1990) makes between photographs that are idealized (posed to communicate a particular impression, such as the happiness of couples in a wedding photograph), those that are naturalistic (showing the subject behaving as they would normally, in their own setting), and those that aim to demystify the viewer (such as candid shots of celebrities that expose aspects of their lifestyle in order to discredit their carefully constructed public image). In each of these, however, there is an implicit assumption that the photograph reveals something genuine about its subjects which could not be captured by any other means: 'the camera doesn't lie'. As Barthes (1972 [1957]) argues, we presume that a photograph simply records information rather than transforms or interprets it, and that this mechanical (rather than human) procedure guarantees objectivity.

In Cultural Studies, visual data are often explored critically as texts through which dominant values and ideologies are said to be transmitted (see chapter 2). For example, Moran (2005) deciphers the meaning of a bus shelter, photographed on an urban street. This apparently mundane artefact is in fact a symbol of social control, he argues, insofar as it acts as an ecological support (cf. Schwartz 1975) to guide queuing behaviour and enforce schedules. Furthermore, the advertisements pasted onto bus shelters can be read critically as embodying themes of consumer capitalism: they represent the colonization of urban spaces by market forces. You may find it interesting to photograph some of your own everyday scenes and decode them in this way!

The Mass Observation archive houses some examples of researcher-generated photographs. For example, respondents to the Autumn 2006 Directive about 'Home' provided not only written accounts of people's homes but also photographs of the rooms they were describing. Another example is the magazine *Picture Post*, which was produced in the UK between 1938 and 1957. This was a pioneering venture into the then new genre of photojournalism, as it contained politically driven articles about forms of social inequality, illustrated by photographic images (Hall 1972). The magazine was extremely popular and influential in the mid-twentieth century, leading campaigns against anti-Semitism in the Second World War and against inequalities of health, education and housing in 1940s Britain. As Hall explains, the power of these documents lay in their authenticity as markers of social reality:

> Picture Post captured for the still commercially-produced 'news' photograph a new social reality: the domain of everyday life ... [There was] a passion to present. Above all, to present people to themselves in wholly recognisable terms: terms which acknowledged their commonness, their variety, their individuality, their representativeness ... (Hall 1972: 83)

Over the last twenty years or so, Internet-based research has become increasingly common as a way of accessing first-person accounts

(Stein 2003). For example, in chapter 7, we saw how narrative analyses have elucidated the meanings behind patients' lived experience of chronic illness and its effects upon their everyday lives. This topic is one that lends itself well to online research, for, by the very nature of such conditions, participants may not feel well enough to attend a face-to-face interview but may be willing to talk online as and when they feel able. Jamie Lewis (2006) found this technique particularly helpful in his study of people living with Crohn's disease and inflammatory bowel syndrome: he created a chat room to which he recruited sufferers of these illnesses from existing self-help fora, and encouraged them to discuss experiences that they held in common. Williams and Robson (2003) suggest that, in this way, traditional focus group methodology can be transferred to cyberspace through insightful 'virtual' discussions. In other studies, researchers have pointed to the value of asynchronous online communication (such as email), in that this makes it easier for participants who are frail, vulnerable, or simply too busy, to take part in live discussions: they can write at a time that suits them, and are therefore more likely to respond (Markham 1998; O'Connor and Madge 2001).

In addition, the relative anonymity afforded by online communication can help to make respondents feel disinhibited about discussing embarrassing or sensitive issues (Joinson 1998; Markham 1998) more generally. In chapter 3, we saw how Scott (2004b) found this to be the case with self-defined 'shy' people, who paradoxically became quite vocal online! This in turn helped to elicit a counter-discourse of resistance (or 'Shy Pride') against the dominant cultural representation of shyness as a problem (Scott 2004b, 2007). Thus innovative methods can uncover unexpected data that challenge the taken for granted.

Visual data can also be used to put a new spin on the traditional method of ethnography. Sarah Pink (2001) describes how social researchers can conduct a visual ethnography, using photographs, video recordings and online imagery rather than the more conventional techniques of interviews and observations written up after the event. She distinguishes between two ways of reading visual data: the 'realist' assumption that they authentically portray social reality, and the 'reflexive' approach, which recognizes the researcher's role in placing an interpretive theoretical framework upon the data. This corresponds to Scott's (1990) distinction between extant, naturalistic and demystifying photographs, and to the challenges posed by the narrative turn.

Dicks et al. (2006) go further in suggesting that visual material can be incorporated into a wider research design – the multi-modal ethnography. That is, one might conduct an ethnographic study of a particular subculture by observing people directly in the field, but complement this by taking photographs, filming, or creating a website, to which the participants themselves can post text or images. Dicks et al. suggest that each of these modalities contributes something different in terms of the type and quality of the data, their semiotic meanings, and the implications for analysis. With increasing amounts of research being conducted online, the use of visual material and digital media may soon become a common way of conducting ethnographic research.

Ethics and politics

A final question to address is the moral one, of whether or not we should be trying to find out about other people's lives and reducing them to 'data'. What are the political implications of representing the everyday worlds of 'others'?

Earlier in this chapter, we saw how the narrative turn in the late twentieth century created a shift in attention from the content of research findings to the manner of their production (Samuel and Thompson 1990). This means that, in order to understand fully the meaning of an empirical study, we need to consider how and why it was conducted, by whom, and in whose interests: the author has a presence in the text through their narrative voice. This can be understood in the context of postmodernist and post-structuralist arguments about the impossibility of neutral, objective knowledge about the social world; all truth claims are partial, selective and provisional (Lyotard 1984). Thus even if we are studying a specific, localized social setting, as with many studies of everyday life, the way in which this world is represented may be only one story among many possible alternatives.

Social factors affect every stage of the research process, from the choice of topic to the methodological design, the analysis of the data, and the way in which findings are reported. For example, we might question who has funded the research and how their interests are addressed by the collection and reporting of the data. Writing, in particular, has been acknowledged as a means by which the researcher can create a version of events which, while appearing true to him or her, might not make sense to the research participants, as we saw in the example of Borland (1991), above. More cynically, narrative analysts have argued that such texts are written with an audience in mind, and so involve strategies of self-presentation, selective use of data and biased versions of events (Richardson 1990). There has been a recent move towards performance ethnography, which uses poetry, drama and experimental writing forms explicitly to acknowledge – and celebrate – the autobiographical bias inherent in social research (Denzin 2003).

Meanwhile, researchers themselves are encouraged to be reflexive about the ways in which their own personal values, beliefs and attitudes will have influenced their approach. Gouldner (1970) argued for a reflexive sociology, whereby researchers study themselves as much as 'other' social groups. Thus we might ask ourselves, why did I choose this topic, setting or group of people to study and not others, how have my theoretical leanings shaped my interpretation of the data, and what kind of story am I trying to tell? This in turn raises questions about the reliability of the data: if another researcher were to observe the same setting with the same research questions, how might their data set and version of events be different? Does this invalidate the meaning of the account that the present researcher has produced?

Further ethical debates surround the question of how, and indeed whether, we should write about other people's lives and social situations. Who has the right to speak for whom (Clough 2000)? If only some groups are selected to be studied, why is this, and who else's views are not being represented? Are we researching a particular social group because their culture is genuinely revelatory, or are we doing so to 'prove' a theoretical hunch and demonstrate our own academic prowess? The researcher may therefore have to address some uncomfortable questions about whether they might be exploiting their participants, albeit unintentionally, for their own benefit. What right do we have to write about 'other' people's lives and reduce them to a data set? Would they agree with our interpretation of events and representation of their characters?

Questions such as these were raised in various postcolonial and feminist critiques of social research in the late twentieth century, which pointed out how knowledge could be used as a tool of oppression. For example, Said's (1978) postcolonial critique of anthropological work on 'Oriental' cultures highlighted the way in which 'the East' had been depicted as a strange, exotic part of the world, by contrast with the implicitly 'normal' West. This ethnocentric 'othering' of social groups contributes to their marginalization, he argued, for readers are presented with an outsider's view that is by definition partial and limited. Thus the researcher stands in a position of power in being able to decide whose views are listened to, whose voices are represented. Out of these debates emerged new forms of participant-driven, collaborative research, which showed a greater respect for indigenous epistemologies – for example, the spoken word 'Red Pedagogy' of Native Americans, which is based on oral traditions of stories and poetry (Grande 2000; cf. Denzin 2003).

An important debate about the politics of representation began in the 1960s following an influential paper by Howard Becker (1967). As an interpretivist sociologist, he argued that the idea of value freedom and objectivity in social research was a myth, for every researcher had their own theoretical and political agenda. Becker famously argued that 'the question is not whether we should take sides, since we inevitably will, but rather whose side are we on?' (1967: 239). Thus all sociological knowledge was partisan, or biased. Significantly, however, he pointed out that accusations of such political bias were not made on an equal basis: research that addressed the situation of deviant or oppressed social groups tended to be recognized immediately as biased and subjective, whereas research that reflected the interests of the powerful was seen as simply neutral. This meant that much of what passed for objective, factual knowledge about the social world was really only one interpretation of events, as viewed from a relatively privileged position.

It was therefore the sociologist's responsibility to represent 'the other side': the views of marginalized groups and those in less powerful positions, whose voices would not otherwise be heard. Becker believed that the social researcher had an ethical duty to examine and present the perspectives of the 'underdogs' of society, to counteract the received wisdom of dominant ideologies. While denying the possibility of 'pure' objective knowledge, he did believe that social research could still be theoretically and methodologically rigorous. Drawing on Weber's (1949 [1904]) epistemology, he argued that the researcher should explicitly acknowledge their sources of bias, but that, having done so, they could critically examine the evidence for and against the theories they presented. This idea lies at the heart of reflexivity, and is an approach taken by many interpretivist social researchers today.

The questions of how we can research the social world, and indeed whether we should, raise issues of ontology, epistemology and methodology. What the researcher believes exists 'out there' in the social world determines what they think is worth studying, how they choose to examine it, and how they produce knowledge about it. The interpretivist stance encourages us also to consider how each of these aspects is shaped by personal values, beliefs and political agendas. When studying local settings of everyday life, therefore, it is important to reflect not only on the meanings of the data, but also on the social context of their discovery, interpretation and representation.

Designing your own research

Where does this leave us? At the beginning of this chapter, I suggested that it could be viewed as a methodological toolkit, to complement the theoretical toolkit in chapter 2 – that is, an array of different approaches from which you may choose when designing your own research. Some techniques may be most suited to exploring questions of social order, while others help more to document rituals and routines, or to reveal alternative, challenging ways of seeing the everyday world. However, it is possible that whichever topic interests you will relate to more than one of these themes, and so triangulation – a combination of methods and/or perspectives – may provide the most comprehensive picture. Furthermore, each method may generate data in line with more than one of our themes, and so even a single-method research design is likely to reveal aspects of order, routines and challenges.

If you are reading this book as an undergraduate or postgraduate student, the chances are you will be about to embark on your own research project. There are many excellent textbooks designed to help you through this process – see, for example, Denscombe (2003), Robson (2006) and Bryman (2008) – and this is not the place to rehearse such advice. Nevertheless, it is worth considering some issues that pertain to researching everyday life. Here I shall draw upon the guidelines presented in the Online Resource Centre (ORC) for Bryman's aforementioned textbook, which can be accessed at http://www.oup.com/uk/orc/bin/9780199202959/. I am biased because I wrote it, but it does contain a variety of pedagogic resources – from multiple choice questions to web links, case studies and sample data – relating to the plethora of methods outlined in Bryman's textbook. Most pertinently, you may find the Student Researcher's Toolkit section useful in summarizing the kinds of practical, theoretical and ethical issues involved at each stage of a project.

Let us suppose that you are interested in the forms of behaviour found in a mundane social space, such as waiting rooms. The first task is to narrow this down into a more manageable topic, by identifying a specific context – let's say airport departure lounges – that generates specific research questions, such as 'How do people manage prolonged, unstructured time in the company of strangers?' This kind of question implies a micro-social, interpretivist interest in the meanings people give to their behaviour and their constructions of reality. You could then revisit the theoretical perspectives of Symbolic Interactionism, phenomenology and ethnomethodology (see chapter 2) and use them to inform a literature search for relevant empirical studies, such as Goffman's *Behavior in Public Places* (1963b) and Schwartz's *Queuing and Waiting* (1975).

The next stage would be to decide what kind of data to collect and how to do so, drawing on the methodological toolkit in this chapter. These choices would depend upon which of our three themes interest you the most in this setting. For example, you may be intrigued by the rituals and routines of waiting behaviour, such as non-verbal gestures, gaze aversion and exaggerated performances of interest in a task, which people use to communicate their lack of 'accessibility' (Goffman 1963b) to others. This would lend itself well to the method of covert participant observation, which promises to offer the most valid insights into 'natural' behaviour, but which does raise ethical concerns about deception.

You might then be required to justify your choice of method(s) to an ethical review committee: students are increasingly required to submit research proposals to the institutional review board (IRB) of their college or university. Each institution will have its own administrative procedures, but typical questions you might be asked include: How exactly are you going to do this research? Why is it important? What are your aims, and are they ethically sound? How will the research affect your participants, and what kind of risks will you need to assess? What measures will you take to safeguard the welfare of your participants, and indeed yourself, in the field? Who will have access to the data produced, and where will you publish the findings? In each of these questions, the core principles are informed consent, anonymity, confidentiality, avoiding harm to participants, and the right to withdraw from the study. These are detailed further in the subject-specific ethical codes of professional bodies such as the British Sociological Association (BSA 2002) and the American Psychological Association (APA 2002).

Assuming that your project receives ethical approval and that the observations go well, you will then have to analyse your data. This might take the form of immersing yourself in fieldnotes and search-ing for emergent themes (qualitative analysis) or using a behavioural checklist to count the frequencies of different events or occurrences (quantitative analysis). The former is arguably more common in studies of everyday life, insofar as it lends itself to the interpretivist principles of *verstehen* and the subjective meanings of behaviour held by the actors concerned (see chapter 2). Bearing in mind the research question for this hypothetical project, it is likely that the first thing you would extract from the data would be the actions and gestures of indi-viduals in the waiting room – a documentary record of what people do (rituals and routines). However, this might lead you to consider why they are doing it and the functions it serves, for example to regulate personal space, manage the boundaries between self and others, mini-mize the embarrassment of spending time with strangers, and so on – questions of social order. Finally, you might observe some individuals breaking these rules (challenging the taken for granted), for example by staring or talking too much: how do those around them react?

This overlap between our three themes might lead you back to the theoretical toolkit in chapter 2, to explore other literature: an initial leaning towards Symbolic Interactionism could shift towards an inter-est in Structural Functionalism or neo-Marxism. As your theoretical interests diverge, you may be inspired to return to the field and collect more data pertaining to social order or challenges, and here different methods might become appropriate – a questionnaire, perhaps, or a breaching experiment? Thus, by dipping into the theoretical toolkit, you may be inspired to rummage deeper into the methodological toolkit. Such an iterative approach – moving back and forth between theory and data collection – is central to the model of grounded theory (Glaser and Strauss 1967), whereby researchers build an interpretive understanding of the context they are studying by allowing ideas to emerge from the research process. It is important, too, to be reflexive about your own role in this process: when writing up the study, con-sider the ways in which your own values, biases and prior assumptions might have shaped the way that you interpreted the data.

A final aspect of being an ethical researcher is that of 'leaving the field clean' when you finish the investigation. This means making sure that you have not caused your participants any distress or changed the setting for its future inhabitants. In the case of the waiting room, with its transient populations, this is unlikely, but it may well be relevant to other studies that involve examining people's home environments, health, eating habits, or any other personal affairs. Leaving the field clean should also involve an element of reflexivity: as you are part of the world that you are studying, have you affected the behaviour of your participants, and have their responses affected you? The research process and its outcomes may have a profound effect upon your own understanding of everyday life and the way in which you make sense of your own social reality. Thus to return to a question posed in chapter 1, this is no mundane or trivial subject matter!

Summary points

- Different research methods are suitable for exploring questions of social order, rituals and routines, and challenges to the taken for granted. These can be thought of as comprising a 'toolkit' from which one selects the best method(s) for one's topic.
- Primary data is information collected by the researcher themselves, for the purpose of the current project. Examples include responses to the Mass Observation directives and researcher-driven diaries.
- Secondary data analysis entails the examination of data produced or collected by another researcher, lay person or organization for a different original purpose. This might include official statistics, personal letters and diaries, and policy documents.
- Ethnography is a methodological approach that is often used by interpretivists. It aims to develop an in-depth understanding of a specific social setting from an 'insider's' perspective. It may involve a combination of methods, such as interviews, participant observation and documentary analysis.
- Visual data are those that involve images or graphics rather than text, such as photographs, diagrams and digital media.
- The 'narrative turn' in the late twentieth century led researchers to be more critically aware of the social context in which life stories, interviews and other forms of qualitative data were produced.
- Reflexive social researchers consider how their own values and biases may have affected their approach to data collection, analysis and writing. This involves an awareness of the ethical and political implications of listening to particular voices and recounting 'other' people's lives.

References

Acton, C., and Hird, M. (2004) 'Toward a sociology of stammering', *Sociology*, 38/3: 495–513.

Adam, B. (2004) *Time*. Cambridge: Polity.

Adamson, C. (1997) 'Existential and clinical uncertainty in the medical encounter', *Sociology of Health and Illness*, 19/2: 133–60.

Allan, G., and Crow, G. (1991) 'Privatisation, home-centredness and leisure', *Leisure Studies*, 10: 19–32.

ANRED (Anorexia Nervosa and Related Eating Disorders) (2007) 'Statistics: how many people have eating disorders?', http://www.anred.com/stats.html.

APA (American Psychological Association) (2002) *Ethical Principles of Psychologists and Code of Conduct*, http://www.apa.org/ethics/code2002.html.

Archer, M. (1995) *Realist Social Theory: The Morphogenetic Approach*. Cambridge: Cambridge University Press.

Archibald, K. (1947) *Wartime Shipyard*. Berkeley and Los Angeles: University of California Press.

Argyle, M. (1994) *The Psychology of Interpersonal Behaviour*. London: Penguin.

Ariès, P. (1979) 'The family and the city in the old world and the new', in V. Tufte and B. Meyerhoff (eds), *Changing Images of the Family*. London: Yale University Press.

Armstrong, D. (1989) *An Outline of Sociology as Applied to Medicine*. London: Wright.

Armstrong, D. (1995) 'The rise of surveillance medicine', *Sociology of Health and Illness*, 17/3: 393–404.

Arnould, E. J., and Price, L. L. (2000) 'Authenticating acts and authoritative performances', in S. Ratneshwar, D. Glen Mick and C. Huffman (eds), *The Why of Consumption*. London: Routledge, pp. 140–63.

Atchison, S. K. (2003) Review of L. Spitale, *Prison Ministry: Understanding Prison Culture Inside and Out* (Nashville, TN: Broadman & Holmann, 2002), http://findarticles.com/p/articles/mi_m1058/is_13_120/ai104681916.

Atkins, L. (2002) 'It's better to be thin and dead than fat and living', *The Guardian*, 22 July.

Augé, M. (1995) *Non-places: Introduction to an Anthropology of Supermodernity*, trans. J. Howe. London: Verso.

Australian Bureau of Statistics (2006) *Social Trends 2006*, http://www.abs.gov.au/.

Bagozzi, R. P., Gürhan-Canli, Z., and Priester, J. R. (2002) *The Social Psychology of Consumer Behaviour*. Buckingham: Open University Press.

Bakhtin, M. (1968) *Rabelais and his World*. Cambridge, MA: MIT Press.

Barker, K. (2002) 'Self-help literature and the making of an illness identity: the case of fibromyalgia syndrome (FMS)', *Social Problems*, 49/3: 279–300.

Barnes, C. (1991) *Disabled People in Britain and Discrimination*. London: Hurst.

Barrett, M., and McIntosh, M. (1991) *The Antisocial Family*. London: Verso.

Barthes, R. (1972 [1957]) *Mythologies*. London: Paladin.

Bartlett, V. (1969) *The Past of Pastimes*. London: Chatto & Windus.

Baudelaire, C. (1986 [1863]) *The Painter of Modern Life and Other Essays*. New York: Da Capo Press.

Baudrillard, J. (1975) *The Mirror of Production*. St Louis: Telos Press.

Baudrillard, J. (1989) *America*. London: Verso.

Baum, S., and Hassan, R. (1999) 'Home owners, home renovation and residential mobility', *Journal of Sociology*, 35/1: 23–41.

Bauman, Z. (1996) 'From pilgrim to tourist – or a short history of identity', in S. Hall and P. Du Gay (eds), *Questions of Cultural Identity*. London: Sage, pp. 18–36.

BBC (2004) 'Pub-goers facing Burberry ban', 20 August, http://news.bbc.co.uk/1/hi/england/leicestershire/3583900.stm.

Beardsworth, A. D., and Keil, E. T. (1992) 'The vegetarian option: varieties, conversions, motives and careers', *Sociological Review*, 40: 253–93.

B-EAT (Beating Eating Disorders) (2007a) 'Some statistics', http://www.b-eat.co.uk/NewsEventsPressMedia/PressMediaInformation/Somestatistics (accessed 15 February 2008).

B-EAT (Beating Eating Disorders) (2007b) 'Men get eating disorders too', http://www.b-eat.co.uk/AboutEatingDisorders/Mengeteatingdisorderstoo (accessed 3 March 2008).

Becker, H. S. (1951) 'The professional dance musician and his audience', *American Journal of Sociology*, 57: 136–44.

Becker, H. S. (1963) *Outsiders: Studies in the Sociology of Deviance*. New York: Free Press.

Becker, H. S. (1967) 'Whose side are we on?', *Social Problems*, 14: 239–47.

Bell, D. (1973) *The Coming of Post-Industrial Society*. New York: Basic Books.

Bendelow, G., and Williams, S. J. (eds) (1998) *Emotions in Social Life*. London: Routledge.

Bennett, A. (1999) 'Subcultures or neo-tribes? Rethinking the relationship between youth, style and musical taste', *Sociology*, 33: 599–617.

Bennett, T. (2002) 'Home and everyday life', in T. Bennett and D. Watson, *Understanding Everyday Life*. Oxford: Blackwell, pp. 1–50.

Bennett, T. (2004) 'The invention of the modern cultural fact: towards a critique of the critique of everyday life', in E. Silva and T. Bennett (eds), *Contemporary Culture and Everyday Life*. Durham: Sociologypress, pp. 21–36.

Bennett, T., and Watson, D. (2002) *Understanding Everyday Life*. Oxford: Blackwell.

Bennett, T., Emmison, M., and Frow, J. (1999) *Accounting for Tastes: Australian Everyday Cultures*. Melbourne: Cambridge University Press.

Benney, M., and Hughes, E. C. (1956) 'Of Sociology and the interview', *American Journal of Sociology*, 62: 137–42.

Berger, P., and Luckmann, T. (1967) *The Social Construction of Reality*. Harmondsworth: Penguin.

Bhatti, M., and Church, A. (2001) 'Cultivating natures: homes and gardens in late modernity', *Sociology*, 35/2: 365–83.

Birenbaum, A., and Sagarin, E. (1973) 'The deviant actor maintains his right to be present: the case of the non-drinker', in A. Birenbaum and E. Sagarin (eds), *People in Places: The Sociology of the Familiar*. New York: Nelson, pp. 68–79.

Black, P. (2004) *The Beauty Industry*. London: Routledge.

Blakemore, C. (1988) *The Mind Machine*. London: BBC.

Blauner, R. (1964) *Alienation and Freedom: The Factory Worker and his Industry*. Chicago: University of Chicago Press.

Blaxter, M., and Paterson, C. (1983) 'The goodness is out of it: the meaning of food to two generations', in A. Murcott (ed.), *The Sociology of Food and Eating*. Aldershot: Gower, pp. 95–105.

Blumer, H. (1969) *Symbolic Interactionism: Perspective and Method*. Englewood Cliffs, NJ: Prentice-Hall.

Boorstin, D. (1992 [1962]) *The Image: A Guide to Pseudo-Events in America*. New York: Vintage.

Bordo, S. (1993) *Unbearable Weight: Feminism, Western Culture and the Body*. Berkeley: University of California Press.

Borland, K. (1991) '"That's not what I said!": Interpretive conflict in oral narrative research', in S. B. Gluck and D. Patai (eds), *Women's Words: The Feminist Practice of Oral History*. London: Routledge, pp. 63–75.

Bourdieu, P. (1984) *Distinction: A Social Critique of the Judgement of Taste*, trans. R. Nice. London: Routledge.

Bowlby, R. (1993) *Shopping With Freud*. London: Routledge.

Brannen, J. (2005) 'Time and the negotiation of work–family boundaries: autonomy or illusion?', *Time and Society*, 14/1: 113–31.

Broad, R., and Fleming, S. (eds) (2006) *Nella Last's War: The Second World War Diaries of 'Housewife 49'*. London: Profile Books.

Brown, R. (1986) *Social Psychology*. 2nd edn, New York: Free Press.

Bryman, A. (1995) *Disney and his Worlds*. London: Routledge.

Bryman, A. (2008) *Social Research Methods*. 3rd edn, Oxford: Oxford University Press.

BSA (British Sociological Association) (2002) *Statement of Ethical Practice*, http://www.britsoc.co.uk/equality/Statement+Ethical+Practice.htm.

Bunch, B. (2006) 'Hardly Fair Trade', *Business Today*, 19 October, http://www.businesstoday.org/index.php?option=com_content&task=view&id=167&Itemid=38.

Bureau of Labor Statistics (2006) *American Time Use Survey 2006*. Washington, DC: US Department of Labor; http://www.bls.gov/tus/home.htm.

Bury, M. (1982) 'Chronic illness as biographical disruption', *Sociology of Health and Illness*, 4: 167–82.

Bury, M. (2004) 'Chronic illness and disability', in J. Gabe, M. Bury and M. Elston (eds), *Key Concepts in Medical Sociology*. London: Sage, pp. 77–81.

Busfield, J. (1996) *Men, Women and Madness: Understanding Gender and Mental Disorder*. London: Macmillan.

Busfield, J. (ed.) (2001) *Rethinking the Sociology of Mental Health*. Oxford: Blackwell.

Butler, J. (1999 [1990]) *Gender Trouble: Feminism and the Subversion of Identity*. London: Routledge.

Byrne, P. (1976) 'Teaching and learning verbal behaviors', in B. Tanner (ed.), *Language and Communication in General Practice*. London: Hodder & Stoughton, pp. 52–70.

Calnan, M. (1983) 'Social networks and patterns of help-seeking behavior', *Social Science and Medicine*, 17: 25–8.

Calnan, M. (1987) *Health and Illness: The Lay Perspective*. London: Routledge & Kegan Paul.

Calnan, M., Wainwright, D., O'Neill, C., Winterbottom, A., and Watkins, C. (2007) 'Illness action rediscovered: a case study of upper limb pain', *Sociology of Health and Illness*, 29/3: 321–46.

Certeau, M. de (1984) *The Practice of Everyday Life*, trans. S. F. Rendell. Berkeley and Los Angeles: University of California Press.

Chamberlain, K. (2004) 'Food and health: expanding the agenda for health psychology', *Journal of Health Psychology*, 9/4: 467–81.

Chaplin, D. (2002) 'Time for life: time for being and time for becoming', in G. Crow and S. Heath (eds), *Social Conceptions of Time: Structure and Process in Work and Everyday Life*. Basingstoke: Palgrave, pp. 215–29.

Chapman, T., and Hockey, J. (1999) 'The ideal home as it is imagined and as it is lived', in T. Chapman and J. Hockey (eds), *Ideal Homes: Social Change and Domestic Life*. London: Routledge.

Charles, N. (1995) 'Food and family ideology', in S. Jackson and S. Moores (eds), *The Politics of Domestic Consumption*. Hemel Hempstead: Prentice-Hall/Harvester Wheatsheaf, pp. 100–15.

Charles, N., and Kerr, M. (1988) *Women, Food and Families*. Manchester: Manchester University Press.

Charmaz, K. (1991) *Good Days, Bad Days: The Self in Chronic Illness and Time*. New Brunswick, NJ: Rutgers University Press.

Chrisman, N. (1977) 'The health care seeking process: an analysis of the natural history of illness', *Culture, Medicine and Psychiatry*, 1: 351–7.

Cicourel, A. V. (1964) *Method and Measurement in Sociology*. New York: Free Press.

Clough, P. T. (2000) 'Comments on setting criteria for experimental writing', *Qualitative Inquiry*, 6/2: 278–91.

Cockerham, W. (2000) *Medical Sociology*. Upper Saddle River, NJ: Prentice-Hall.

Coffey, A. (1999) *The Ethnographic Self*. London: Sage.

Cohen, S. (1972) *Folk Devils and Moral Panics: The Creation of the Mods and Rockers*. London: MacGibbon & Kee.

Cohen, S., and Taylor, L. (1992) *Escape Attempts*. London: Routledge.

Collins, R. (2005) *Interaction Ritual Chains*. Princeton, NJ: Princeton University Press.

Cooley, C. H. (1983 [1902]) *Social Organization: A Study of the Larger Mind*. New Brunswick, NJ: Transaction Books.

Cooper, L. (1997) 'Myalgic encephalomyelitis and the medical encounter', *Sociology of Health and Illness*, 19/2: 186–207.

Corti, L. (1993) 'Using diaries in social research', *Social Research Update*, 2, http://sru.soc.surrey.ac.uk/SRU2.html.

Craib, I. (1997) 'Social constructionism as psychosis', *Sociology*, 31/1: 1–15.

Crompton, R. (ed.) (1999) *Restructuring Gender Relations and Employment: The Decline of the Male Breadwinner*. Oxford: Oxford University Press.

Crossik, G., and Gaumain, S. (eds) (1999) *Cathedrals of Consumption: European Department Stores, 1850–1939*. Oxford: Ashgate.

Crozier, W. R. (2006) *Blushing and the Social Emotions: The Self Unmasked*. London: Palgrave Macmillan.

Cunningham-Burley, S., and MacLean, U. (1991) 'Dealing with children's illness: mothers' dilemmas', in S. Wyke and J. Hewison (eds), *Child Health Matters*. Milton Keynes: Open University Press, pp. 29–39.

Davidoff, L. (1990) 'The family in Britain', in F. M. L. Thompson (ed.), *People and their Environment* (vol. 2 of *The Cambridge Social History of Britain 1750–1950*). Cambridge: Cambridge University Press.

Davidoff, L., and Hall, C. (1987) *Family Fortunes*. London: Hutchinson

Davidoff, L., and Hawthorn, R. (1976) *A Day in the Life of a Victorian Domestic Servant*. London: Allen & Unwin.

Davies, K. (1990) *Women and Time: The Weaving of the Strands of Everyday Life*. Aldershot: Avebury.

Davis, F. (1964) 'Deviance disavowal: the management of strained interaction by the visibly handicapped', in H. S. Becker (ed.), *The Other Side: Perspectives on Deviance*. London: Collier-Macmillan, pp. 119–38.

Dawkins, R. (2006 [1976]) *The Selfish Gene*. Oxford: Oxford University Press.

Delamont, S. (2004) 'Ethnography and participant observation', in C. Seale, G. Gobo, J. F. Gubrium and D. Silverman (eds), *Qualitative Research Practice*. London: Sage.

Denscombe, M. (2003) *The Good Research Guide for Small-Scale Social Research Projects*. 2nd edn, Maidenhead: Open University Press.

Denzin, N. K. (1987) *The Alcoholic Self*. Beverly Hills, CA: Sage.

Denzin, N. K. (1989) *Interpretive Biography*. London: Sage.

Denzin, N. K. (2003) 'Reading and writing performance', *Qualitative Research*, 3/2: 243–68.

Denzin, N. K. (2007) *On Understanding Emotion*. Edison, NJ: Transaction Books.

Derrida, J. (1978 [1967]) *Writing and Difference*. London: Routledge.

DeVault, M. L. (1991) *Feeding the Family: The Social Organization of Caring as Gendered Work*. Chicago and London: University of Chicago Press.

Dicks, B., Soyinka, B., and Coffey, A. (2006) 'Multimodal ethnography', *Qualitative Research*, 6/1: 77–96

Dittmar, H. (1992) *The Social Psychology of Material Possessions*. Hemel Hempstead: Harvester Wheatsheaf.

Ditton, J. (1977) *Part-Time Crime: An Ethnography of Fiddling and Pilferage*. London: Macmillan.

Dobash, R. E., and Dobash, R. P. (1998) *Rethinking Violence against Women*. London: Sage.

Douglas, J. (1967) *The Social Meanings of Suicide*. Princeton, NJ: Princeton University Press.

Douglas, J. (ed.) (1981 [1971]) *Understanding Everyday Life*. London: Routledge & Kegan Paul.

Douglas, M. (1966) *Purity and Danger*. London: Routledge & Kegan Paul.

Douglas, M. (1975 [1972]) 'Deciphering a meal', in M. Douglas, *Implicit Meanings: Essays in Anthropology*. London: Routledge.

Douglas, M., and Isherwood, B. (1996 [1979]) *The World of Goods*. London: Routledge.

Duck, S. (1988) *Relating to Others*. Milton Keynes: Open University Press.

Duncombe, J., and Marsden, D. (1993) 'Love and intimacy: the gender division of emotion and "emotion work"', *Sociology*, 27/2: 221–41.

Durkheim, E. (1976 [1912]) *The Elementary Forms of the Religious Life*. London: Allen & Unwin.

Durkheim, E. (1982 [1895]) *The Rules of Sociological Method*. New York: Free Press.

Durkheim, E. (1984 [1893]) *The Division of Labour in Society*. London: Macmillan.

Edelmann, R. J. (1987) *The Psychology of Embarrassment*. Chichester: Wiley.

Ekman, P., and Friesen, W. V. (1969) 'Non-verbal leakage and clues to deception', *Psychiatry*, 32: 88–106.

Elder, A., and Samuel, O. (eds) (1987) *'While I'm Here, Doctor': A Study of the Doctor–Patient Relationship*. London: Tavistock.

Elias, N. (1994) *The Civilizing Process*. Oxford: Blackwell

Elliott, H. (1997) 'The use of diaries in sociological research on health experience', *Sociological Research Online*, 2/2, http://www.socresonline.org.uk/2/2/7.html.

Evans, J. (1997) 'Introduction to "Nation, Mandate, Memory"', in J. Evans (ed.), *The Camerawork Essays: Context and Meaning in Photography*. London: Rivers University Press, pp. 145–7.

Evans, M. (2003) *Love: An Unromantic Discussion*. Cambridge: Polity.

Fagan, C. (2001) 'The temporal reorganization of employment and the household rhythm of work schedules: the implications for class and gender relations', *American Behavioral Scientist*, 44/7: 1199–212.

Fagan, C. (2002) 'How many hours? Work-time regimes and preferences in European societies', in G. Crow and S. Heath (eds), *Social Conceptions of Time: Structure and Process in Work and Everyday Life*. Basingstoke: Palgrave, pp. 69–87.

Fairclough, C. A., Boylstein, C., Rittman, M., Young, M. E., and Gubrium, J. (2004) 'Sudden illness and biographical flow in narratives of stroke recovery', *Sociology of Health and Illness*, 26/2: 242–61.

Farmer, B. (2003) 'The ideologies of everyday life', in F. Martin (ed.), *Interpreting Everyday Culture*, London: Edward Arnold, pp. 15–31.

Featherstone, M. (1982) 'The body in consumer culture', *Theory, Culture and Society*, 1: 18–33.

Feifer, M. (1985) *Tourism in History: From Imperial Rome to the Present*. New York: Stein & Day.

Fein, E., and Schneider, S. (1995) *The Rules: Time-Tested Secrets for Capturing the Heart of Mr. Right*. Lebanon, IN: Warner Books.

Felski, R. (1999) 'The invention of everyday life', *New Formations*, 39: 15–31.

Ferreday, D. (2003) 'Unspeakable bodies: erasure, embodiment and the pro-ana community', *International Journal of Cultural Studies*, 6/3: 277–95.

Fetterman, D. M. (1998) *Ethnography: Step by Step*. 2nd edn, London: Sage.

Fielding, N. (1993) 'Qualitative interviewing', in N. Gilbert (ed.), *Researching Social Life*. London: Sage, pp. 135–53.

Fine, G. (1996) *Kitchens: The Culture of Restaurant Work*. Berkeley: University of California Press.

Fiske, J. (1989) *Reading the Popular*. London: Unwin Hyman.

Foucault, M. (1977 [1975]) *Discipline and Punish*. London: Allen Lane.

Foucault, M. (1980 [1976]) *The History of Sexuality*, Vol. 1: *An Introduction*. New York: Vintage.

Fox, K. (2004) *Watching the English: The Hidden Rules of English Behaviour*. London: Hodder & Stoughton.

Fox, N., Ward, K., and O'Rourke, A. (2005a) 'Pro-anorexia, weight-loss drugs and the Internet: an "anti-recovery" explanatory model of anorexia', *Sociology of Health and Illness*, 27/7: 944–71.

Fox, N., Ward, K., and O'Rourke, A. (2005b) 'The "expert patient": empowerment or medical dominance? The case of weight loss, pharmaceutical drugs and the Internet', *Social Science and Medicine*, 60/6: 1299–309.

Frank, A. W. (1991) *At the Will of the Body: Reflections on Illness*. Boston: Houghton-Mifflin.

Freidson, E. (1970) *Profession of Medicine: A Study of the Sociology of Applied Knowledge*. New York: Dodd, Mead.

French, S., and Swain, J. (2004) 'Whose tragedy? Towards a personal non-tragedy view of disability', in J. Swain, S. French, C. Barnes and C. Thomas (eds), *Disabling Barriers, Enabling Environments*. 2nd edn, London: Sage, pp. 34–40.

Freud, S. (1975a [1901]) *The Psychopathology of Everyday Life*. Harmondsworth: Penguin.

Freud, S. (1975b [1920]) *Beyond the Pleasure Principle*. London: W. W. Norton.

Freud, S. (1984 [1923]) *The Ego and the Id*. Harmondsworth: Penguin.

Freud, S. (2004 [1930]) *Civilization and its Discontents*. London: Penguin.

Fulcher, J., and Scott, J. (2007) *Sociology*. 3rd edn, Oxford: Oxford University Press.

Garfinkel, H. (1967) *Studies in Ethnomethodology*. Englewood Cliffs, NJ: Prentice-Hall.

Geertz, C. (1975) *The Interpretation of Cultures*. London: Hutchinson.

Geller, D. (1934) 'Lingo of the shoe salesman', *American Speech*, 9/4: 283–6; cited in E. Goffman, *The Presentation of Self in Everyday Life*. Harmondsworth: Penguin, 1959, p. 176.

Gergen, K. J. (1991) *The Saturated Self: Dilemmas of Identity in Contemporary Life*. New York: Basic Books.

Gershuny, J. (2000) *Changing Times: Work and Leisure in Postindustrial Society*. Oxford: Oxford University Press.

Giddens, A. (1984) *The Constitution of Society: Outline of the Theory of Structuration*. Cambridge: Polity.

Giddens, A. (1991) *Modernity and Self-Identity*. Cambridge: Polity.

Giddens, A. (1992) *The Transformation of Intimacy*. Cambridge: Polity.

Giles, D. (2000) *Illusions of Immortality: A Psychology of Fame and Celebrity*. New York: St Martin's Press.

Glaser, B. G., and Strauss, A. L. (1967) *The Discovery of Grounded Theory: Strategies for Qualitative Research*. Chicago: Aldine.

Glenton, C. (2003) 'Chronic back pain sufferers: striving for the sick role', *Social Science and Medicine*, 57: 2243–52.

Goffman, E. (1956) 'Embarrassment and social organization', *American Journal of Sociology*, 62/3: 264–74; repr. in Goffman, *Interaction Ritual*, New York: Pantheon, 1967, pp. 97–112.

Goffman, E. (1959) *The Presentation of Self in Everyday Life*. Harmondsworth: Penguin.

Goffman, E. (1961a) *Asylums: Essays on the Social Situation of Mental Patients and other Inmates*. Garden City, NY: Anchor Books.

Goffman, E. (1961b) *Encounters: Two Studies in the Sociology of Interaction*. Indianapolis: Bobbs-Merrill.

Goffman, E. (1963a) *Stigma: Notes on the Management of Spoiled Identity*. Harmondsworth: Penguin.

Goffman, E. (1963b) *Behavior in Public Places: Notes on the Social Organization of Gatherings*. New York: Free Press.

Goffman, E. (1967a) 'On facework', in Goffman, *Interaction Ritual*, New York: Pantheon, pp. 7–45.

Goffman, E. (1967b) 'Where the action is', in Goffman, *Interaction Ritual*, New York: Pantheon, pp. 149–270.

Gold, R. L. (1958) 'Roles in sociological fieldwork', *Social Forces*, 36: 217–23.

Gouldner, A. W. (1970) *The Coming Crisis of Western Sociology*. New York: Basic Books.

Government Office for Science (2007) *Tackling Obesities: Future Choices. Modelling Future Trends in Obesity and the Impact on Health*. 2nd edn, London: HMSO.

Graham, H., and Oakley, A. (1981) 'Competing ideologies of reproduction: medical and maternal perspectives on pregnancy', in H. Roberts (ed.), *Women, Health and Reproduction*. London: Routledge & Kegan Paul.

Grande, S. (2000) 'American Indian identity and intellectualism: the quest for a new Red Pedagogy', *International Journal of Qualitative Studies in Education*, 13/4: 343–59.

Gray, D. E. (2002) '"Everybody just freezes. Everybody is just embarrassed": felt and enacted stigma among parents of children with high-functioning autism', *Sociology of Health and Illness*, 24/6: 734–49.

Gregory, S. (2005) 'Living with chronic illness in the family setting', *Sociology of Health and Illness*, 27/3: 372–92.

Gross, E., and Stone, G. (1973) 'Embarrassment and the analysis of role requirements', in A. Birenbaum and E. Sagarin (eds), *People in Places: The Sociology of the Familiar*. London: Nelson, pp. 101–19.

Gross, R. D. (2005) *Psychology: The Science of Mind and Behaviour*. 5th rev. edn, London: Hodder Arnold.

Gusfield, J. (1987) 'Passage to play: rituals of drinking time in American society', in M. Douglas (ed.) *Constructive Drinking: Perspectives on Drink from Anthropology*. Cambridge: Cambridge University Press.

Hall, C. (1982) 'The butcher, the baker, the candlestickmaker: the shop and the family in the Industrial Revolution', in E. Whitelegg, A. Arnot, E. Bartels, V. Beechey, L. Birke, S. Himmelweit, D. Leonard, S. Ruehl and M. Speakman (eds), *The Changing Experience of Women*. Oxford: Blackwell.

Hall, S. (1972) 'The social eye of Picture Post', *Working Papers in Cultural Studies*, no. 2, University of Birmingham.

Hall, S. (1997) *Representation: Cultural Representations and Signifying Practices*. London: Sage.

Hall, T. (2003) *Better Times than This: Youth Homelessness in Britain*. London: Pluto Press.

Hammersley, M., and Atkinson, P. A. (1995) *Ethnography: Principles in Practice*. London: Routledge.

Harré, R. (1990) 'Embarrassment: a conceptual analysis', in W. R. Crozier (ed.), *Shyness and Embarrassment: Perspectives from Social Psychology*. Cambridge: Cambridge University Press, pp. 181–204.

Hart, N. (1985) *The Sociology of Health and Medicine*. Ormskirk: Causeway Press.

Hebdige, D. (1979) *Subculture: The Meaning of Style*. London: Methuen.

Heider, F. (1958) *The Psychology of Interpersonal Relations*. New York: Wiley.

Helman, C. G. (2007) *Culture, Health and Illness*. 5th edn, London: Hodder Arnold.

Herzlich, C. (1973) *Health and Illness: A Social Psychological Analysis*. London: Academic Press.

Hetherington, K. (1992) 'Stonehenge and its festival: spaces of consumption', in R. Shields (ed.), *Lifestyle Shopping*. London: Routledge, pp. 83–98.

Highmore, B. (2002) *Everyday Life and Cultural Theory: An Introduction*. London: Routledge.

Hinton, J. (1987) *Performance*. Basingstoke: Macmillan.

Hislop, J., Arber, S., Meadows, R., and Venn, S. (2005) 'Narratives of the night: the use of audio diaries in researching sleep', *Sociological Research Online*, 10/4, http://www.socresonline.org.uk/10/4/hislop.html (accessed 5 December 2007).

Hochschild, A. R. (1983) *The Managed Heart: Commercialization of Human Feeling*. Berkeley: University of California Press.

Hogben, S. (2006) 'Life's on hold: missing people, private calendars and waiting', *Time and Society*, 15/2–3: 327–42.

Hoggart, R. (1994) 'A walk along the sceptred aisles', *The Independent*, 4 November, p. 21.

Hollows, J. (2003) 'Feeling like a domestic goddess: postfeminism and cooking', *European Journal of Cultural Studies*, 6/2: 179–202.

Holstein, J. A., and Gubrium, J. F. (1995) *The Active Interviewer*. London: Sage.

Homans, G. C. (1974) *Social Behavior: Its Elementary Forms*. 2nd edn, New York: Harcourt, Brace, Jovanovich.

Hornbacher, M. (1998) *Wasted: A Memoir of Anorexia and Bulimia*. London: HarperCollins.

Hughes, B. (2000) 'Medicalized bodies', in P. Hancock, B. Hughes, E. Jagger, K. Paterson, R. Russell, E. Tulle-Winton and M. Tyler (eds), *The Body, Culture and Society*. Milton Keynes: Open University Press, pp. 12–28.

Hurdley, R. (2006) 'Dismantling mantelpieces: narrating identities and materializing culture in the home', *Sociology*, 40/4: 717–33.

Illich, I. (1975) *Medical Nemesis*. London: Calder & Boyars.

Izard, C. E. (1972) *The Face of Emotion*. New York: Appleton Century Crofts.

Jäckel, M., and Wollscheid, S. (2007) 'Time is money and money needs time? A secondary analysis of time-budget data in Germany', *Journal of Leisure Research*, http://findarticles.com/p/articles/mi_qa3702/is_200701/ai_n19198739.

Jackson, S. (1993) 'Even sociologists fall in love: an exploration in the sociology of emotions', *Sociology*, 27/2: 201–20.

Jahoda, M., Lazarsfeld, P., and Zeisel, P. (1972) *Marienthal: The Sociography of an Unemployed Community*. London: Tavistock.

James, W. (1890) *The Principles of Psychology*,Vol. 1. New York: Holt.

Jenkins, H. (1992) *Textual Poachers: Television Fans and Participatory Culture*. London: Routledge.

Johnson, T. (1972) *Professions and Power*. London: Macmillan.

Joinson, A. (1998) 'Causes and implications of disinhibited behavior on the Internet', in J. Gackenbach (ed.) (1998), *Psychology and the Internet: Intrapersonal, Interpersonal and Transpersonal Implications*. San Diego and London: Academic Press, pp. 43–59.

Jolly, A. (1999) *Lucy's Legacy: Sex and Intelligence in Human Evolution*. Cambridge, MA: Harvard University Press.

Jones, E. E., and Nisbett, R. E. (1971) 'The actor and the observer: divergent perceptions of the causes of behavior', in E. E. Jones, D. E. Kanouse, H. H. Kelley, R. E. Nisbett, S. Valins and B. Weiner (eds), *Attribution: Perceiving the Causes of Behavior*. Morristown, NJ: General Learning Press, pp. 79–94.

Kant, I. (2003 [1781]) *Critique of Pure Reason*, trans. N. K. Smith. Basingstoke: Palgrave Macmillan.

Kelly, H. H. (1967) 'Attribution theory in social psychology', in D. Levine (ed.), *Nebraska Symposium on Motivation*, Vol. 15. Lincoln: University of Nebraska Press, pp. 192–238.

Kelly, M. P. (1992) *Colitis*. London: Routledge.

Kemmer, D. (2000) 'Tradition and change in domestic roles and food preparation', *Sociology*, 34/2: 323–33.

Kleinman, A. (1980) *Patients and Healers in the Context of Culture: An Exploration of the Borderland between Anthropology, Medicine and Psychiatry*. Berkeley: University of California Press.

Kleinman, A. (1988) *The Illness Narratives: Suffering, Healing and the Human Condition*. New York: Basic Books.

Knight, W. (2005) 'Email forwarding amounts to gift exchange', *New Scientist*, 12 July.

Kumar, K (1997) '"Home": the problem and predicament of private life at the end of the twentieth century', in J. Weintraub and K. Kumar (eds), *Public and Private in Thought and Practice*. Chicago: University of Chicago Press, pp. 204–36.

Kvale, S. (1996) *InterViews: An Introduction to Qualitative Research Interviewing*. London: Sage.

Laing, R. D., Phillipson, H., and Lee, A. R. (1966) *Interpersonal Perception*. London: Tavistock.

Lancaster, B. (1995) *The Department Store: A Social History*. Leicester: Leicester University Press.

Langman, L. (1992) 'Neon cages: shopping for subjectivity', in R. Shields (ed.), *Lifestyle Shopping: The Subject of Consumption*. London: Routledge, pp. 40–82.

Larsson, J., and Sanne, C. (2005) 'Self-help books on avoiding time shortage', *Time and Society*, 14/2–3: 213–30.

Leary, M. R. (1996) *Self-Presentation: Impression Management and Interpersonal Behavior*. Oxford: Westview Press.

Leary, M. R., Britt, T. W., Cutlip, W. D. H., and Templeton, J. L. (1992) 'Social blushing', *Psychological Bulletin*, 112: 446–60.

Lefebvre, H. (1971 [1968]) *Everyday Life in the Modern World*, trans. S. Rabinovitch. London: Allen Lane.

Lefebvre, H. (2008 [1947]) *Critique of Everyday Life*, Vol. 1. London: Verso.

Lever, J. (2006) 'Office romance: are the rules changing?', *Conference Board Review*, March–April: 1–6, http://www.conference-board.org/articles/atb_article.cfm?id=344.

Lévi-Strauss, C. (1963) *Structural Anthropology*. New York: Basic Books.

Lewis, J. (2006) 'Making order out of a contested disorder: the utilisation of online support groups in social science research', *Qualitative Researcher*, 1/3: 4–7.

Lincoln, Y. S., and Guba, E. (1985) *Naturalistic Inquiry*. Beverly Hills, CA: Sage.

Lukács, G. (1977 [1923]) *History and Class Consciousness*. London: Merlin Press.

Lupton, D. (1995) *The Imperative of Health: Public Health and the Regulated Body*. London: Sage.

Lupton, D. (1996) *Food, the Body and the Self*. London: Sage.

Lupton, D. (1998) *The Emotional Self*. London: Sage.

Lury, C. (1996) *Consumer Culture*. Cambridge: Polity.

Lyotard, J. (1984) *The Postmodern Condition*. Minneapolis: University of Minnesota Press.

McAdams, D. P. (1993) *The Stories We Live By: Personal Myths and the Making of the Self.* New York: Williams & Morrow.

McCaffrey, J. (2006) 'The time of your lives', *Daily Mirror*, 22 June, http://www.mirror.co.uk/news/tm_objectid=17272126&method=full&siteid=94762&headline=the-time-of-your-lives--name_page.html.

MacCannell, D. (1976) *The Tourist: A New Theory of the Leisure Class.* New York: Schocken.

McDaniel, P. A. (2003) *Shrinking Violets and Caspar Milquetoasts: Shyness, Power and Intimacy in the United States, 1950–1995.* New York: New York University Press.

Maclagan, I. (1994) 'Food and gender in a Yemeni community', in S. Zubaida and R. Tapper (eds), *Culinary Cultures of the Middle East.* London: Taurus.

Madge, C., and Harrisson, T. (1939) *Britain by Mass Observation.* London: Penguin.

Maleuvre, D. (1999) *Museum Memories: History, Technology, Art.* Palo Alto, CA: Stanford University Press.

Malinowski, B. (1984 [1922]) *Argonauts of the Western Pacific.* Prospect Heights, IL: Waveland Press.

Marcuse, H. (1955) *Eros and Civilization: A Philosophical Inquiry into Freud.* Boston: Beacon Press.

Markham, A. N. (1998) *Life Online: Researching Real Experience in Virtual Space.* Oxford: AltaMira Press.

Marsh, P., Rosser, E., and Harré, R. (1994) *The Rules of Disorder.* London: Routledge.

Martin, F. (2003) 'Introduction', in Martin, *Interpreting Everyday Culture.* London: Edward Arnold.

Marx, K. (1959 [1844]) *Economic and Philosophical Manuscripts.* London: Lawrence & Wishart.

Mass Observation (1987 [1943]) *The Pub and the People: A Worktown Study.* London: Cresset Library.

Mauss, M. (1990 [1925]) *The Gift: The Form and Reason for Exchange in Archaic Societies*, trans. W. D. Halls. London: Routledge.

May, C. (2001) 'Pathology, identity and the social construction of alcohol dependence', *Sociology*, 35/2: 385–401.

May, C., and Mead, N. (1999) 'Patient-centredness: a history', in C. Dowrick and L. Frith (eds), *Ethical Issues in General Practice: Uncertainty and Responsibility.* London: Routledge.

May, C., Allison, G., Chapple, A., Chew-Graham, C., Dixon, C., Gask, L., Graham, R., Rogers, A., and Roland, M. (2004) 'Framing the doctor–patient relationship in chronic illness: a comparative study of general practitioners' accounts', *Sociology of Health and Illness*, 26/2: 135–58.

Mayhew, H. (1950 [1861]) *London Labour and the London Poor.* London: Frank Cass; repr. in P. Quennell (ed.), *Mayhew's London.* London: Spring Books.

Mead, G. H. (1934) *Mind, Self and Society from the Standpoint of a Social Behaviorist*. Chicago: University of Chicago Press.

Mechanic, D. (1978) *Medical Sociology*. 2nd edn, New York: Free Press.

Mechanic, D., and Volkart, E. (1961) 'Stress, illness behaviour and the sick role', *American Sociological Review*, 26: 51–8.

Mellinger, W. (2008) 'Critical interactionism: the microsociology of domination', http://waynemellinger.blogs.friendster.com/doing_moder nity/2008/05/critical_intera.html (accessed 31 July 2008).

Meštrović, S. G. (1997) *Postemotional Society*. London: Sage.

Miller, D. (1998) *A Theory of Shopping*. Cambridge: Polity.

Miller, D., Jackson, P., Thrift, N., Holbrook, B., and Rowlands, M. (1998) *Shopping, Place and Identity*. London: Routledge.

Miller, R. S. (1996) *Embarrassment: Poise and Peril in Everyday Life*. London: Guilford Press.

Mills, C. W. (1959) *The Sociological Imagination*. New York: Oxford University Press.

Mintel (2000) *Pub Visiting*. London: Mintel International Group.

Mishler, E. (1981) 'Viewpoint: critical perspectives on the biomedical model', in E. Mishler, L. Amarasingham, S. Osherson, S. Hausler, N. Waxler and R. Liem (eds), *Social Contexts of Health, Illness, and Patient Care*. Cambridge: Cambridge University Press, pp. 1–23.

Monaghan, L. F. (2007) 'McDonaldizing men's bodies? Slimming, associated (ir)rationalities and resistances', *Body and Society*, 13/2: 67–93.

Moran, J. (2005) *Reading the Everyday*. London: Routledge.

Morgan, R. (2002) 'Imprisonment: a brief history, the contemporary scene, and likely prospects', in M. Maguire, R. Morgan and R. Reiner (eds), *Oxford Handbook of Criminology*. 3rd edn, Oxford: Oxford University Press, pp. 1113–67.

Morris, M. (1988) 'Things to do with shopping centres', in S. Sheridan (ed.), *Grafts: Essays in Feminist Cultural Criticism*. London: Verso, pp. 193–224.

Mukerji, C. (2002) 'Artwork: collection and contemporary culture', in D. Weinberg (ed.), *Qualitative Research Methods*. Oxford: Blackwell, pp. 313–28.

Murcott, A. (1982) '"It's a pleasure to cook for him": food, meal times and gender in South Wales households', in E. Gamarnikow et al. (eds), *The Public and the Private*. London: Heinemann.

Murcott, A. (1997) 'Family meals: a thing of the past?', in P. Caplan (ed.), *Food, Health and Identity*. London: Routledge, pp. 32–49.

Murcott, A. (2000) 'Understanding life-style and food use: contributions from the social sciences', *British Medical Bulletin*, 56: 121–32.

Muzzetto, L. (2006) 'Time and meaning in Alfred Schütz', *Time and Society*, 15/1: 5–31.

Nayak, A. (2006) 'Displaced masculinities: chavs, youth and class in the post-industrial city', *Sociology*, 40/5: 813–31.

Nazroo, J. (1995) 'Uncovering gender differences in the use of marital violence: the effect of methodology', *Sociology*, 29/3: 475–94.

NCA (National Coffee Association) (2000) *Coffee Drinking Trends Survey 2000*. New York: NCA.

Neal, M. (1998) '"You lucky punters!" A study of gambling in betting shops', *Sociology*, 32/3: 581–600.

Nettleton, S. (1995) *The Sociology of Health and Illness*. Cambridge: Polity.

Newcomb, M. D. (1986) 'Cohabitation, marriage and divorce among adolescents and young adults', *Journal of Social and Personal Relationships*, 3: 473–94.

Nixon, C. (2007) 'A life coloured red', *The Guardian*, 4 June.

Nixon, S. (1996) *Hard Looks: Masculinities, the Visual and Practices of Consumption*. London: Routledge.

Norton, A. J., and Moorman, J. E. (1987) 'Current trends in marriage and divorce among American women', *Journal of Marriage and the Family*, 49: 3–14.

Novell, J. (1987) 'Uses and abuses of the consultation', in A. Elder and O. Samuel (eds), *'While I'm Here, Doctor': A Study of the Doctor–Patient Relationship*. London: Tavistock.

Nowotny, H. (1994) *Time: The Modern and Postmodern Experience*. Cambridge: Polity.

Oakley, A. (1974) *Housewife*. London: Allen Lane.

Oakley, A. (1981) 'Interviewing women: a contradiction in terms?', in H. Roberts (ed.), *Doing Feminist Research*. London: Routledge & Kegan Paul, pp. 30–61.

O'Connor, H., and Madge, C. (2001) 'Cyber-mothers: online synchronous interviewing using conferencing software', *Sociological Research Online*, 5/4, http://www.socresonline.org.uk/5/4/oconnor.html.

Oliver, M. (1990) *The Politics of Disablement*. Basingstoke: Macmillan.

Oliver, M. (1996) *Understanding Disability: From Theory to Practice*. Basingstoke: Macmillan.

Oliver, M. (2004) 'The social model in action: if I had a hammer', in C. Barnes and G. Mercer (eds), *Implementing the Social Model of Disability*. Leeds: Disability Press.

ONS (Office for National Statistics) (2006) 'Lifestyles' (Time Use Survey 2005), *National Statistics Online*, http://www.statistics.gov.uk/CCI/nugget.asp?ID=1659&Pos=3&ColRank=2&Rank=432.

ONS (Office for National Statistics) (2007a) 'Divorces', *National Statistics Online*, http://www.statistics.gov.uk/cci/nugget.asp?id=170.

ONS (Office for National Statistics) (2007b) *Social Trends*, 37, http://www.statistics.gov.uk/socialtrends.

O'Reilly, K. (2007) 'Intra-European migration and the mobility enclosure dialectic', *Sociology*, 41/2: 277–93.

Orbach, S. (1986) *Hunger Strike*. London: Faber & Faber.

Packard, V. (1959) *The Status Seekers*. Harmondsworth: Penguin.

Parker, H., Williams, L., and Aldridge, J. (2002) 'The normalization of "sensible" recreational drug use: further evidence from the North West England Longitudinal Study', *Sociology*, 36/4: 941–64.

Parry, N., and Coalter, F. (1982) 'Sociology and leisure: a question of root or branch', *Sociology*, 16/2: 220–31.

Parsons, T. (1951) *The Social System*. London: Routledge & Kegan Paul.

Parsons, T., and Bales, R. F. (1956) *Family, Socialization and Interaction Process*. London: Routledge & Kegan Paul.

Paterson, M. (2006) *Consumption and Everyday Life*. London: Routledge.

Patterson, S. (1963) *Dark Strangers*. London: Tavistock.

Payer, L. (1988) *Medicine and Culture*. New York: Holt.

Picton, T. (1978) 'A very public espionage', *Camerawork*, 11/2.

Pilgrim, D., and Rogers, A. (2005) *A Sociology of Mental Health and Illness*. 3rd edn, Buckingham: Open University Press.

Pink, S. (2001) *Visual Ethnography*. London: Sage.

Pitkin, W. B. (1932) *The Consumer: His Nature and His Changing Habits*. New York: McGraw-Hill.

Plummer, K. (2001) *Documents of Life 2: An Invitation to a Critical Humanism*. 2nd edn, London: Sage.

Potter, J., and Wetherell, M. (1987) *Discourse and Social Psychology*. London: Sage.

Pringle, R. (1983) 'Women and consumer capitalism', in C. V. Baldock and B. Cass (eds), *Women, Social Welfare and the State in Australia*. Sydney: Allen & Unwin.

Radley, A. (1994) *Making Sense of Illness: The Social Psychology of Health and Disease*. London: Sage.

Rafalovich, A. (2005) 'Exploring clinician uncertainty in the diagnosis and treatment of attention deficit hyperactivity disorder', *Sociology of Health and Illness*, 27/3: 305–23.

Reed-Danahay, D. (1997) *Auto/Ethnography: Rewriting the Self and the Social*. Oxford: Berg.

Reekie, G. (1993) *Temptations: Sex, Selling and the Department Store*. Sydney: Allen & Unwin.

Rich, E. (2006) 'Anorexic dis(connection): managing anorexia as an illness and an identity', *Sociology of Health and Illness*, 28/3: 284–305.

Richardson, L. (1990) *Writing: Reaching Diverse Audiences*. Newbury Park, CA: Sage.

Ritzer, G. (1996) *Modern Sociological Theory*. 4th edn, New York: McGraw-Hill.

Ritzer, G. (1999) *Enchanting a Disenchanted World: Revolutionizing the Means of Consumption*. New York: Pine Forge Press.

Ritzer, G. (2004) *The McDonaldization of Society*. Rev. edn, London: Sage.

Roberts, H. (1985) *The Patient Patients: Women and their Doctors*. London: Routledge & Kegan Paul.

Roberts, K. (2002) 'Are long or unsocial hours of work bad for leisure?', in G. Crow and S. Heath (eds), *Social Conceptions of Time: Structure and Process in Work and Everyday Life*. Basingstoke: Palgrave, pp. 165–78.

Robinson, J., and Godbey, G. (1997) *Time for Life: The Surprising Ways that Americans Use their Time*. University Park: Pennsylvania State Press.

Robson, C. (2006) *How to Do a Research Project*. Oxford: Blackwell.

Rothman, D. J. (1997) *Beginnings Count: The Technological Imperative in American Health Care*. New York: Oxford University Press.

Rowntree, S. (1901) *Poverty: A Study of Town Life*. London: Longmans Green.

Roy, D. (1958) 'Banana time: job satisfaction and informal interaction', *Human Organization*, 18: 158–68.

Rubin, Z. (1973) *Liking and Loving*. New York: Holt, Rinehart & Winston.

Russell, D. E. H. (1990) *Rape in Marriage*. 2nd edn, Bloomington: Indiana University Press.

Ryan, M. (2006) 'Have family meals gone out of fashion?', BBC News, 10 February, http://news.bbc.co.uk/1/hi/uk/4356992.stm.

Rybczynski, W. (1991) *Waiting for the Weekend*. London: Penguin.

Sacks, H. (1987) 'You want to find out if anybody really does care', in G. Button and J. R. E. Lee (eds), *Talk and Social Organisation*. Clevedon: Multilingual Matters, pp. 219–25.

Sacks, H. (1992) *Lectures in Conversation*, ed. G. Jefferson. Oxford: Blackwell.

Sacks, O. (1996) *An Anthropologist on Mars*. London: Picador.

Said, E. (1978) *Orientalism*. New York: Pantheon.

Samuel, R., and Thompson, P. (1990) *The Myths We Live By*. London: Routledge.

Sartre, J. P. (1957 [1943]) *Being and Nothingness*. London: Methuen.

Saunders, D. M., and Turner, D. E. (1987) 'Gambling and leisure: the case of racing', *Journal of Leisure Studies*, 6: 281–99.

Saunders, P. (1990) *A Nation of Homeowners*. London: Unwin Hyman.

Saussure, F. de (1974 [1916]) *Course in General Linguistics*, trans. W. Baskin. London: Fontana.

Scambler, A., and Scambler, G. (1992) *Menstrual Disorders*. London: Routledge.

Scambler, G. (2004) 'Re-framing stigma: felt and enacted stigma and challenges to the sociology of chronic and disabling conditions', *Social Theory & Health*, 2/1: 29–46.

Scambler, G., and Hopkins, A. (1986) 'Being epileptic: coming to terms with stigma', *Sociology of Health and Illness*, 8: 26–43.

Scheff, T. J. (1984 [1966]) *Becoming Mentally Ill: A Sociological Theory*. New York: Aldine.

Scherer, K. R. (1974) 'Acoustic concomitants of emotional dimensions: judging affect from synthesized tone sequences', in S. Weitz (ed.), *Nonverbal Communication*. New York: Oxford University Press.

Schütz, A. (1962) *Collected Papers*, Vol. 1: *The Problem of Social Reality*. The Hague: Martinus Nijhoff.

Schütz, A. (1964) *Collected Papers*, Vol. 2: *Studies in Social Theory*. The Hague: Martinus Nijhoff.

Schütz, A. (1972) *The Phenomenology of the Social World*. London: Heinemann.

Schwartz, B. (1975) *Queuing and Waiting: Studies in the Social Organization of Access and Delay*. Chicago: University of Chicago Press.

Scott, J. (1990) *A Matter of Record*. Cambridge: Polity.

Scott, J. (2001) 'If class is dead, why won't it lie down?', in A. Woodward and M. Kohli (eds), *Inclusions and Exclusions in European Society*. London: Routledge.

Scott, J. (2006) *Social Theory: Central Issues in Sociology*. London: Sage.

Scott, M. B., and Lyman, S. M. (1968) 'Accounts', *American Sociological Review*, 33: 46–62.

Scott, S. (2004a) 'The shell, the stranger and the Competent Other: towards a sociology of shyness', *Sociology*, 38/1: 121–37.

Scott, S. (2004b) 'Researching shyness: a contradiction in terms?', *Qualitative Research*, 4/1: 91–105.

Scott, S. (2005) 'The red, shaking fool: dramaturgical dilemmas in shyness', *Symbolic Interaction*, 28/1: 91–110.

Scott, S. (2007) *Shyness and Society: The Illusion of Competence*. Basingstoke: Palgrave.

Seedhouse, D. (1986) *Health: Foundations for Achievement*. Chichester: Wiley.

Shakespeare, T. (2006) 'The social model of disability', in L. Davis (ed.), *The Disability Studies Reader*. Oxford: Taylor & Francis, pp. 197–204.

Shaw, C. (1930) *The Jack Roller: A Delinquent Boy's own Story*. Chicago: University of Chicago Press.

Shaw, J. (1994) 'Punctuality and the everyday ethics of time: some evidence from the Mass-Observation Archive', *Time and Society*, 3/1: 79–97.

Shaw, J. (2009) *Shopping: Social and Cultural Perspectives*. Cambridge: Polity.

Sheller, M., and Urry, J. (2003) 'Mobile transformations of "public" and "private" life', *Theory, Culture and Society*, 20/3: 107–25.

Sheridan, D., Street, B., and Bloome, D. (2000) *Writing Ourselves: Mass Observation and Literary Practices*. London: Hampton Press.

Shields, R. (ed.) (1992a) *Lifestyle Shopping*. London: Routledge.

Shields, R. (1992b) 'Spaces for the subject of consumption', in R. Shields (ed.), *Lifestyle Shopping*. London: Routledge, pp. 1–20.

Shorter, E. (1976) *The Making of the Modern Family*. London: Collins.

Shove, E. (2003) *Comfort, Cleanliness and Convenience.* Oxford: Berg.

Silva, E. (1999) 'Transforming housewifery: dispositions, practices and technologies', in E. Silva and C. Smart (eds), *The 'New' Family?* London: Sage, pp. 46–65.

Silva, E., and Bennett, T. (eds) (2004) *Contemporary Culture and Everyday Life.* Durham: Sociologypress.

Simmel, G. (1950a [1902–3]) 'The metropolis and mental life', in *The Sociology of Georg Simmel*, ed. and trans. K. H. Wolff. London: Free Press, pp. 409–24.

Simmel, G. (1950b [1908]) 'The isolated individual and the dyad', in *The Sociology of Georg Simmel*, ed. and trans. K. H. Wolff. London: Free Press, pp. 118–44.

Simmel, G. (1950c [1917]) 'Fundamental problems of sociology (individual and society)', in *The Sociology of Georg Simmel*, ed. and trans. K. H. Wolff. London: Free Press, pp. 3–57.

Simpson, M. (2002) 'Meet the metrosexual', 22 July, http://dir.salon.com/story/ent/feature/2002/07/22/metrosexual/index.html.

Sneijder, P., and Te Molder, H. F. M. (2004) '"Health should not have to be a problem": talking health and accountability in an Internet forum on veganism', *Journal of Health Psychology*, 9/4: 599–616.

Solomon, N. (1996) *Judaism: A Very Short Introduction.* Oxford: Oxford University Press.

Southerton, D. (2003) 'Squeezing time: allocating practices, co-ordinating networks and scheduling society', *Time and Society*, 12/1: 12–25.

Southerton, D. (2006) 'Analyzing the temporal organization of daily life: social constraints, practices and their allocation', *Sociology*, 40/3: 435–54.

Squire, C. (2000) 'Situated selves: the coming out genre and equivalent citizenship in narratives of HIV', in P. Chamberlayne, J. Bornat and T. Wengraf (eds), *The Turn to Biographical Methods in Social Science.* London: Routledge.

Stacey, J. (1993) *Star Gazing: Hollywood Cinema and Female Spectatorship.* London: Routledge.

Stanley, L. (1984) *The Diaries of Hannah Cullwick, Victorian Maidservant.* London: Virago.

Steger, B. (2006) 'Introduction: timing daily life in Japan', *Time and Society*, 15/2–3: 171–5.

Stein, S. (2003) *Sociology on the Web.* Harrow: Pearson Education.

Stockman, N., Bonney, N., and Xuewen, S. (1995) *Women's Work in East and West.* London: Routledge.

Stones, R. (2005) *Structuration Theory.* Basingstoke: Palgrave.

Straus, M. A., and Gelles, R. J. (1986) 'Societal change and change in family violence from 1975 to 1985 as revealed by two national surveys', *Journal of Marriage and the Family*, 48: 465–79.

Strauss, A. L. (1978) *Negotiations: Varieties, Contexts, Processes and Social Order*. San Francisco: Jossey-Bass.

Stryker, S. (1980) *Symbolic Interactionism: A Social Structural Version*. Menlo Park, CA: Benjamin/Cummings.

Sullivan, O. (1997) 'Time waits for no (wo)man: an investigation of the gendered experience of domestic time', *Sociology*, 31/2: 231–9.

Sullivan, S. (1999) *Falling in Love*. Basingstoke: Macmillan.

Summer Institute of Linguistics (2006) 'What is interactional competence?', http://www.sil.org/lingualinks/LANGUAGELEARNINGOtherResources/GudlnsFrALnggAndCltrLrnngPrgrm/WhatIsInteractionalCompetence.htm.

Szasz, T., and Hollander, M. (1956) 'A contribution to the philosophy of medicine: the basic models of the doctor–patient relationship', *Journal of the American Medical Association*, 97: 585–8.

Tangney, J. P., and Fischer, K. W. (eds) (1995) *Self-Conscious Emotions*. New York: Guilford Press.

Thomas, M. (2000) 'Exploring the contexts and meanings of women's experiences of sexual intercourse on holiday', in S. Clift and S. Carter (eds), *Tourism and Sex: Culture, Commerce and Coercion*. London: Pinter, pp. 200–20.

Thomas, M. (2005) '"What happens in Tenerife stays in Tenerife": understanding women's sexual behaviour on holiday', *Culture, Health and Sexuality*, 7/6: 571–84.

Thomas, W. I. (1923) *The Unadjusted Girl*. Boston: Little, Brown.

Thomas, W.I. and Thomas, D.S. (1970 [1928]) 'Situations defined as real are real in their consequences', in G. Stone and H Farberman (eds), *Social Psychology Through Interaction*, Waltham, MA: Ginn-Blasidell, pp. 154–55.

Thomas, W. I., and Znaniecki, F. (1958 [1918–20]) *The Polish Peasant in Europe and America*, 5 vols. New York: Dover.

Thompson, E. P. (1963) *The Making of the English Working Class*. Harmondsworth: Penguin.

Thompson, P. (1975) *The Edwardians: The Remaking of British Society*. London: Weidenfeld & Nicolson.

Thornton, S. (1995) *Club Cultures: Music, Media and Subcultural Capital*. Cambridge: Polity.

Thrasher, F. (1927) *The Gang*. Chicago: University of Chicago Press.

Tijdens, K. G. (2003) 'Employees' and employers' preferences for working time reduction and working time differentiation: a study of the 36 hour working week in the Dutch banking sector', *Acta Sociologica*, 46/1: 69–82.

Tomkins, S. S. (1962) *Affect, Imagery and Consciousness*, Vol. 1: *The Positive Affects*. New York: Springer.

Tomkins, S. S. (1963) *Affect, Imagery and Consciousness*, Vol. 2: *The Negative Affects*. New York: Springer.

Tuckett, D. (1976) *An Introduction to Medical Sociology*. London: Tavistock.

Turner, B. S. (1995 [1987]) *Medical Power and Social Knowledge*. London: Sage.

Turner, B. S. (1996) *The Body and Society*. 2nd edn, London: Sage.

Turner, V. (1967) 'Betwixt and between: the liminal period in *rites de passage*', in *The Forest of Symbols: Aspects of Ndembu Ritual*. Ithaca, NY: Cornell University Press, pp. 93–111.

Turton, J. (2006) *Child Abuse, Gender and Society*. London: Routledge.

Twigg, J. (1983) 'Vegetarianism and the meanings of food', in A. Murcott (ed.), *The Sociology of Food and Eating*. Aldershot: Gower, pp. 18–30.

Underhill, P. (1999) *Why We Buy*. London: Orion Books.

Urry, J. (2002) *The Tourist Gaze*. 2nd edn, London: Sage.

Urry, J. (2006) 'Travelling times', *European Journal of Communication*, 21/3: 357–72.

US Bureau of Justice Statistics (2007) 'Prison statistics', http://www.ojp.usdoj.gov/bjs/prisons.htm (accessed 22 February 2008).

US Census Bureau (2000) 'Profiles of general demographic characteristics: 2000 Census of Population and Housing, United States', http://www.census.gov/prod/cen2000/dp1/2kh00.pdf.

US Department of Housing and Urban Development (2007) 'Federal definition of homeless', http://www.hud.gov/homeless/index.cfm (accessed 22 February 2008).

US Temporal Trends (2007) 'Most overweight countries in the world: ranking', *Epidemiologic Inquiry*, 20 February, http://www.epidemiologic.org/2007/02/most-overweight-countries-in-world.html.

Veatch, R. (1972) 'Models for ethical medicine in a revolutionary age', *Hastings Center Report*, 2: 5–7.

Veblen, T. (2005 [1899]) *The Theory of the Leisure Class*. New York: Dodo Press.

Vegetarian Society (2008) '21st century vegetarianism – through the ages', http://www.vegsoc.org/news/2000/21cv/ages.html (accessed 7 January 2008).

Ville, I. (2005) 'Biographical work and returning to employment following a spinal cord injury', *Sociology of Health and Illness*, 27/3: 324–50.

Wajcman, J. (1995) 'Domestic technology, labour saving or enslaving?', in S. Jackson and S. Moores (eds), *The Politics of Domestic Consumption*. London: Prentice-Hall, pp. 217–29.

Walby, S. (2004) *The Cost of Domestic Violence*. London: Department of Trade and Industry.

Walby, S., and Allen, J. (2004) *Domestic Violence, Sexual Assault and Stalking: Findings from the British Crime Survey*. London: Home Office.

Walmsley, R. (2006) *World Prison Population List*. 7th edn, King's College London, International Centre for Prison Studies, http://www.kcl.ac.uk/

depsta/law/research/icps/download/world-prison-pop-seventh.pdf (accessed 23 September 2008).

Walter, T. (1991) 'The mourning after Hillsborough', *Sociological Review*, 39/3: 599–625.

Walvin, J. (1978) *Beside the Seaside: A Social History of the Popular Seaside Holiday*. London: Allen Lane.

Ward, C., and Hardy, D. (1986) *Goodnight Campers!: The History of the British Holiday Camp*. London: Mansell.

Warde, A. (1997) *Consumption, Food and Taste: Culinary Antinomies and Commodity Culture*. London: Sage.

Warde, A., and Martens, L. (2000) *Eating Out: Social Differentiation, Consumption, and Pleasure*. Cambridge: Cambridge University Press.

Wardhaugh, J. (1999) 'The unaccommodated woman: home, homelessness and identity', *Sociological Review*, 47: 91–109.

Warner, W. L. (1953) *American Life: Dream and Reality*. Chicago: University of Chicago Press.

Warren, S., and Brewis, J. (2004) 'Matter over mind? Examining the experience of pregnancy', *Sociology*, 38/2: 219–36.

Waters, L. E., and Moore, K. A. (2002) 'Reducing latent deprivation during unemployment: the role of meaningful leisure activity', *Journal of Occupational and Organizational Psychology*, 75/1: 15–32; http://www.ingentaconnect.com/content/bpsoc/joop/2002/00000075/00000001/art00002.

Watson, D. (2002) '"Home from home": the pub and everyday life', in T. Bennett and D. Watson (2002), *Understanding Everyday Life*. Oxford: Blackwell, pp. 183–228.

Weber, M. (1949 [1904]) '"Objectivity" in social science and social policy', in M. Weber, *The Methodology of the Social Sciences*. New York: Free Press.

Weber, M. (1985 [1904–5]) *The Protestant Ethic and the Spirit of Capitalism*. London: Routledge.

Westenholz, A. (2006) 'Identity, times and work', *Time and Society*, 15/1: 33–55.

WHO (World Health Organization) (1946) 'Preamble to the constitution of the World Health Organization', *International Health Conference*, New York, 19–22 June.

WHO (World Health Organization) (1998) *Obesity: Preventing and Managing the Global Epidemic*. Geneva: World Health Organization.

WHO (World Health Organization) (2007) 'Obesity and overweight', http://www.who.int/mediacentre/factsheets/fs311/en/index.html.

Whyte, W. F. (1955) *Street Corner Society: The Social Structure of an Italian Slum*. 2nd edn, Chicago: University of Chicago Press.

Wickham, G. (1992) *A History of the Theatre*. London: Phaidon.

Widerberg, K. (2006) 'Embodying modern times: investigating tiredness', *Time and Society*, 15/1: 105–20.

Wiggins, S. (2004) 'Good for "you": generic and individual healthy eating advice in family mealtimes', *Journal of Health Psychology*, 9/4: 535–48.

Williams, G. H. (1984) 'The genesis of chronic illness: narrative reconstruction', *Sociology of Health and Illness*, 6: 175–200.

Williams, J., and Neatrour, J. (2001) 'Football and families', University of Leicester: Sir Norman Chester Centre for Football Research, http://www.le.ac.uk/sociology/css/resources/factsheets/fs14.pdf.

Williams, M., and Robson, K. (2003) 'Re-engineering focus group methodology for the online environment', in S. Sarina Chen and J. Hall (eds), *Online Social Research: Methods, Issues & Ethics*. New York: Peter Lang.

Williams, R. (1958) *Culture and Society*. London: Chatto & Windus.

Williams, S. J. (1999) 'Is anybody there? Critical realism, chronic illness and the disability debate', *Sociology of Health and Illness*, 21/6: 797–819.

Williams, S. J., and Bendelow, G. (1996) 'The "emotional" body', *Body and Society*, 2: 125–39.

Williamson, J. (1978) *Decoding Advertisements*. London: Boyars.

Willmott, P., and Young, M. D. (1960) *Family and Class in a London Suburb*. London: Routledge & Kegan Paul.

Wilson, M. S., Weatherall, A., and Butler, C. (2004) 'A rhetorical approach to discussions about health and vegetarianism', *Journal of Health Psychology*, 9/4: 567–81.

Winch, P. (1958) *The Idea of a Social Science and its Relation to Philosophy*. London: Routledge & Kegan Paul.

Wolf, N. (2007 [1990]) *The Beauty Myth: How Images of Beauty are Used against Women*. New York: Vintage.

Woolf, H. (1991) *Prison Disturbances April 1990: Report of an Inquiry by the Rt Hon. Lord Justice Woolf (Parts I and II) and His Honour Judge Stephen Tumin (Part II)*, Cm 1456. London: HMSO.

World of Tea (2008) 'World tea consumption percentages', http://coffeetea.about.com.

Wrong, D. (1961) 'The oversocialized conception of man in modern sociology', *American Sociological Review*, 26: 183–93.

Young, J. T. (2004) 'Illness behaviour: a selective review and synthesis', *Sociology of Health and Illness*, 26/1: 1–31.

Yue, A. (2003) 'Shopping', in F. Martin (ed.), *Interpreting Everyday Culture*. London: Edward Arnold, pp. 124–39.

Zerubavel, E. (1981) *Hidden Rhythms: Schedules and Calendars in Social Life*. Chicago: University of Chicago Press.

Zimbardo, P. G. (1977) *Shyness: What It Is and What to Do about It*. London: Pan Books.

Zola, I. K. (1972) 'Medicine as an institution of social control', *Sociological Review*, 20: 487–503.

Zola, I. K. (1973) 'Pathways to the doctor – from person to patient', *Social Science and Medicine*, 7: 677–89.

Zukin, S. (1995) *The Cultures of Cities*. Oxford: Blackwell.

Zukin, S. (2004) *Point of Purchase: How Shopping Changed American Culture*. New York: Routledge.

Index

CPSIA information can be obtained
at www.ICGtesting.com
Printed in the USA
BVHW01*0017160118
505311BV00005B/54/P